D1393988

SUPPLEMENTARY VOLUME LXXXII
2008

THE
ARISTOTELIAN
SOCIETY

THE SYMPOSIA READ AT THE JOINT SESSION
OF THE ARISTOTELIAN SOCIETY
AND THE MIND ASSOCIATION
AT THE UNIVERSITY OF ABERDEEN
JULY 2008

PUBLISHED BY
The Aristotelian Society
2008

First published 2008 by
The Aristotelian Society

© The Aristotelian Society 2008

ISBN 0 907111 58 0
ISSN 0309-7013

Printed in Great Britain by 4 Word Page and Print Production, Bristol.

EDITOR
Mark Eli Kalderon, University College London

ASSISTANT EDITOR
David Harris, University College London

EXECUTIVE SECRETARY
Rachel Carter, University of London, Room 281, Stewart House,
Russell Square, London WC1B 5DN

ACTIVITIES AND PUBLICATIONS
The Society, founded in 1880, meets fortnightly in London to hear
and discuss philosophical papers. The Society's website is at
www.aristoteliansociety.org.uk. The *Proceedings* is published as a
journal in one annual printed edition, with three online journals ap-
pearing via Blackwell Synergy in March, June and September. The
Supplementary Volume, published annually in June, contains the
papers to be read at the Joint Session of the Aristotelian Society and
the Mind Association in July. Information about institutional subscription rates, back copies and other Aristotelian Society publications is available at the end of this volume. Information for
individual members can be found on the Aristolian Society website
at http://www.aristoteliansociety.org.uk.

CONTENTS

PROGRAMME

JOINT SESSION OF THE ARISTOTELIAN SOCIETY AND
THE MIND ASSOCIATION, UNIVERSITY OF ABERDEEN
11–13 JULY 2008

Friday 11 July	5:00 pm	Sarah Broadie The Inaugural Address: *Theological Sidelights from Plato's* Timaeus Chair: Dorothy Edgington
Saturday 12 July	9:00 am	Duncan Pritchard and Martijn Blaauw *Scepticism and Epistemic Value* Chair: Alan Millar
	11:00 am	Michelle Kosch and John Lippitt *Kierkegaard's* Fear and Trembling Chair: Dan Watts
	2:00 pm	*Graduate Papers*
	4:30 pm	*Submitted Papers—Open Sessions*
	8:00 pm	Kit Fine and John Divers *Material Coincidence* Chair: Paul Noordhof
Sunday 13 July	9:00 am	Elizabeth Anderson and John Skorupski *Equality and Bureaucracy* Chair: Dudley Knowles
	11:00 am	Peter Goldie and Dominic McIver Lopes *Virtues of Art* Chair: Berys Gaut
	2:00 pm	*Submitted Papers—Open Sessions*
	4:30 pm	*Submitted Papers—Open Sessions*
	8:00 pm	Ned Block and Cynthia Macdonald *Phenomenal and Access Consciousness* Chair: Bill Brewer

The Inaugural Address
Sarah Broadie

Theological Sidelights from Plato's *Timaeus*

Plato's account of the making of the world by a supreme divinity has often been felt to foreshadow the natural theology associated with orthodox western religion. This paper examines some significant ways (having more than merely antiquarian interest, it is hoped) in which the *Timaeus* scheme differs from more familiar orthodoxy.

I

Introduction. They are 'sidelights', because the *Timaeus* account is eccentric in relation to what westerners think of as mainstream theology, without being off the map; and because the account is illuminating for anyone fascinated by sheer possibilities of theological thinking.

If I focus on the eccentric aspects, it is precisely with a view to bringing out some of the less familiar possibilities, and not at all because I question the magnitude of mainstream theology's debt to Platonism.

I shall arrange most of the discussion round two themes. One is what I call the monistic polytheism of the *Timaeus*; the other is the question of what light is shed by that dialogue on the notion of divine transcendence. Finally, I shall point very briefly towards what the *Timaeus* can offer by way of religious consolation.

II

Monistic Polytheism. The *Timaeus* is a dialogue set in Athens, and Socrates speaks first, opening the proceedings. Socrates in a sense presides over all that follows, but the bulk of the work is in fact a cosmological monologue spoken by the fictitious character Timaeus. Timaeus is a visitor from southern Italy, and he is described as a consummate philosopher and deeply versed in astronomy (*Timaeus* 17a ff., 27a).

©2008 The Aristotelian Society
Proceedings of the Aristotelian Society Supplementary Volume LXXXII
doi: 10.1111/j.1467-8349.2008.00159.x

According to Timaeus's cosmology, the physical world as we see it today is an organized system—a cosmos—fashioned by a divine craftsman from pre-existing inanimate materials, in light of an intelligible paradigm (*Timaeus* 29a). In the actual story as Plato writes it, the materials which went into the world's construction were not at that point completely untouched by divinity, for they were already themselves the product of a divine ordering. The materials were fire, earth, water and air; but these, according to the account, are masses of minute particles shaped in accordance with four of the geometrically regular solids; and a divinity had already done this shaping in advance of the process of world-making (*Timaeus* 53a–b, 56c). What was it that was replaced by the geometrically pleasing partiles? We are told only that it was chaotic 'vestiges' of earth, fire, water and air. Was the divinity that ordered the vestiges into regular particles the same as the one that then used these to fashion the cosmos? This is left indefinite; what is clear is that the ordering of the particles belongs to the same divine project as the construction of the cosmos. The divinity that does the first is on the same side as the divinity that does the second: for example, each strives to implement beautiful mathematical forms wherever possible. Plainly, what matters to Plato is the fact that they are completely in harmony, not whether they are two gods or one god with two functions. If we read them as two gods, this is an example of what I am calling 'monistic polytheism', and we shall see other examples in the *Timaeus*. What matters for Plato is the self-harmony of the divine. He rejects not the *polytheism* of his culture, but those ancient cosmogonic myths according to which the divine regime we have today came about through the overthrow of a more primal regime, and is maintained only through continual repression of the overthrown divinities.

Thus the text of the *Timaeus* itself gives very little purchase, if any, to the widespread interpretation that the divine craftsman had to deal with 'recalcitrant' matter when he crafted the cosmos.[1] The materials with which he deals are not just brutishly there, but are already themselves the product of processing by a thoroughly congenial divinity. Their fiery, earthy, watery and airy natures are not alien to his enterprise, but are present in full actuality because of the ordering into particles that prepared them for it. As for the yet more primal vestiges, they had too little by way of positive character to be

---

[1] The interpretation is alive and well today: see, for example, Hasker (1998, §2).

©2008 THE ARISTOTELIAN SOCIETY
Proceedings of the Aristotelian Society Supplementary Volume LXXXII
doi: 10.1111/j.1467-8349.2008.00159.x

recalcitrant to ordering. The god who regulated them geometrically no more faced resistance than the orthodox god who creates *ex nihilo*. If this is right, we should be wondering what the advantage is (from the point of view of natural theology) of conceiving god as a creator literally *ex nihilo*, over conceiving god as producing order from something unordered and without character. Or at any rate we should be wondering what difference the distinction makes. In neither case does god have to fight matter and subdue it so as to accomplish what is required. So perhaps the difference is this: in the one case we have a rescue operation whereby something chaotic, characterless, and in itself completely pointless, is saved from this predicament by being divinely ordered, whereas in the case of creation *ex nihilo* the divine act is more purely spontaneous, being triggered by absolutely nothing external.

We have broached the question of polytheism in the *Timaeus* by considering the relation between the divinity that crafts the cosmos from positively-natured materials and the divinity that produced positively-natured materials by ordering something more primal. But before continuing on the theme of polytheism, it is worth taking a parenthetical look at what the *Timaeus* account achieves through *not* postulating creation *ex nihilo*. Here I shall consider the stage that consists in world-making from the fully developed materials fire, earth, water and air. Now, by speaking of the account as simply *not* postulating creation *ex nihilo*, I may seem to suggest that Plato could have availed himself of that concept but deliberately set it aside. No doubt that is historically absurd. However, when explicating the *Timaeus*, the more we emphasize the fact that a doctrine of creation *ex nihilo* would simply have seemed inadmissible to any Greek mind of this period, the more we risk ignoring or underrating a positive feature of great interest, namely the seamless way in which the work integrates theology and physical science. The Timaean story of divine world-making is designed to be a deeply penetrating and detailed account of the composition, structures and workings of a vast range of physical entities. Far from showing only *that* divinity is responsible for the things of each kind, the story sets out to explain precisely *how* they were made and *why* the distinctly described physical features are as they are. In every case, divinity is represented forming something complex from pre-existing empirical materials, the natures of which are important for the explanation, since they make distinctive contributions to the results. In short, the

©2008 THE ARISTOTELIAN SOCIETY
Proceedings of the Aristotelian Society Supplementary Volume LXXXII
doi: 10.1111/j.1467-8349.2008.00159.x

story of divine world-making is essentially also a scientific analysis
of physical complexes in terms of matter, form and function. What
seems a limitation from the point of view of orthodox theology—
namely, crafting divinity's dependence on distinct materials—is
nothing but a strength from the Timaean point of view, according to
which a *theologically* appropriate account of the coming into being
of the world essentially incorporates the most advanced physical science. Contrast, in particular, the first creation story in the book of
Genesis, the purpose of which is presumably to teach to everyone
the immediate dependence of all natural things on the will of God.
The key words of the imperatives by which God there creates the ar-
ray of familiar components of our world are not analytical formulae
indicating that such-and-such structures are to be realized in one or
another carefully specified type of matter: they are the same ordinary simple terms that the uneducated use.

This contrast with the *Timaeus* is particularly obvious as we look
at the later sections of the Timaean cosmology, the ones that deal
with the physics and chemistry of the sublunary world. Let us, however, return to the beginning. Here, Timaeus lays it down as an axiom, which will control everything that follows, that this physical
universe is as good and beautiful as anything in the realm of becoming can be. In fact, he states that it would be impious even to frame
an opinion to the contrary (*Timaeus* 29a). One may wonder in pass-
ing, 'Impious against whom?', and the fact that Timaeus immediately infers from the excellence of the cosmos around us to its origin in
a divine maker working from an intelligible paradigm may lead us
to think straight away that the god implied by the spectre of impiety
is none other than the Timaean equivalent of the god of orthodox
theology, the transcendent being who in the beginning created the
heavens and the earth. We may feel at this point a logical misgiving:
surely Timaeus has begged the question. For presumably he is pre-
senting a version of the argument from design, whereby we argue
from the supposed excellence of nature to the conclusion that god
exists, on the ground that divine creation is the best, or the only
possible, explanation of the order of nature. In that case, Timaeus
should not be shoring up his premiss that nature is as good and
beautiful as possible by the consideration that one would blaspheme
against the author of nature in supposing otherwise.

The presumption, however, would be mistaken. From the point of
view of orthodox theology, design arguments are meant to establish

the existence of an author of nature in order to establish the existence of a god at all. If our design arguments fail, then to that extent
we have failed in the bid to prove by reason that we are not in a
godless universe. That is why it would be begging the question to
appeal to a point of piety in order to set up the premiss about nature
from which one's design argument begins. Timaeus, however, does
not infer to a distinct maker of the universe in order to have
grounds for theism as such. For it soon becomes apparent that his
axiom about the excellence of the world already by itself yields a
god: a god that is identical with the all-embracing natural whole itself. This emerges when Timaeus depicts the divine world-maker
thinking out the nature of what he is about to construct (*Timaeus*
30a ff.). Given that it is to be maximally excellent, the maker deduced that it would have to be alive and intelligent; that it must contain all matter and all physical kinds within itself and therefore is to
be the one and only physical cosmos; that it must be ageless and
self-sufficient. All this was in the divine plan, and the universe was
made accordingly. What the world-maker's reason told him in advance to make is what Timaeus's reason anyway tells him is what
the already existing world is like, with both reasoners basing their
pictures on the axiom that the world must be as excellent as possible. Now, taken together, the features deduced from the axiom are
the attributes of *divinity*. Hence Timaeus more than once, and very
deliberately, calls the cosmic system a god, blessed (or: happy) and
perfect (*Timaeus* 34b, 68e, 92c; cf. 34a, matched by *Critias* (the
companion dialogue) 106a, 36e). Any human suggestion that the
physical world is less than perfect would therefore be first and foremost impiety towards the world-god.

The main point for present consideration is that Timaeus does not
argue for the maker in order to prove the reality of the divine, or in
order to establish that religion and worship have an object. In starting from this world Timaeus starts from what he already implicitly
knows is divine. Then why does he argue to a distinct intelligent
maker at all? The answer lies in the purely Platonic assumptions that
even a divine physical cosmos is in the realm of becoming, and that
nothing in the realm of becoming can be metaphysically ultimate.

We are faced, then, with the Timaean doctrine furthest removed
from orthodox theology: that in making the universe, the transcendent god made a god, and a god having a body made of the materials
of nature. According to this perspective, the physical cosmos is not a

©2008 THE ARISTOTELIAN SOCIETY
Proceedings of the Aristotelian Society Supplementary Volume LXXXII
doi: 10.1111/j.1467-8349.2008.00159.x

secular thing, since 'secular' is contrary to 'divine' and 'sacred'; nor
can we even call it 'the world' if we think of this term as meaning
something 'worldly' in the sense of 'secular'.

Even though we may feel the notions *created god* and *physical
god* to be self-contradictory, the idea of gods that are brought into
being was rife in the mythological background of Plato's culture,
and the idea of nature or physical principles as impersonal divinities
was central to the systems of several of his philosophical predeces-
sors. Again, what matters to Plato is not that god be unique and
purely spiritual, but that whatever is divine is in perfect harmony
with whatever is divine. Thus if one could contrive the notion of a
god who is somehow racked by internal conflict, a sort of self-tor-
menting god, Plato would reject this as the height of blasphemy; and
his rejection would remain unfaltering even if one told him that the
notional god is the unique divinity and completely non-physical.

At one point in Timaeus's story, the transcendent and purely intellectual world-making god is shown delighting in the beauty of the
cosmic system he has constructed entirely in accordance with his
own values (and he then even thinks of a way of making it more
beautiful still; *Timaeus* 37c ff.). We may be reminded of the succes-
sive moments in Genesis I when, stage by stage, God sees that what
he has created is good. But the resemblance is perhaps superficial.
For surely behind the Timaean account stands a contrast unthinka-
ble in biblical terms: namely, the ancient stories like those in Hesiod
(whose cultural importance was second, if that, only to Homer's) of
gods who by a kind of biological necessity gave birth to new gods
and then tried to destroy them as rivals bent on subverting the old
gods' values.

This point illuminates the famous passage where Timaeus states
the divine world-maker's motive for making a cosmos from the materials that were at hand: because he was good he harboured no ves-
tige of jealousy or grudgingness (*phthonos*), hence wanted everything to be as like himself as possible (*Timaeus* 29d–30a). Orthodox
theologians have sometimes seen this as prefiguring the idea that
monotheistic creation *ex nihilo* is an overflowing of divine perfection, or the idea that God created the world because he wanted
something non-divine to love and even to redeem. That Timaeus's
explanation feeds into this tradition should not, however, blind us
to its non-orthodox edge: *this* world-maker was so wholly removed
from jealousy that he actually made, not merely something else, but

another *god*. From the orthodox point of view it is of particular interest that this new god, the cosmic god, rather upstages the maker-god when it comes to being an object of religious attention. For Timaeus begins his monologue with a prayer to the gods and goddesses in general that his account will be pleasing to them, and he ends it[2] with a prayer uniquely directed to the cosmic god 'who has come into being just now in our discourse, although long ago in reality'; but neither Timaeus nor any other character ever singles out the maker-god in prayer.[3]

If I had to identify what from our own cultural perspective is probably the strangest aspect of Timaean theology, I would not pinpoint the concept *god that is brought into being*, nor the concept *corporeal god*. For Christians, at any rate, these ideas are not completely beyond the pale. It may be a theological *mistake* to venerate X as a god while at the same time believing that X was in some sense generated and had physical existence; but as attitudes or states of mind these clearly can be combined—one does not drive the other out—whether or not conjoining their contents is rationally or religiously acceptable. What I think for many of us is much harder to take on board, and enter into as a genuinely possible outlook (even if we consider it to be theologically mistaken), is one that integrates *venerating X as a god* with *treating X as the object of physical research*. We find such an outlook in some of the earlier Greek philosophies, and in Aristotle's treatise *On the Heavens*. It is, very markedly, the outlook of the *Timaeus* with respect to the overall world-system. Timaeus's monologue does not separate religious celebration of this cosmic god's nativity from the scientific detailing of its nature.

III

Transcendence. I turn now to the question of the transcendence of the Timaean world-maker. It is clear, if we take the account at face value, that the divine world-maker is a wholly incorporeal intellect wholly distinct from the world-god. Thus the account depicts the world-maker as constructing the soul of the world-god from incor-

---

[2] At the start of the *Critias*.

[3] Cf. Cornford (1935, p. 35): 'Neither in the *Timaeus* nor anywhere else is it suggested that the Demiurge should be an object of worship: he is not a religious figure.'

©2008 THE ARISTOTELIAN SOCIETY
Proceedings of the Aristotelian Society Supplementary Volume LXXXII
doi: 10.1111/j.1467-8349.2008.00159.x

poreal and highly abstract ingredients, just as he constructs the
world-god's body from the four elements. Interpreters imbued with
the tradition of biblical monotheism have tended, I suspect, to accept rather too easily the transcendence of the Timaean world-maker. I suspect that acceptance can come easily because it fits nicely
with the transcendence of the biblical god. We are used to thinking
of God in this way, as beyond and prior to the natural world he has
made. But there ought to be a rationale for the Platonic account;
and the, to us, most obvious rationale is not available. By the rationale most obvious to us I mean, of course, the thought that it belongs to the very nature of the divine to be completely incorporeal
and transcendent. But we have seen that Plato is uninhibited in supposing that the overall system of the physical world is itself a great
and blessed god. Hence, in so far as his account postulates a transcendent world-maker, it is not on the basis of assumptions about
the nature of divinity as such.

The question to be asked is functional: what theoretical or religious purpose is served by the notion of transcendence here? Pursuing this forces us to become clearer about the import of *divine
transcendence* itself. The transcendence in question is clearly in relation to the natural universe. We are thinking of the natural universe
and its natural contents as not the whole of reality. But the quasi-
spatial and -temporal imagery of *above*, *beyond*, *before* and *outside*
earns its keep, I think, only on either of two conditions: either we
must think that nature itself is such that it could not exist except in
dependence on something utterly dissimilar to itself and to any
feature of itself; or we must think that the divine first principle of
nature has some other function besides that of being the divine first
principle of nature. When both conditions are fulfilled, and one and
the same divinity is assumed to fulfil them, there results a complex
and rich notion of transcendence.

We can illustrate the first condition by reference to the fact that in
the Genesis accounts of creation nothing explicit is said to the effect
that nature in and of itself is a single organized system. In both accounts we are shown the different kinds of physical things being created in succession. This sort of account could (I am not claiming
that it necessarily in fact did) combine its observation of the multi-
plicity of things with a sense that, although hang together they do,
none of them, and nothing in any of them, has the power to produce
or conserve the others, and nothing in them by themselves has the

©2008 The Aristotelian Society
Proceedings of the Aristotelian Society Supplementary Volume LXXXII
doi: 10.1111/j.1467-8349.2008.00159.x

power to make them all hang together. This outlook would naturally lead to postulating one divine being as the source of all of them,
whose power unites them in the single system they could never of
themselves establish; and since (on pain of regress) this being has a
unity and self-connectedness that owes nothing to anything other
than itself, this being is of a kind wholly apart from them, and hence
can be deemed transcendent. Its transcendence corresponds to the
intuition that nothing about what we call the physical world can account for its unity. Since the problem of its unity is an ongoing one,
extending through the 'seasons, days and years' which the sun,
moon and stars were created to mark, the same transcendent power
that created nature is seen as also upholding it at every instant. Thus
a supposedly naïve feature of the Genesis accounts, namely the plu-
ralizing way they exhibit nature as a catalogue of distinctly localized
entities, makes them amenable to the grandest theological development.

From the perspective of our first condition, the *Timaeus* account
as actually presented is not entirely stable. For what the supposedly
transcendent maker makes is conceived of from the start as an all-
embracing organic system, intelligent and divine. So understood,
nature easily seems to have all that it takes to be self-sufficient. It
easily seems to contain its active ordering principle within itself.
What deepens this impression is that if we take seriously the account as Timaeus states it, the transcendent world-maker is shown
finishing his work and then, in some sense, retiring (*Timaeus* 42e).
Once the cosmic system is up and running under the governance of
the world-soul, the world-soul itself seems to do all that is needed to
keep it going. Nature, as long as it is fully animated by the world-
soul, is fully alive and in no way tending of itself to sink into chaos
or non-existence. Nor is there any external threat. The maker, we
are told, would dissolve the cosmos only if *per impossibile* he ceased
to be pleased with it (*Timaeus* 41a–b); this makes its continuance a
matter of divine transcendent inaction rather than action.

It starts to seem only rational to question the need for any distinct
maker; all the more so given that, almost as soon as the *Timaeus*
was finished, various of Plato's disciples were not only agreeing with
Aristotle that the universe is everlasting in both temporal directions,
but were claiming that this was the hidden meaning of the *Timaeus*.
For once one does away with the assumption that the world had a
sort of proto-historical beginning, it cannot be pictured as the work

of a transcendent maker-god operating on actually unordered materials: but if the materials have always been ordered into a cosmos
(even if this means that they have always been in process of being effectively ordered), and if the ongoing maintenance of this order is
due to the world-soul, it becomes redundant to postulate a transcendent workman. One can then move all the way to the Stoic position, according to which the world is totally ultimate, being
governed by an imminent intelligence structured by reference to
nothing beyond itself. Alternatively, one can retain an important element of Platonism by postulating that the otherwise self-sufficient
world-soul operates in accordance with an intelligible paradigm
conceived of as a distinct and more ultimate principle.[4]

The second condition under which it can make sense to postulate
a god transcendent over nature was that we invest this divinity with
a function other than being the source of nature. The way this idea
is played out for the biblical god is so familiar that brief mention is
enough. God the creator of the world is immediately also represented as standing in an ethical and personal relation to a certain people, and then through it to the whole of humanity. It now becomes
the task of detailed monotheistic theology to show how these two
functions are coherently integrated. Philosophical work is also necessary to explicate the intuition supporting our sense that these are
genuinely distinct functions: the intuition, namely, that the sphere of
nature is different from, and does not in an obvious or automatic
way include as a straightforward part of itself the whole sphere of
human religion and ethics. To return to the Timaean world-maker:
this divinity too is more than simply the source of nature; hence the
second condition of transcendence turns out to be satisfied. Before
turning to the demonstration of this claim we should note that the
truth of some such claim is needed to vindicate the Timaean world-
maker's transcendence at all, given that fulfilment of the first condition proved in this case to be metaphysically rather unstable. The
present interpretation will uncover an interesting fact: the very doctrine that destabilized fulfilment of the first condition turns out to
play a crucial part in accounting for the fulfilment of the second
one. This is the doctrine that the cosmic system is itself a god.

To proceed, I must report more of Timaeus's account, which will

---

[4] Gabriela Carone (2005, ch. 2) has argued the *Timaeus* should be understood as identifying
the divine world-maker with the world-soul.

©2008 The Aristotelian Society
Proceedings of the Aristotelian Society Supplementary Volume LXXXII
doi: 10.1111/j.1467-8349.2008.00159.x

involve introducing yet more gods. The world-maker not only created the all-embracing cosmic god, body and soul, but also various
other kinds of gods whose effects show up *within* this world. Some
of these further gods are visible, being identified with the earth, the
moon, the sun, the five recognized planets, and the fixed stars; their
activity is astronomical, and of course perfectly coordinated
(*Timaeus* 40a–d). But we are also told of created gods whose special
task is to carry out the work of creating mortal animals. These ancillary gods are necessary for a double reason: first, there have to be
mortal animals, since the world would be incomplete without them;
and, secondly, the supreme uncreated world-maker cannot himself
make anything that is subject to death (*Timaeus* 41a–d; cf. 39e–
40a). Significantly, he is shown communicating this double reason
to the ancillary divine workers when he assigns them their task. He
gives them a sketch of all that the world must contain if it is to be
complete; hence they understand their function in light of the sovereign world-project. The intelligible paradigm that guided the supreme maker informs in its wholeness the guidance he gives *them*,
from which they will then operate. In short, they will not be acting
as tunnel-visioned animistic forces, but as gods, although lesser
gods.

The animals which these gods create are not mortal in every respect. Each has an immortal rational element which the supreme god
has already created in much the same way as he created the intellect
of the all-embracing cosmic god. In much the same way, but not in
the identical act: for as Timaeus tells the story, it turns out that after
the cosmic god had been constructed, body and soul, some ingredients had been left over—incorporeal ingredients—from the operation in which the supreme god had mixed and organized the
immortal world-soul. The supreme god turned to these leftovers,
made them into a new though less perfect version of the same mix-
ture, and divided this into intellects that were to be joined to mortal
bodies (*Timaeus* 41d). The task of the ancillary makers is to build
suitable bodies, at the same time planting in them, or fitting them for,
the various additional psychic powers necessary for mortals.

Mortal animals are not autonomous and invulnerable: they depend on the physical environment for nutrition and respiration, and
they receive from it all kinds of violent shocks and disturbances. To
live at all they have to be endowed with sense-perception and a gamut of non-rational impulses and emotions, but all this sets a tremen-

dous problem for the immortal part of their soul: its natural rhythm is distorted and obstructed.

Thus the completeness of the cosmos comes at painful cost to mortals and to the immortal souls within them. But obviously it cannot be supposed that the world-maker instigates this programme because he wants to torture these creatures' immortal souls for no reason. Moreover, in the story as Timaeus tells it, there is no room for the theory that these immortal souls are mortalized as a punishment. They are not given any chance actually to do anything, to distinguish themselves for good or ill, before they are first placed in bodies. However, something did happen to them before the initial embodiment. The supreme god assigned each one to a star, and 'mounting them as it were on chariots, he showed them the nature of the universe, and declared to them the laws of Destiny' (*Timaeus* 41e). He told them:

> There would be appointed a first incarnation, *the same for all, that none might suffer disadvantage at his hands*, and they ... [were] to be born as the most god-fearing of living creatures. When, therefore, they should *of necessity* have been implanted in bodies, and of their bodies some part should always be coming in and some part passing out, *there must needs* be innate in them, first, sensation, the same for all, arising from violent impressions; second, desire blended with pleasure and pain, and besides these fear and anger and all the feelings that accompany these and all that are of a contrary nature: and if they should master these passions they would live in righteousness; if they were mastered by them, in unrighteousness. And he who should live well for his due span of time should journey back to the habitation of his consort star and there live a happy and congenial life; but failing of this, he should shift at his second birth into a woman;[5] and if in this condition he still did not cease from wickedness, then according to the character of his depravation, he should constantly be changed into some beast of a nature resembling the formation of that character, and should have no rest from the travail of these changes, until letting the revolution of the Same and uniform within himself draw into its train all that turmoil of fire and water and earth and air that had later grown about it, he should control its irrational turbulence by discourse of reason and return once more to his first and best condition. (*Timaeus* 41e–42d)

---

[5] Here Plato unfortunately loses some of the credit he acquired for admitting female philosopher rulers in the *Republic* (reprised at *Timaeus* 17d). On reincarnation downwards see also *Timaeus* 90e–92c.

©2008 The Aristotelian Society
Proceedings of the Aristotelian Society Supplementary Volume LXXXII
doi: 10.1111/j.1467-8349.2008.00159.x

Timaeus continues:

> *When he had delivered to them all these ordinances to the end that he* *might be guiltless of the wickedness of any one of them,* he sowed them, some in the Earth, some in the Moon, some in all the other instruments of time [i.e. the sun and the planets]. After this sowing he left it to the newly made gods to mould mortal bodies, to fashion all that part of a human soul that there was still need to add and all that these things entail, and *to govern and guide the mortal creature to the* *best of their powers, save in so far as it should be a cause of evil to itself.* (*Timaeus* 42d–e)[6]

There is too much to discuss in all this, but let me pick out two points. The first is the stress on the individual responsibility of each immortal soul for how it fares on embodiment. The second is the way in which, at this stage of the account, the cosmic god has completely faded into the background.

(1) It is emphasized that the souls destined for mortal embodiment receive the best possible start. The supreme god creates them as individuals on equal footing, giving them all the same vision, warning, and assurance that they can make progress. The ancillary gods will do everything possible to forward it; we see many examples when Timaeus reaches the detailed anatomy and physiology of the first animals, i.e. humans.[7] Even so, the account stresses the enormous difficulty of the challenges facing our rational souls. Significantly, however, this theme of the difficulty makes its first appearance in the supreme god's address to the pre-embodied souls, by which he prepares them. In first dividing a sort of primal psychic material into these individual souls, he set them up as, so to speak, repositories of responsibility. However, by his subsequent communication to them, which, it is implied, they cannot fail to take in, he puts them in a position to take, themselves, responsibility, thereby becoming actually responsible. First: by giving them the vision of the universe he lets them know that they will always be more than bundles of dispositions to react to the dangers and lures of their partial circumstances and their embodiment. Then: for it to be true that they can make progress, it has to be true not only that they will if they try, but also that they have a will to try; and in order to have a

---

[6] Translated by Cornford (1935), with one minor change; italics added.

[7] Our physical design facilitates rational functioning under mortal conditions: cf. 47a–d on vision and hearing, 69d–71e on anatomical arrangements for the psychic powers that subserve reason, 72e–73a on the alimentary system, 75a–c on head and mouth.

will to try, they have to carry with them the belief that they can succeed, even if only incrementally. Thus he assures them that they can.
Finally: in order to make the maximum effort, they must not get
stuck in the acquiescent delusion that the gods—or even their own
pre-embodied selves—positively desire them to flounder, or have
left them to do so through neglect. Thus by emphasizing to them
that these great natural difficulties arise through natural necessity,
hence not through anyone's fault, the god turns them away from
blaming, and disposes them to regard these as things that can be
worked through by them. His communication to them is an act of
not neglecting them, by which they are in a position to know that
they have not been neglected.

(2) Earlier it seemed that Timaeus's transcendent world-maker
trembled on the edge of becoming redundant because nature seemed
adequately accounted for by the mighty cosmic god, or more exactly
by the soul of this god ordering the body of the cosmos in light (no
doubt) of the Platonically indispensable intelligible paradigm. But
once human beings come into the picture as centres of ultimate responsibility, even if only on a limited scale, the idea that the cosmic
god's soul is a sufficient principle becomes unattractive. For the
most natural view to take, if the cosmic god alone is the source of
everything, is the pantheistic one whereby we are transient and local
manifestations of it. On such a view, our immortal souls are, so to
speak, rays of the cosmic soul; our thoughts and actions are in the
end its; and our historic story—a topic in which we know Plato was
distinctly interested when he composed the *Timaeus*—is simply an
aspect of the life of cosmic nature. In short: it may perhaps be possible, but it is certainly difficult, to make sense of us as individual centres of responsibility if our only source is the cosmos itself, even if,
or perhaps especially if, the cosmos is itself a god. It is easier, perhaps, to think that centres of limited but ultimate responsibility
have emerged from a completely non-divine world (such as the
world of contemporary naturalism), than to make room for them in
a pervading world-god to which they owe their being. But Timaeus
holds fast to the tenet of the world-god. Thus precisely this tenet,
given his commitment to individual responsibility, sets up the theoretical need for a distinct divine agency with the function of forming
our immortal rational souls, and (by proxy in the *Timaeus*) our
mortal bodies. Now, theoretically Plato in his monistic polytheism
might have postulated a completely self-sufficient cosmic god plus

another god responsible for making us. Instead, however, he has chosen to attribute to a single god the role of accounting for us and the role of accounting for the cosmos. (We and the cosmic god are, after all, parts of a single divine plan.) Therefore, since the god that accounts for us is necessarily other than the cosmic god, and other, also, than the cosmic god's soul, the god that accounts for the cosmic god cannot be the cosmic god itself or its soul.

In this way transcendence is established for the divine source of the cosmos, and we reach a position in this respect reminiscent of biblical theism. But the rationale of the Platonic position, if my reconstruction is not off target, crucially involves the biblically alien doctrine that the physical cosmos is itself a blessed god.

So the Timaean picture allows the elaboration of a distinction between physical nature and the sphere of ethics. This difference in the *Timaeus* does not arise simply from the fact that we, in that account, incorporate an immortal incorporeal element. After all, just such an element is an essential aspect of the natural cosmos: it is not something supernatural introduced contrary to nature. Similarly, the immortal soul of a mortal individual is an aspect of its nature, as much part of its natural endowment as its body and mortal capacities. The crucial point is that these mortalized immortal souls are individual centres of responsibility. The fact that, once embodied, they live in the very real possibility of making bad choices instead of good ones is what opens up space for ethical differences and human ethical concern about those differences.[8] No doubt it is due to our common natural endowment that we can choose better and worse; but how we actually do choose on a given occasion is not a working out of our common natural endowment. Plato is scientific about nature, and like any scientist he assumes that, barring external interferences, nature necessarily works in the same way. But ethically we do not necessarily work in the same way under the same natural circumstances. This, I think, is his view.

The distinction between natural and ethical spheres implies, I think, that Timaeus's original axiom that the physical world is as good as possible is limited to it *qua* natural universe. The cosmogonic gods have done the best possible job, but it does not follow that this world is as good as possible *simpliciter*, i.e. that every state

---

[8] This distinction between *natural* and *human-ethical* is not undermined by the fact that Plato tends to use the same vocabulary of 'symmetry', 'proportion', 'measure', 'balance', etc., in explaining both naturally good arrangements and ethically good ones.

©2008 THE ARISTOTELIAN SOCIETY
Proceedings of the Aristotelian Society Supplementary Volume LXXXII
doi: 10.1111/j.1467-8349.2008.00159.x

of affairs is superior to all possible alternatives. Plato surely holds
that in any generation wrongs are committed, foolish political decisions taken, crass measures followed in bringing up children, where
the choice could have gone better.[9,10] Nor does anything in Timaeus's account commit him to holding that the consequences of every
human action inevitably by some secret connection make this world
better *simpliciter* than it would have been otherwise.

IV

The Cosmic God and Us. We have looked at the transcendent
world-maker's relation to the cosmic god; also at the way (partly direct and partly by proxy) in which the former gives rise to us. Let
me end by sketching the relation in which we stand to the cosmic
god. (a) Our bodies, we are told, have been fashioned by the ancillary gods from materials 'borrowed' from nature at large (*Timaeus*
42e–43a). Thus our bodily materials are straightforwardly parts of
the physical world, and are subject to the laws of nature. (b) Our rational souls, by contrast, are made of generically the same stuff as
the cosmic soul, but from a distinct portion. Hence we creatures
that result when these rational souls are joined to mortal bodies are
not parts of the cosmic living being, even though we necessarily in-
habit it. Our parts are not all parts of it, since one of our parts, the
rational soul, is not a part of it at all. (c) Our bodies, too, as distinct
from the materials of our bodies, are not parts of the cosmic god.
They were not fashioned as organs for it, but so as to embody *our*
distinct rational souls. (d) Nor do we as wholes stand to the cosmic
god as an animal's organs or limbs to the animal, since our governing principles and our lives are distinct from its. (e) Given its and
our common origin and similar nature, it seems right to say that we
stand to it rather as younger and necessarily dependent siblings.

Its astronomical movements, the perfect expressions of its soul,
constitute for us, Timaeus says, a vital source of salvation. For our

---

[9] This is consistent with holding that for some, given their upbringing and other social circumstances, it is much more difficult to make good choices than for those better placed (cf.
Timaeus 87a–b).

[10] In fact, since the physical completeness of the universe requires that it always contain
every kind of mortal animal, there can never be a time when all rational souls of mortals
have passed beyond reincarnation and returned each to its star. Thus cosmic completeness
necessitates the incompleteness of ethical goodness.

©2008 The Aristotelian Society
Proceedings of the Aristotelian Society Supplementary Volume LXXXII
doi: 10.1111/j.1467-8349.2008.00159.x

cognition of those regularities strengthens the rhythms of our cognate element, immunizing it against the afflictions of embodiment, and making it more godlike (*Timaeus* 90a–d; cf. 47a–c). There never has been, nor will be, a great redeemer from heaven whose arrival in history transforms by a single stroke mankind's relationship with God; nor for this immortal world will there be an end of days when God takes over completely. Still, the Timaean believer can presumably draw a comfort unavailable to the atheist. The thought that, very probably, in view of what experience shows, rational life in the universe will never be anything but faulty, stumbling, and completely at the mercy of nature and history, cannot gnaw at Timaean believers. They think they behold in the cosmic god the magnificent and invulnerable triumph of an embodied reason not completely different from ours.

School of Philosophical, Anthropological, and Film Studies
University of St Andrews
The Scores
St Andrews
Fife KY16 9AL
Scotland
UK

REFERENCES

Carone, Gabriela 2005: *Plato's Cosmology and its Ethical Dimensions.* Cambridge: Cambridge University Press.

Cornford, F. M. 1937: *Plato's Cosmology: The* Timaeus *of Plato Translated with a Running Commentary.* London: Kegan Paul.

Hasker, W. 1998: 'Creation and Conservation, Religious Doctrine of'. *Routledge Encyclopedia of Philosophy*, ed. Edward Craig, <http://www.rep. routledge. com>.

Plato 1900–07: *Platonis Opera*, 5 vols.. ed. J. Burnet. Oxford: Clarendon Press.

©2008 THE ARISTOTELIAN SOCIETY
Proceedings of the Aristotelian Society Supplementary Volume LXXXII
doi: 10.1111/j.1467-8349.2008.00159.x

Scepticism and Epistemic Value
Duncan Pritchard and Martijn Blaauw

I — Duncan Pritchard

Radical Scepticism, Epistemic Luck, and Epistemic Value

It is argued that it is beneficial to view the debate regarding radical scepticism through the lens of epistemic value. In particular, it is claimed that we should regard radical scepticism as aiming to deprive us of an epistemic standing that is of special value to us, and that this methodological constraint on our dealings with radical scepticism potentially has important ramifications for how we assess the success of an anti-sceptical strategy.

Suppose we take it as a starting-point in our dealings with radical sceptical arguments that they are trying to demonstrate that the epistemic standing in question which, they claim, is unavailable to us—knowledge, typically—is an epistemic standing that is of distinctive value. This is a sensible enough working assumption, after all, since if the epistemic standing that is, it seems, snatched from us by the (successful) radical sceptical argument is not of special value, then it is hard to see why anyone should particularly care. Put another way, if the epistemic standing in question is not distinctively valuable, then why is our response to the sceptical argument not simply a resigned shrug?

On the face of it, such a working assumption may seem pretty benign, since we tend to take it for granted that the targets of radical sceptical arguments are indeed of special value to us. Suppose, however, that it could be demonstrated that the relevant epistemic standing is not of distinctive value: what then? As it happens, I am suspicious of the idea that knowledge *simpliciter* is distinctively valuable (at least in the way that we typically suppose), and I will sketch why I think this in a moment. Accordingly, this issue looms large for me. What I propose to explore here is how such a perspective on the value of knowledge impacts on our understanding of the radical sceptical argument. More generally, I want to argue that

©2008 The Aristotelian Society
Proceedings of the Aristotelian Society Supplementary Volume LXXXII
doi: 10.1111/j.1467-8349.2008.00160.x

considerations about epistemic value can potentially have important ramifications for the debate regarding radical scepticism.

I

Following most contemporary epistemologists, I will take radical scepticism to be primarily concerned with knowledge. Such scepticism has been formulated in various ways, but the overarching formulation in recent times has been along the lines of the following template, where '*E*' is some 'everyday' proposition (i.e. a proposition which we all tend to think that we know, such as that one has two hands), and '*SH*' is a radical sceptical hypothesis which is logically inconsistent with the everyday proposition (e.g. that one is a brain in a vat (BIV)):

> *The Template Radical Sceptical Argument*
> (s1) *S* does not know not-SH.
> (s2) If *S* does not know not-*SH*, then *S* does not know *E*.
> (sc) *S* does not know *E*.[1]

The motivation for the first premiss concerns the fact that there is, so the argument goes at any rate, nothing available to us to indicate that we are not the victims of a radical sceptical hypothesis. Since, for example, my experience of being a BIV who merely seems to have two hands would be subjectively indistinguishable from my experience of actually having two hands in normal circumstances, the thought goes that one cannot possibly know that one is not envatted. The same goes for other radical sceptical hypotheses.

The motivation for the second premiss comes from the 'closure' principle for knowledge, which we can formulate as follows:

> *The Closure Principle for Knowledge*
> If *S* knows that *p*, and *S* competently deduces *q* from *p* (thereby coming to believe *q* while retaining her knowledge that *p*), then *S* knows that *q*.[2]

---

[1] For further discussion of this template radical sceptical argument, and its role in contemporary epistemology, see Pritchard (2002*a*). For a critical discussion of whether the sceptical argument is best expressed in this fashion, see Pritchard (2005*b*).

[2] This formulation of the closure principle is essentially that offered by Williamson (2000, p. 117) and Hawthorne (2005, p. 29).

©2008 THE ARISTOTELIAN SOCIETY
Proceedings of the Aristotelian Society Supplementary Volume LXXXII
doi: 10.1111/j.1467-8349.2008.00160.x

This principle is clearly highly intuitive. Moreover, given that we can legitimately suppose that any reasonably reflective agent is at least in a position to know the relevant entailment once prompted (i.e. that the target E-type proposition entails the target not-SH-type proposition), it follows from closure that our inability to know the denials of sceptical hypotheses is able to undermine our putative knowledge of E-type propositions. Indeed, given that the epistemic standing of our belief in just about any E-type proposition can be threatened in this way—one would just need to vary the sceptical hypothesis to suit—it follows that radical scepticism quickly ensues.

We thus have two highly intuitive premises as part of a valid argument which generates a sceptical conclusion. Given that the sceptical conclusion is so counterintuitive, what we have on our hands is thus a paradox.

II

There are various ways of responding to this argument. One approach, advanced by Fred Dretske (1970) and Robert Nozick (1981) amongst others, is to block the argument by denying the closure principle. Given the intuitive nature of this principle, however, this is more easily said than done, and this proposal has since fallen into disfavour. Accordingly, I won't explore it further here.[3] With closure intact, however—at least in a form in which it can appropriately support (s2) of the sceptical argument—the options for evading radical scepticism of this sort become rather limited. Indeed, a few complications aside, I think most would now agree that the premiss in the sceptical argument that needs to be denied is (s1).[4] The anti-sceptical position that results is one that we might broadly call 'Moorean'.[5]

---

[3] For a recent discussion of the status of the closure principle, see the exchange between Dretske (2005a, 2005b) and Hawthorne (2005).

[4] One complication in this regard is the contrastivist approach as defended, for example, by Schaffer (2005). According to this proposal, there is no such thing as knowing a proposition *simpliciter*; rather, all knowledge is to be understood as relative to a specific set of contrasts (i.e. not-*p* propositions), and this has important ramifications for how one should understand the sceptical argument. I have not the space to explore the contrastivist response to radical scepticism here; for further discussion, see Pritchard (forthcoming a).

[5] Even though, depending on the details of the specific rendering of the view in question, the position may not in practice resemble G. E. Moore's own response to the sceptic very much at all.

©2008 THE ARISTOTELIAN SOCIETY
Proceedings of the Aristotelian Society Supplementary Volume LXXXII
doi: 10.1111/j.1467-8349.2008.00160.x

There are various ways of defending a Moorean anti-sceptical strategy, some more concessive to the sceptic than others. For example, at one end of the spectrum of concessiveness, one might argue that one has merely a standing entitlement to believe in the denials of sceptical hypotheses, even though one lacks any specific grounds to epistemically support such belief.[6] Alternatively, at the other end of the spectrum, one might argue that one has factive epistemic support in favour of one's belief in this regard, such that the epistemic support one has for this belief actually *entails* the target proposition.[7] One could also be more or less concessive to scepticism along a different axis in terms of the extent to which one wishes to accommodate our sceptical intuitions—in particular, our intuition, at least in contexts in which the problem of scepticism is under discussion, that there is *something* right about scepticism. One concessive option in this regard is to adopt some form of contextualism and so argue that in certain contexts what the sceptic claims is true.[8] Still, the point remains that while there are a myriad of anti-sceptical approaches in play here, the step in the radical sceptical argument above that is ultimately objected to is (s1).

Moreover, notice that the concession to the sceptic all Moorean anti-sceptical strategies make is to allow that agents are unable to distinguish between everyday experiences and the sort of sceptical experiences that would be generated by being the victim of a (relevant) sceptical hypothesis. So even if one argues that we do have adequate evidence in favour of our beliefs in the denials of sceptical hypotheses, one still faces the task of treading the delicate path of endorsing this claim while nonetheless conceding that agents lack the relevant discriminatory powers.

Of course, one might be tempted to take the heroic option here of maintaining that there is nothing more to telling the difference between two scenarios than knowing that the one scenario has ob-

---

[6] See, for example, Wright (2004) for an anti-sceptical proposal which is cast along these lines.

[7] This would be one way of reading the brand of anti-scepticism propounded by McDowell (1995), for example, although it is debatable whether McDowell himself would ever put the point in quite these terms. See Pritchard (2008c) for further discussion of this reading. See also Williamson (2000, ch. 8).

[8] The kind of contextualism that I have in mind here is attributer contextualism, of the sort defended by, for example, DeRose (1995), Lewis (1996) and Cohen (2000). Other types of view could also be understood as aiming to accommodate sceptical intuitions along broadly contextualist lines, however, such as a subject contextualism of the sort defended (under a very different name) by Hawthorne (2004) and Stanley (2005).

©2008 THE ARISTOTELIAN SOCIETY
Proceedings of the Aristotelian Society Supplementary Volume LXXXII
doi: 10.1111/j.1467-8349.2008.00160.x

tained rather than the other. After all, with closure in play, it will follow on the Moorean view that one does know both the *E*-type and the not-*SH*-type proposition. For example, one will know that one has hands and that one is not envatted, and thus that one has hands rather than being handlessly envatted. The temptation, then, is to maintain that one can tell the difference between having hands and being a handless BIV after all, since one is able to know that the one possibility has obtained and the other hasn't. I take it that this sort of claim will not stand up to closer scrutiny, however, attractive though it may be given the potential theoretical pay-off involved.

In order to see this, forget about scepticism for a moment, and consider instead an apparently normal situation in which one is at home with one's children. Suppose now that someone raises the error possibility that you are not at home with your children at all, but are instead sitting next to extremely lifelike robots pretending to be your children who were substituted a few moments ago when you were temporarily distracted. Given everything that you know about the plausibility of this scenario, you are surely in a position to rationally dismiss it. Indeed, once you have rationally formed a view as to why you are entitled to dismiss this error possibility we would describe your epistemic situation as being one in which (i) you know that the persons before you are your children, and (ii) you know that the persons before you are not extremely lifelike robots. In short, you know that it is your children who are before you rather than extremely lifelike robots.

Still, all this is entirely compatible with the idea that were there to be extremely lifelike robots before you, you wouldn't be able to tell the difference. That is, your belief in this regard is *insensitive*—viz., you would continue to believe that it is your children before you in such a scenario even though what you are in fact looking at are lifelike robots. After all, your grounds in support of your knowledge that it is your children before you rather than extremely lifelike robots need have nothing to do with whether you can tell the difference between the two, but would in all likelihood instead concern other factors—as noted above, it would probably just concern your grounded judgement of the plausibility of this scenario given the background information available to you. Moreover, given the implausibility of the error possibility in question, we surely wouldn't insist that you should have specific grounds to dismiss it in order to know that you are looking at your children. We wouldn't require,

©2008 THE ARISTOTELIAN SOCIETY
Proceedings of the Aristotelian Society Supplementary Volume LXXXII
doi: 10.1111/j.1467-8349.2008.00160.x

for example, that you should examine your children closely to ensure that they aren't lifelike robots (run a Turing test on them, say).

There is thus more to being able to tell the difference between two competing scenarios than simply knowing that the one scenario has obtained rather than the other.[9] With this in mind, one should resist the temptation to argue that because on the anti-sceptical approach which denies (s1) one is able to know both the *E*-type proposition and the denial of the *SH*-type proposition, one can thereby perform the incredible feat of being able to tell the difference between normal experiences and their sceptical counterparts.

•   III

I noted above that I am suspicious of the idea that knowledge *simpliciter* is distinctively valuable, at least in the way that we typically suppose. I think it is pretty clear that we instinctively regard knowledge as distinctively valuable. If this were not the case, then it would be mysterious why so much of our epistemological theorizing unhesitatingly focuses on knowledge rather than on other lesser epistemic standings. Moreover, various thought-experiments also lend support to this claim. For example, suppose you were faced with the choice between knowing a proposition and, say, merely truly believing it. Suppose further that it is stipulated in advance that there will be no practical implications resting on your decision. Still, wouldn't you prefer to have knowledge?

The latter observation in particular suggests that the way in which we instinctively value knowledge is as something which is good in its own right, regardless of any additional instrumental value it might have. That is, what makes knowledge distinctively valuable, on this view, is that it is non-instrumentally, or *finally*, valuable. Furthermore, notice that if it is right that knowledge—unlike lesser epistemic standings, like reliably formed belief—is finally valuable in this way, then this would surely explain why we unhesitatingly focus on knowledge in our epistemological theorizing, rather than on other epistemic standings. After all, whereas these other epistemic standings may be of great instrumental value, it is only when we get to the epistemic standing picked out by

---

[9] I expand on this point, and its epistemological ramifications, in Pritchard (2008*b*).

©2008 THE ARISTOTELIAN SOCIETY
Proceedings of the Aristotelian Society Supplementary Volume LXXXII
doi: 10.1111/j.1467-8349.2008.00160.x

knowledge that we have something which is good in its own right. Put another way, the difference in value between knowledge and lesser epistemic standings is a difference in kind, and not merely a difference in degree.

In contrast, if knowledge were just instrumentally valuable then it is hard to see how this could explain the way in which we instinctively value knowledge. For example, one might have a picture on which knowledge lay on a continuum of instrumental epistemic value, with lesser epistemic standings generally enjoying lesser degrees of instrumental value and more enhanced epistemic standings generally enjoying greater degrees of epistemic value. On this 'continuum' picture of the value of knowledge, however, it is mysterious why we should fixate on the particular point on the continuum that knowledge marks out, rather than, say, a point just before or just after.

The value that we intuitively attach to knowledge is thus final value, a final value that lesser epistemic standings lack.[10]

IV

Of course, that we treat something as finally valuable does not mean that we are right to do so (think, for example, of the miser). The question, then, is whether we are right to finally value knowledge in the way that we do. I am inclined to think not.

I know of only one proposal in the literature that is able to offer a good argument for why knowledge is finally valuable. This is the virtue-theoretic account of the value of knowledge, which gains its clearest expression in recent work by John Greco (2002, 2007, forthcoming a, forthcoming b). Essentially, Greco argues that once we understand knowledge along virtue-theoretic lines then we see that knowledge—unlike lesser epistemic standings—is a form of achievement, and thus, like achievements more generally, something that is valuable in its own right.[11]

---

[10] I develop this line of argument in more detail in Pritchard (2008d, §1). For more on the general issues surrounding the value of knowledge, see Kvanvig (2003) and Pritchard (2007b, 2007c).

[11] Greco, like other virtue epistemologists who have pursued this general line, actually argues that knowledge is *intrinsically* valuable rather than finally valuable (e.g. Greco forthcoming a, §4). It is clear from what he says about the value of knowledge, however, that it is specifically final value that he has in mind, and so this is how I have expressed his view here.

©2008 The Aristotelian Society
Proceedings of the Aristotelian Society Supplementary Volume LXXXII
doi: 10.1111/j.1467-8349.2008.00160.x

There are two claims in play here. The first, which we will call the *final value thesis*, is that achievements are finally valuable. The second, which we will call the *achievement thesis*, is that knowledge, unlike lesser epistemic standings, is a form of achievement. If both theses can be adequately defended, then that would suffice to support the claim that knowledge is distinctively valuable in the sense that the difference in value between knowledge and that which falls short of knowledge is a matter of kind and not merely degree.

Both theses are, in fact, highly plausible, at least once they are understood in the right way. Greco understands achievements to be successes that are because of ability, where the 'because of' relation is to be read in causal explanatory terms—i.e., roughly, that the ability is the best explanation of the success. This certainly seems right. Consider an archer—let's call him 'Archie'—taking aim at a target and successfully hitting the target. Suppose, however, that Archie lacks any relevant archery abilities, such that his success was simply down to luck. In such a case we would not regard Archie's success as being because of his ability, because he lacks the relevant ability. Equally, we would not regard his success as an achievement.

Interestingly, the same goes even if Archie has the relevant ability and is also successful, but where the success is not appropriately related to—i.e. is not *because of*—his ability. Suppose, for example, that Archie's success is 'gettierized', as would happen, for instance, if a freak gust of wind blew his arrow off course but then a second freak gust of wind blew it back on course again. Even though in this case there is the conjunction of success and ability, the success clearly does not constitute an achievement, and the natural explanation for this is that the success is not because of the ability.

The idea that achievements should be understood as successes that are because of ability thus has a great deal to commend it. With achievements so construed, however, it is likewise plausible to suppose that achievements are finally valuable. In order to see this, suppose that the practical benefits of successfully hitting the target are exactly the same regardless of whether or not the success in question is because of one's ability (and so a *bona fide* achievement). Nevertheless, wouldn't one prefer to be successful because of one's ability rather than because of luck? Given that the instrumental value at issue is the same either way, it follows that the greater value we attribute to achievements in such a case reflects a judgement on our part that achievements are finally valuable in a way that successes which fall short of achievements are not. Moreover, there seems no good reason why we shouldn't take this common-sense judgement about the value of achievements at face value.

The final value thesis thus looks compelling, at first pass at least. What about the achievement thesis? Here is where the virtue-theoretic element of the proposal comes to the fore, for virtue epistemologists like Greco argue that knowledge is to be understood as cognitive success (i.e. true belief) that is because of cognitive ability (i.e. intellectual virtue, broadly conceived). Most epistemologists will agree that there must be some ability component to knowledge, since cognitive success that is unrelated to one's ability—and so just down to luck—would clearly not constitute knowledge. What is distinctive about this proposal, however, is that it in effect exclusively defines knowledge in terms of ability, in that it argues that once the relationship between cognitive ability and cognitive success is understood correctly—in terms of the 'because of' relation—there is no need to introduce any further epistemic component into one's analysis of knowledge.[12]

One can see the appeal of such a proposal by considering how it deals with standard Gettier-style cases. After all, such cases tend to involve agents who exhibit the relevant cognitive ability, and who are in addition cognitively successful, and yet who nonetheless lack knowledge because the cognitive success in question is not because of their cognitive ability. Imagine, for example, a farmer looking into a field who, by using her highly reliable perceptual faculties, comes to believe that there is a sheep in the field because she sees a sheep-shaped object there. Suppose further that she is cognitively successful in this regard, in that there really is a sheep in the field. Finally, however, suppose that the success is gettierized in the sense that what the farmer is in fact looking at is a big hairy dog which looks just like a sheep, and which is obscuring from view the real sheep in the field. We would not class such a success as a cognitive achievement, nor would we class it as knowledge.[13] For Greco, the reason why is the same in both cases: the cognitive success in question is not because of the agent's cognitive ability, but is instead

---

[12] See also Sosa (1988, 1991, 2007) and Zagzebski (1996, 1999) for virtue-theoretic accounts of knowledge that are cast along roughly these lines.

[13] This example is due to Chisholm (1977, p. 105).

©2008 THE ARISTOTELIAN SOCIETY
Proceedings of the Aristotelian Society Supplementary Volume LXXXII
doi: 10.1111/j.1467-8349.2008.00160.x

merely down to luck.

There is thus also a great deal of intuitive support for the achieve-ment thesis as well. With both theses in play, the virtue-theoretic ac-count of the distinctive value of knowledge seems to have much to commend it: knowledge, like achievements more generally, is rightly regarded as distinctively valuable because it is finally valuable.

V

Unfortunately, on closer inspection this proposal does not hold wa-ter. I think that many will probably find the final value thesis to be the weaker of the two claims in play here, on account of how there do seem to be some achievements—such as achievements which are very easy, or trivial, or just plain wicked—which are not valuable at all, much less finally valuable. This problem is, however, tractable, for notice that the claim is only that successes *qua* achievements are finally valuable. In particular, it is not part of the view that the over-all (*ultima facie*) value of a success that constitutes an achievement should be particularly great.

To illustrate this point, consider the case of a trivial cognitive achievement. Suppose, for example, that one devotes one's time to pointlessly counting the pebbles on a beach, a task at which one is very successful. Now, one might say that on this view there is noth-ing stopping such trivial successes counting as achievements, and thus as accruing final value. But notice that there is nothing prob-lematic in itself about supposing that a trivial success, *qua* achieve-ment, is finally valuable. The problem only emerges once one further supposes that if a success is finally valuable then it has a high overall value. This conditional, however, is false; indeed, cases like that of the trivial cognitive achievement represent clear coun-terexamples. After all, given the fact that the instrumental value of this success will inevitably be negligible, and given further that the opportunity cost of engaging in such an endeavour will almost cer-tainly be very high—thereby generating quite a lot of disvalue—it follows that the overall value of this success will be very low (per-haps even negative), even despite the fact that it generates some final value.

Accordingly, I don't think the problem with the virtue-theoretic account of the value of knowledge lies with the final value thesis, at

©2008 The Aristotelian Society
Proceedings of the Aristotelian Society Supplementary Volume LXXXII
doi: 10.1111/j.1467-8349.2008.00160.x

least once that thesis is understood correctly.[14] Instead, I think the real weak point for this proposal lies with the achievement thesis. In particular, on closer analysis it turns out that knowledge is not a cognitive achievement at all. This is because one can possess knowledge without exhibiting a cognitive achievement, and exhibit a cognitive achievement while lacking knowledge.

Cases of the former are easy to come by, but the most straightforward cases concern testimonial knowledge. Consider an example put forward by Jennifer Lackey (2007), albeit to illustrate a slightly different point. Imagine someone getting off the train in an unfamiliar city and asking the first person she meets for directions to a local landmark. Suppose that the person our hero speaks to has first-hand knowledge of the area and communicates this information to our agent, who promptly forms a true belief about the right way to go. Unless we know an awful lot less than we think we do, then we often gain testimonial knowledge in this fashion. Notice, however, that we wouldn't say that it is because of our *agent's* cognitive abilities that she is cognitively successful—i.e. that the explanation for her cognitive success is specifically her cognitive abilities. (We might say that it is because of her informant's cognitive abilities that she is successful, but that's a different matter.) Testimonial knowledge of this sort, then, seems to be available even in the absence of a cognitive achievement.

It's worth spending a little time explaining exactly what the point being made here is. In particular, it is not being denied that our hero is exercising relevant cognitive abilities in this case, such that her cognitive abilities are playing *some* role in that success. We would expect her to be appropriately sensitive to potential defeaters, for example, such as an informant displaying body language which would indicate that she was not trustworthy. The point is only that such cases illustrate that one can gain knowledge by exhibiting a cognitive

---

[14] A second way of defending the final value thesis against this line of objection is to opt for a kind of holism about value. Just as one might hold that pain is the sort of thing which is generally bad but sometimes good, so one might argue that knowledge is the kind of thing which is generally finally valuable but sometimes—e.g. where the cognitive success in question is trivial, etc.—not finally valuable. The reason why such an approach might work is that all the virtue-theoretic account of the value of knowledge is aiming to account for is why knowledge is distinctively valuable in the way that we think it is, and demonstrating that it is *generally* finally valuable would probably suffice in this regard (at least so long as there is no lesser epistemic standing which is also generally finally valuable). I am grateful to Mike Ridge for this suggestion. For further discussion of what is required of an adequate account of the distinctive value of knowledge, see Pritchard (2007*b*, 2007*c*, 2008*d*).

©2008 THE ARISTOTELIAN SOCIETY
Proceedings of the Aristotelian Society Supplementary Volume LXXXII
doi: 10.1111/j.1467-8349.2008.00160.x

success which is not best explained in terms of one's own cognitive ability (and which is thus not because of that cognitive ability). There is thus sometimes less to knowledge than cognitive achievement.

Significantly, there is also sometimes more to knowledge than a cognitive achievement too. In order to see this, consider again the case of Archie described above. This time, though, imagine that Archie selects his target from a range of potential targets entirely at random before skilfully firing his arrow and hitting the target. Let us stipulate that the success here is not subject to Gettier-style luck, in that nothing intervenes between the ability and the success, such as the two freak gusts of wind which fortuitously cancel each other out that were described above. Nevertheless, the success is lucky because, unbeknownst to Archie, all of the other targets that he could have fired at contained force fields which would usually repel arrows. Fortunately, Archie just happened to fire at the one target that lacked such a force field. His success is thus lucky in the sense that he could very easily have been unsuccessful.   .

Interestingly, however, I take it that we have a strong intuition in this case that even though the success in question is lucky, this does not prevent Archie from exhibiting a genuine achievement. Indeed, we would naturally say that his success—his hitting of the target—is because of his skills at archery. What this highlights is that there are two distinct ways in which a success could be lucky, only one of which is incompatible with achievements. On the one hand, there is the kind of luck found in Gettier-style cases in which something intervenes between the ability and the success to ensure that the success is not because of the ability. On the other hand, there is the kind of 'environmental' luck which does not intervene between ability and success in this way but rather simply reflects some unfortunate feature of the environment which would usually prevent success but which does not do so in this case. Environmental luck, it turns out, is compatible with genuine achievements, unlike Gettier-style luck.

The importance of this distinction between two types of luck and their relationship to achievements becomes apparent once one considers the epistemological analogue of the above case. Indeed, the famous 'barn façade' example is structurally analogous to the case involving Archie just described. In particular, unlike a standard Gettier-style case, such as that involving the farmer described above, in the barn façade case nothing intervenes between the agent's cognitive ability and her cognitive success. She really does see a barn after all (and not, say, something that merely looks like a barn but which is obscuring from view a genuine barn, or something like that). Nevertheless, the agent's belief is still lucky in the sense that she could very easily have been mistaken. The luck in question is thus environmental luck. Had the agent been looking at any other barn-shaped object in the area then she would have formed a false belief; it is just fortunate that despite the epistemically unfriendly nature of the environment, she happens nonetheless to be cognitively successful. Moreover, notice that just as in the Archie case involving environmental luck, where we are inclined to say that a genuine achievement is being exhibited, similarly there seems no reason why we should deny that the agent in this case is not exhibiting a genuine cognitive achievement. Wouldn't we say that her cognitive success is because of her cognitive abilities? Even so, she lacks knowledge.

The moral is that there is sometimes more to knowledge than exhibiting a cognitive achievement, and I suggest that this point has been overlooked by proponents of the virtue-theoretic proposal because they have failed to notice the distinction between Gettier-style and environmental epistemic luck (indeed, between Gettier-style and environmental luck more generally).

VI

Now I don't want to deny that there are moves available to someone like Greco when it comes to responding to these problems. He could insist, for example, that the testimonial case described above is an example in which the agent's knowledge does reflect a cognitive achievement, and thus deny our intuitions in this case. Equally, he could also argue that there are relevant disanalogies between the Archer case and the barn façade case which can enable him to resist the conclusion that a cognitive achievement is exhibited in the latter situation even though an achievement is exhibited in the former. And, indeed, there are other potential moves available.

Space prevents me from exploring these responses here.[15] In any case, the line of argument put forward in the last section is not meant to constitute a knock-down argument against the view any-

---

[15] I describe some of the moves that Greco makes in the light of this line of objection and evaluate their merits in Pritchard (2008d, 2008e, forthcoming b).

way. Rather the point of this argument is to show that intuition in
fact points towards a very different conception of knowledge, one
on which knowledge and cognitive achievements come apart (in
both directions).[16]

If the above line of argument is accepted then it should become
clear why I am suspicious about the kind of distinctive value that we
tend to ascribe to knowledge. Assuming that no further argument
can be supplied in defence of the thesis that knowledge is finally valuable, then it seems that all we are entitled to suppose is that cognitive achievement, an epistemic standing which can fall short of
knowledge, is finally valuable. But if that's right, then there is nothing particularly special about knowledge; in particular, knowledge is
not more valuable, as a matter of kind and not merely degree, than
that which falls short of knowledge.

In what follows, I will take it as given that no further argument in
defence of the final value of knowledge is available, and thus conclude that the failure of the virtue-theoretic defence of the final
value of knowledge entails that knowledge is not finally valuable.
Moreover, I will also take it as given that cognitive achievements are
finally valuable. I will then explore what consequences these two
claims have for the problem of radical scepticism.

VII

As explained there, the standard way to resolve the radical sceptical
argument is by arguing—in a broadly 'Moorean' fashion—that we
are able to know the denials of sceptical hypotheses after all, even
though we are unable to distinguish between ordinary circumstances and the corresponding sceptical scenario. Given that we grant
that knowledge is not distinctively valuable in the manner that we
pre-theoretically suppose, the interesting question we now need to
ask is whether the success of such a Moorean anti-sceptical strategy
would ensure that we have thereby rescued from the sceptic's grasp
a distinctively valuable epistemic standing. In particular, assuming

---

[16] In particular, I argue elsewhere that considerations like this point towards what I term an
'anti-luck virtue epistemology'. I expand on what such a view involves in Pritchard (2008a,
2008d). Interestingly, although this view is motivated in a very different way, such a proposal is very close in spirit to the sort of view that Greco defended in earlier work, and
abandoned in favour of the more robust virtue-theoretic proposal discussed here. See, for
example, Greco (1999, 2000).

©2008 The Aristotelian Society
Proceedings of the Aristotelian Society Supplementary Volume LXXXII
doi: 10.1111/j.1467-8349.2008.00160.x

the success of the Moorean strategy, is the kind of knowledge that is preserved potentially of the distinctively valuable sort such that it involves genuine cognitive achievement?

We can get a better handle on what is at issue here by reformulating the template sceptical argument outlined above specifically in terms of a type of knowledge which essentially involves cognitive achievement—let's call it 'knowledge+'—and considering each of the reformulated premises in turn. Here, then, is the new version of the sceptical argument:

> The Template Radical Sceptical Argument Reformulated
> (s1+) S does not know+ not-SH.
> (s2+) If S does not know+ not-SH, then S does not know+ E.
> (sc+) S does not know+ E.

The crux of the matter is that such an argument still has the potential to pose a worrisome sceptical challenge, since while its conclusion is consistent with our having widespread knowledge of E-type propositions, it nevertheless has the capacity to generate a form of scepticism which deprives us of an epistemic standing that is of special value to us.

In order to give the Moorean approach the best run for its money, let us grant for the sake of argument the most robust form of Mooreanism available—i.e. the view that our knowledge, even of the denials of sceptical hypotheses, is typically supported by factive grounds. With this in mind, let us examine first the plausibility of (s1+).

Given the form of Mooreanism in play, there are certainly good grounds for supposing that the agent in question is able to know that she is not the victim of a sceptical hypothesis. In normal circumstances there can be no question that the truth of the target belief—i.e. that one is not the victim of a sceptical hypothesis—is not a matter of luck. After all, in such circumstances a belief of this sort could not very easily be false, since an awful lot would need to change about the world in order to ensure the falsity of this belief. Accordingly, it is plausible to suppose that whatever anti-luck condition one imposed on one's theory of knowledge would be met.[17] Moreover, if the belief is supported by factive grounds, then we ought to be able to allow that this belief would satisfy other constraints we might

---

[17] In particular, the belief would be 'safe'. For more on safety and the extent to which it captures the 'anti-luck' requirement on knowledge, see Sosa (1999) and Pritchard (2002b, 2005a, 2007a).

want to lay down on knowledge possession. The belief would surely be adequately supported by evidence, for example. There is thus a strong *prima facie* case for agreeing with the robust Moorean that one can know the denials of sceptical hypotheses.

Nevertheless, since we have already seen that one can have knowledge without thereby exhibiting a cognitive achievement— and that it is cognitive achievements which are distinctively valuable—that the conditions for knowledge are satisfied does not ensure that the kind of knowledge in question is distinctively valuable. In short, it does not ensure that one has knowledge+, which is the kind of knowledge specifically at issue in (s1+). Moreover, there is every reason for supposing that the kind of knowledge in play here is not knowledge+. For recall, in order to exhibit a cognitive achievement the truth of one's belief needs to because of the exercise of one's relevant cognitive abilities. It is, however, wholly unintuitive to suppose that the truth of an agent's belief that she is not, say, a BIV is *because of* her cognitive ability (even if we are willing to grant that her cognitive ability plays some substantive role in this cognitive success). Indeed, if anything, it seems that the cognitive success in question here is more creditable to the good fortune of being in an epistemically friendly environment than it is to the agent's cognitive abilities.

That we lack the relevant discriminatory abilities is key to understanding why this is so. If one is unable to discriminate between ordinary scenarios and sceptical scenarios, and one is in addition unable to rationally adduce independent epistemic support in favour of the target belief, then it can hardly be the case that one's cognitive success when one believes truly that one is not the victim of a sceptical hypothesis is because of one's own cognitive ability.

This claim requires some development, and part of the reason for this is that one might think that whether or not this is so depends on the kind of Moorean proposal in question. That is, one might argue that provided one's Mooreanism is of the robust type that we are interested in, such that it allows that one's beliefs in the denials of sceptical hypotheses could be supported by factive grounds, then there is no reason to deny that one's cognitive success in such a case is because of one's cognitive ability.

In order to explore this issue it will be helpful to return to the example given in §11 which was meant to illustrate that one can have better evidence for believing that one scenario has obtained rather

than an alternative scenario, and thereby for knowing that the one
scenario has obtained rather than the alternative scenario, even
though one cannot discriminate between the two scenarios.[18] The
example I offered concerned being able to come to know, in normal
circumstances, that one is presently looking at one's children rather
than extremely lifelike robots. The thought was that given the excellent background evidence one possesses, which indicates that the error possibility in question is so remote as to be discountable, it
follows that one is in a position to rationally dismiss this error possibility, and thereby have adequate grounds to support one's knowledge that one is presently looking at one's children rather than
extremely lifelike robots. Crucially, however, it was pointed out that
knowledge of this sort can be possessed—and, indeed, will usually
be possessed—even though one is unable to discriminate between
one's children and extremely lifelike robots.

The relevance of this example for our present discussion is that an
agent who knows, on this evidential basis, that she is not presently
looking at extremely lifelike robots which are masquerading as her
children surely *does* exhibit a cognitive achievement. While it is un-
deniable that her cognitive success is not because of the operation of
her relevant discriminative abilities, that doesn't undermine the fact
that the truth of her belief (that she is not presently looking at extremely lifelike robots) does seem to be because of her cognitive
ability more generally. After all, she has weighed up the evidence
available to her in order to form an informed judgement on the matter. If this is right, however, then one might naturally wonder why a
Moorean response to the sceptical problem which allowed our
knowledge of the denials of sceptical hypotheses to be supported by
adequate evidence could not similarly argue that such knowledge
also involves a cognitive achievement.

There is, however, a crucial disanalogy between the two cases,
and this is that the agent in the 'robot' case, while lacking the relevant discriminatory capacities, is nevertheless able to rationally adduce independent grounds in favour of her belief. Such independent
grounds are not, however, rationally available to the agent in the
sceptical case, even assuming a robust form of Mooreanism.

In the robot case, even though the agent cannot discriminate between the two alternative scenarios she is nonetheless able to ration-

---

[18] Recall that for the purposes of this example we were setting sceptical worries to one side.

©2008 THE ARISTOTELIAN SOCIETY
Proceedings of the Aristotelian Society Supplementary Volume LXXXII
doi: 10.1111/j.1467-8349.2008.00160.x

ally enhance the epistemic support for her belief that the target error possibility does not obtain by reflecting on relevant background information that is available to her and which is not itself called into question by that error possibility (and which is thus in this sense *independent* of that error possibility). Indeed, were our agent to be unable to rationally adduce independent grounds in favour of her belief, then we would not regard her belief as being true because of her cognitive abilities at all, and hence we would not regard it as a cognitive achievement. After all, such an agent would be in a position of being aware of the target error possibility and believing that it does not obtain, and yet regarding herself as lacking any independent rational basis for holding this belief. In effect, she would simply be groundlessly trusting that she is in the kind of epistemically friendly environment that she takes herself to be in; but if that's right, then the truth of her belief cannot be because of her cognitive abilities.

Crucially, in the sceptical case the agent lacks both the discriminatory capacities *and* is unable to undertake the kind of rational process that is possible in the robot case. We have already noted that the discriminatory capacities are lacking, so the crux of the matter is the unavailability of the relevant rational process. The reason why this is unavailable is that sceptical error possibilities by their nature call into question the evidential support one possesses for one's beliefs *en masse*. Accordingly, there is no rational route by which the agent can adduce independent grounds in favour of her belief that she is not the victim of a sceptical hypothesis, since whatever background evidence she might appeal to will be itself problematized by the sceptical hypothesis.

From a rational perspective, then, all one can do is simply reflect that so long as one is indeed in the normal circumstances that one takes oneself to be in, then one has excellent evidence in support of one's belief that one is not a victim of a sceptical hypothesis. But that is just to grant that whether or not one's belief in this regard is true is to a substantive degree down to the good fortune of being in an epistemically friendly environment rather than being due to one's own cognitive ability. In effect, one's epistemic position is akin to that of the agent in the robot case who is aware of a certain error possibility but who is unable to rationally form a judgement as to why she is entitled to dismiss it. Just as this agent's true belief that she is not a victim of this error possibility does not constitute a cognitive achievement, neither does one's true belief that one is not the victim of a sceptical hypothesis.

So in order to exhibit a cognitive achievement, one must either appropriately exercise one's discriminative capacities or else be in a position to rationally adduce independent grounds in favour of what one's believes in order to compensate for the lack of such discriminatory capacities. Since one is unable to meet either condition when it comes to one's belief that one is not the victim of a sceptical hypothesis, it follows that such a belief, when true, does not constitute a cognitive achievement. So even if the Moorean is right that one can know such propositions, it does not follow that one can have knowledge+ of them, and hence (s1+) is on strong ground.

VIII

Still, one might argue that even though one's knowledge that one is not the victim of a sceptical hypothesis does not involve a cognitive achievement, it doesn't follow that one's knowledge of E-type propositions also doesn't involve a cognitive achievement. Couldn't it be the case that the cognitive success involved in the latter case does constitute a cognitive achievement, even though the cognitive success in the former case doesn't? In effect, the point in play here is that it is (s2+) that is the contentious premise in the reformulated sceptical argument.

One could regard (s2+) as being motivated by a sister principle to the closure principle that motivated (s2) which explicitly focuses on knowledge+:

> *The Closure Principle for Knowledge+*
> If S knows+ that p, and S competently deduces q from p (thereby coming to believe q while retaining her knowledge+ that p), then S knows+ that q.

With this principle in play, it would not be hard to make a strong case for (s2+). Moreover, there does seem to be a great deal of intuitive support for such a principle. After all, if the truth of one's belief in a (known) proposition is because of one's cognitive ability, and so constitutes a cognitive achievement, then it is hard to see why any further knowledge which one competently deduces from that knowledge should involve a belief the truth of which is related to one's cognitive ability to any lesser degree. Indeed, if anything, shouldn't the presence of the competent deduction actually *enhance* the extent to which the truth of one's belief is creditable to one's own cognitive abilities?

One might think that one could adapt the robot case to generate a counterexample to this principle. Suppose, for example, that at time t_1 our hero knows+ that the persons before her are her children. Suppose now, however, that at t_2 she becomes aware of the error possibility that she might instead be looking at extremely lifelike robots and that she lacks the background information that would enable her to rationally adduce independent grounds in favour of her belief in the denial of this error possibility. Nevertheless, she does recognize that this error possibility is inconsistent with something that she believes (indeed knows+), and so she competently deduces on this basis that this error possibility is false. Given what we have said earlier, while she might come to know the denial of the error possibility on this basis, she cannot come to know+ this proposition, because her true belief would not constitute a cognitive achievement. Given that by hypothesis she does know+ the antecedent proposition, however, then it seems we have a counterexample to the closure principle for knowledge+.

On closer inspection, however, such a putative counterexample fails to convince. After all, if we really are to suppose that the agent is unable to rationally adduce independent grounds in support of her belief in the denial of the error possibility, then why would we continue to grant that she has knowledge+ of the antecedent proposition? Indeed, wouldn't the fact that someone was struck dumb by the presentation of an error possibility of this sort indicate that their knowledge of the antecedent proposition (in so far as we continue to grant that they do have knowledge of this proposition) is far more 'brute' than it first appeared? (It's not as if such independent grounds are hard to come by, after all).

With this point in mind, there is a lot of *prima facie* support for the knowledge+ closure principle. The problem, of course, is that with a closure principle of this sort in play, (s2+) immediately follows. Moreover, since we have already noted that there is a strong case in favour of (s1+), the sceptical conclusion (sc+) also follows.

IX

No doubt there will be moves available to the anti-sceptic in this respect; the point of this paper has not been to supply a definitive basis for a new form of scepticism, but rather to demonstrate that viewing the problem of scepticism through the lens of epistemic value highlights a very different sceptical challenge that needs responding to—viz., that while we might well have much of the knowledge that we typically suppose ourselves to have, the type of knowledge that we possess may not be of the specially valuable variety. Perhaps this is a conclusion that we can ultimately grant to the sceptic; granting it certainly won't be as intellectually disastrous as allowing that widespread knowledge is impossible. Nevertheless, it is clearly a conclusion that is, to say the least, uncomfortable. By definition, if the sceptic deprives us of something that is of special value to us, then that is something that should concern us.[19]

Department of Philosophy
University of Edinburgh
David Hume Tower
George Square
Edinburgh EH9 9JX
Scotland
UK

REFERENCES

Chisholm, Roderick M. 1977: *Theory of Knowledge*, 2nd edn. Englewood Cliffs, NJ: Prentice-Hall.
Cohen, Stewart 2000: 'Contextualism and Skepticism'. *Philosophical Issues*, 10, pp. 94–107.
DeRose, Keith 1995: 'Solving the Skeptical Problem'. *Philosophical Review*, 104, pp. 1–52.
Dretske, Fred I. 1970: 'Epistemic Operators'. *Journal of Philosophy*, 67, pp. 1007–23.
——2005a: 'The Case Against Closure'. In Ernest Sosa and Michael Steup (eds.), *Contemporary Debates in Epistemology*, pp. 13–26. Oxford: Blackwell.

[19] I am grateful to Adam Carter and John Turri for detailed comments on an earlier version of this paper. Thanks also to Jennifer Lackey and Mike Ridge.

——2005*b*: 'Reply to Hawthorne'. In Ernest Sosa and Michael Steup (eds.), *Contemporary Debates in Epistemology*, pp. 43–6. Oxford: Blackwell.

Greco, John 1999: 'Agent Reliabilism'. *Philosophical Perspectives*, 13, pp. 273–96.

——2000: *Putting Skeptics in their Place: The Nature of Skeptical Arguments and their Role in Philosophical Inquiry*. Cambridge: Cambridge University Press.

——2002: 'Knowledge as Credit for True Belief'. In Michael DePaul and Linda Zagzebski (eds.), *Intellectual Virtue: Perspectives from Ethics and Epistemology*. Oxford: Oxford University Press.

——2007: 'The Nature of Ability and the Purpose of Knowledge' (typescript).

——forthcoming *a*: 'The Value Problem'. In Adrian Haddock, Alan Millar and Duncan Pritchard (eds.), *The Value of Knowledge*. Oxford: Oxford University Press.

——forthcoming *b*: 'What's Wrong With Contextualism?' *Philosophical Quarterly*.

Hawthorne, John 2004: *Knowledge and Lotteries*. Oxford: Clarendon Press.

——2005: 'The Case for Closure'. In Ernest Sosa and Michael Steup (eds.), *Contemporary Debates in Epistemology* , pp. 26–43. Oxford: Blackwell.

Kvanvig, Jonathan L. 2003: *The Value of Knowledge and the Pursuit of Understanding*. Cambridge: Cambridge University Press.

Lackey, Jennifer 2007: 'Why We Don't Deserve Credit for Everything We Know'. *Synthese*, 158(3), pp. 345–61.

Lewis, David 1996: 'Elusive Knowledge'. *Australasian Journal of Philosophy*, 74, pp. 549–67.

McDowell, John 1995: 'Knowledge and the Internal'. *Philosophy and Phenomenological Research*, 55, pp. 877–93.

Nozick, Robert 1981: *Philosophical Explanations*. Oxford: Oxford University Press.

Pritchard, Duncan 2002*a*: 'Recent Work on Radical Skepticism'. *American Philosophical Quarterly*, 39, pp. 215–57.

——2002*b*: 'Resurrecting the Moorean Response to the Sceptic'. *International Journal of Philosophical Studies*, 10, pp. 283–307.

——2005*a*: *Epistemic Luck*. Oxford: Oxford University Press.

——2005*b*: 'The Structure of Sceptical Arguments'. *Philosophical Quarterly*, 55, pp. 37–52.

——2007*a*: 'Anti-Luck Epistemology'. *Synthese*, 158(3), pp. 277–97.

——2007*b*: 'Knowledge, the Value of'. *Stanford Encyclopaedia of Philosophy*, ed. E. Zalta, <http://plato.stanford.edu/entries/knowledge-value/>.

——2007*c*: 'Recent Work on Epistemic Value'. *American Philosophical Quarterly*, 44, pp. 85–110.

——2008*a*: 'Anti-Luck Virtue Epistemology' (typescript).

©2008 THE ARISTOTELIAN SOCIETY
Proceedings of the Aristotelian Society Supplementary Volume LXXXII
doi: 10.1111/j.1467-8349.2008.00160.x

——2008b: 'Relevant Alternatives, Perceptual Knowledge and Discrimination'. Forthcoming in *Noûs*.

——2008c: 'McDowellian Neo-Mooreanism'. In Adrian Haddock and Fiona Macpherson (eds.), *Disjunctivism: Perception, Action, Knowledge*. Oxford: Oxford University Press.

——2008d: 'Virtue Epistemology and Epistemic Luck, Revisited'. *Metaphilosophy*, 38, pp. 66–88.

——2008e: 'The Value of Knowledge' (typescript).

——forthcoming a: 'Contrastivism, Evidence and Scepticism'. *Social Epistemology*.

——forthcoming b: 'Greco on Knowledge: Virtues, Contexts, Achievements'. *Philosophical Quarterly*.

Schaffer, Jonathan 2005: 'Contrastive Knowledge'. In Tamar Szabó Gendler and John Hawthorne (eds.), *Oxford Studies in Epistemology*, Volume 1. Oxford: Oxford University Press.

Sosa, Ernest 1988: 'Beyond Skepticism, to the Best of our Knowledge'. *Mind*, 97, pp. 153–89.

——1991: *Knowledge in Perspective: Selected Essays in Epistemology*. Cambridge: Cambridge University Press.

——1999: 'How to Defeat Opposition to Moore'. *Philosophical Perspectives*, 13, 141–54.

——2007: *A Virtue Epistemology: Apt Belief and Reflective Knowledge*. Oxford: Oxford University Press.

Stanley, Jason 2005: *Knowledge and Practical Interests*. Oxford: Clarendon Press.

Williamson, Timothy 2000: *Knowledge and Its Limits*. Oxford: Oxford University Press.

Wright, Crispin 2004: 'Warrant for Nothing (and Foundations for Free)?' *Proceedings of the Aristotelian Society Supplementary Volume* 78, pp. 167–212.

Zagzebski, Linda Trinkaus 1996: *Virtues of the Mind: An Inquiry into the Nature of Virtue and the Ethical Foundations of Knowledge*. Cambridge: Cambridge University Press.

——1999: 'What is Knowledge?' In John Greco and Ernest Sosa (eds.), *The Blackwell Guide to Epistemology*, pp. 92–116. Oxford: Blackwell.

©2008 THE ARISTOTELIAN SOCIETY
Proceedings of the Aristotelian Society Supplementary Volume LXXXII
doi: 10.1111/j.1467-8349.2008.00160.x

II — Martijn Blaauw

Epistemic Value, Achievements, and Questions

A central intuition many epistemologists seem to have is that knowledge is distinctively valuable. In his paper 'Radical Scepticism, Epistemic Luck and Epistemic Value', Duncan Pritchard rejects the virtue-theoretic explanation of this intuition. This explanation says that knowledge is distinctively valuable because it is a cognitive achievement. It is maintained, in the first place, that the arguments Pritchard musters against the thesis that knowledge is a cognitive achievement are unconvincing. It is argued, in the second place, that even if the arguments against the thesis that knowledge is a cognitive achievement *were* convincing, there is another explanation of the intuition that knowledge has final value available: the question-relative treatment of knowledge.

Two of the most prominent debates in contemporary epistemology are the debate surrounding the value of knowledge and the debate surrounding the problem of radical scepticism. As to the first debate, one key question (the *value question*) is: what, if anything, makes knowledge more valuable than mere true belief?[1] As to the second debate, one key challenge (the *sceptical challenge*) is to find a convincing answer to the closure-based problem of radical scepticism.[2]

These two debates have for the most part been treated separately. In his contribution to this symposium, however, Duncan Pritchard (2008) connects them by asking what the consequences for addressing the sceptical challenge will be if we uphold a particular answer to the value question. Pritchard argues that we can distinguish between two types of knowledge: knowledge where no cognitive achievement is involved (knowledge *simpliciter*) and knowledge where a cognitive achievement *is* involved (knowledge *plus*). He then argues that

---

[1] There is a enormous amount of literature on this problem. For a useful overview of the various issues related to the value problem, see Greco (forthcoming *a*) and Pritchard (2007*a*, forthcoming *a*).

[2] There is an equally enormous amount of literature on this problem. For useful overviews of the various issues related to the problem of radical scepticism, see DeRose (1999*b*), Greco (2000) and Pritchard (2002).

©2008 The Aristotelian Society
Proceedings of the Aristotelian Society Supplementary Volume LXXXII
doi: 10.1111/j.1467-8349.2008.00161.x

knowledge *simpliciter* is not distinctively valuable although knowledge *plus* is distinctively valuable. And he continues to argue that even if we are able to solve the problem of radical scepticism when this problem is formulated in terms of knowledge *simpliciter*, we will not be not able to solve this problem when it is formulated in terms of knowledge *plus*. Thus the only thing we can save from the hands of the sceptic is something that is not that valuable at all.

Pritchard raises many interesting issues in his paper, and I cannot possibly do justice to them all. In what follows, then, I will focus on the following two issues. In the first place, I will argue, *contra* Pritchard, that the arguments he puts forward against the thesis that knowledge implies a cognitive achievement are unconvincing (§§ II–III). In the second place, I will argue that even if Pritchard's arguments to the effect that knowledge does not imply a cognitive achievement were convincing, this does not establish the conclusion that knowledge has no final value—there are ways other than the virtue-theoretic proposal to accommodate the intuition that knowledge is distinctively valuable. Specifically, I will argue that the question-relative treatment of knowledge—as recently defended by Jonathan Schaffer (2004, 2005, 2007)—can also explain this intuition (§IV). I will end this paper by making some remarks about the way in which the question-relative treatment of knowledge is able to respond to the problem of radical scepticism (§V). But I will begin this paper by quickly explaining Pritchard's overall argument so as to make it as clear as possible on which elements of this argument I will focus (§I).

I

Pritchard's Argument. Many epistemologists have noted that there is a near-universal intuition that knowledge is something that is distinctively valuable. Here is how Pritchard explains what it means for knowledge to be distinctively valuable:

> [T]he way in which we instinctively value knowledge is as something which is good in its own right, regardless of any additional instrumental value it might have. That is, what makes knowledge distinctively valuable, on this view, is that it is non-instrumentally, or *finally*, valuable. (Pritchard 2008, p. 24)

Call this intuition the *value intuition*. Given the pervasiveness of the

©2008 The Aristotelian Society
Proceedings of the Aristotelian Society Supplementary Volume LXXXII
doi: 10.1111/j.1467-8349.2008.00161.x

value intuition, we might well think that theories of knowledge should at least explain this intuition.[3] According to Pritchard, the best candidate in this respect is the virtue-theoretic explanation of the value intuition as recently defended by, amongst others, John Greco.[4] The basic idea of this specific explanation is that knowledge should be seen as a cognitive achievement, where a cognitive achievement is a successful (i.e. *true*) belief because of one's own abilities. And since achievements in general have final value, *cognitive* achievements take over this final value.

More specifically, the virtue-theoretic explanation of the value intuition consists of the following two claims: (i) achievements are finally valuable (the *final value thesis*); and (ii) knowledge is a form of achievement (the *achievement thesis*). And from (i) and (ii) it follows, of course, that knowledge is itself finally valuable. Now, Pritchard holds that knowledge is *not* finally valuable and so he has to deny either (i) or (ii). And the premiss Pritchard ultimately rejects is (ii)—knowledge is *not* an achievement. He offers two arguments against (ii), and since they will prove important in what follows I will quickly rehearse them.

In the first place, Pritchard argues that one can sometimes know *without* any cognitive achievement on the part of the knowing subject. The example he uses to support this is the testimony example originally due to Jennifer Lackey (2007). In this example, you get off the train in an unfamiliar city and ask the first person you meet for directions. The testifier knows the area well, and gives you the requested information, upon which you form a true belief. It seems intuitive to say that you have acquired knowledge. In this case, however, there is no cognitive achievement on the part of the knowing subject. Rather, or so the argument goes at any rate, it is a cognitive achievement on the part of the testifier that is relevant here. Thus, knowledge on the basis of testimony does not require a cognitive achievement on the part of the subject.

In the second place, Pritchard argues that one can sometimes fail to know *even though* one exhibits a cognitive achievement. In order to illustrate this, Pritchard asks us to imagine Archie the archer who arbitrarily selects his target and skilfully fires his arrow, hitting the

---

[3] But see Jason Baehr (forthcoming) for an interesting discussion about what exactly this intuition is supposed to constrain.

[4] See, for instance, Greco (2002, 2007a, forthcoming a, forthcoming b). See also Sosa (1991, 1999, 2007) for a related view.

target. Unbeknownst to Archie, all the other potential targets contain force fields that would have repelled his arrow—and as a consequence, Archie would not have hit the target had he fired his arrow at any of them. Fortunately, Archie happened to have chosen the target that is force field-free. Thus, his success is lucky in the sense that he could easily have been unsuccessful. According to Pritchard, however, in this case we will still have the intuition that Archie exhibits a genuine achievement, even though the success is lucky. Moreover, Pritchard argues that the Archie case is structurally analogous to the fake barn case. Thus, if we think that there is an achievement in the Archie case, we should also think that there is an achievement in the fake barn case.

So suppose Henry is in fake barn county and drives past the one real barn in the county. He brings the car to a halt, stares at the barn, and forms the belief that there is a barn in front of him—and this belief is true. Still, he might easily have been wrong: he might just as well have pulled over next to a fake barn. Now, in this case, or so Pritchard argues, we would say that even though Henry's believing the truth is a cognitive achievement, the belief is intuitively *not* an instance of knowledge.

The upshot of these two arguments against the achievement thesis is that '... intuition in fact points towards a very different conception of knowledge, one on which knowledge and cognitive achievements come apart (in both directions)' (Pritchard 2008, pp. 31–2). And if that is the case, then the virtue-theoretic explanation of the value intuition has lost its explanatory power. Now one could defend several possible moves in response to this conclusion. Pritchard sets out to defend a view of knowledge according to which knowledge is not distinctively valuable, but that at the same time explains why we have the intuition that knowledge *is* distinctively valuable. In the following two sections, however, I will argue that we can save the virtue-epistemological explanation of the value intuition from the two problems introduced above. There is no need to go revisionist just yet.

II

Cognitive Achievements. The fake barn objection to the achievement thesis has not received all that much attention in the literature. Greco himself, however, has recently put forward a reply to the ob-

jection, and it might prove useful to start by considering his proposal.[5] According to Greco (2007*b*), we should *deny* that the Archie
case and the fake barn case are structurally analogous, and thus we
should also deny that Henry exhibits a cognitive achievement (or
'success from ability', as Greco calls it). Even though Henry has a
true belief, and even though this true belief certainly is not the product of a lucky guess, we should deny that Henry's belief equals success through ability. Greco motivates this line of thought by arguing
that abilities are always to be relativized to conditions and specific
environments. Not being able to play the violin under water, for instance, does not count against someone having the ability to play
the violin; this ability can only be exercised in the appropriate conditions. Now the barn facade case is a case in which Henry's relevant cognitive abilities do not function properly—and according to
Greco, the relevant cognitive ability in this case is the ability to discriminate between fake barns and real barns.

I agree with Greco that the two cases are disanalogous. First off,
in the Archie case, if Archie had chosen another target (one that was
protected by a force field) and had consequently missed the target,
Archie would not have missed the target due to a failure on his part.
In contrast, in the fake barn case, if Henry had pulled over next to
another barn and would have consequently formed a false belief,
Henry *would* have formed a false belief due to a failure on his part:
in this case, a failure to discriminate between real barns and fake
barns. Secondly, in the Archie case there seems to be no inclination
to negatively qualify Archie's success. In the fake barn case, however, there is an inclination to negatively qualify Henry's true belief: it
falls short of knowledge. So we should ask: is there a better analogous case? Consider the following case:

> *Archie Modified.* Archie is participating in an archery contest.
> In this contest, there are six objects that look like targets. Five
> of these objects are holograms, but one of them is the real tar-
> get. The archers face a twofold challenge: to find the target and
> to hit the bull's-eye. From where Archie is standing, the six ob-
> jects look exactly the same. Archie randomly chooses a target,
> and the one he chooses happens to be the real target. He fires
> his arrow and hits the bull's-eye.

---

[5] This reply, given at a Stirling conference on virtue epistemology, has thus far not been published.

©2008 The Aristotelian Society
Proceedings of the Aristotelian Society Supplementary Volume LXXXII
doi: 10.1111/j.1467-8349.2008.00161.x

In this case, if Archie had chosen another object as target, he would have missed the target, and he would have missed the target due to a failure on his part: in this case, a failure to discriminate between real targets and fake targets. Moreover, Archie's hitting the target qualifies, I think, as success from ability. Even so, however, we can also negatively qualify his success through ability: Archie's hitting the real target is not completely due to his own abilities. *Archie Modified*, therefore, seems to me to be a better analogous case than Pritchard's original Archie case. And therefore, if we are inclined to think that in *Archie Modified* there is an achievement (or success through ability), we should also think that there is an achievement (or success through ability) in the fake barn case.

Now, even though I agree with Greco that the two cases—the original Archie case and the fake barn case—are disanalogous, I still object to his solution to the fake barn objection first and foremost by saying that it seems to me to be counterintuitive. Even if there were no case analogous to the fake barn case in which we have the intuition that there was an achievement, I would still intuit that Henry exhibits a cognitive achievement of some sort. After all, he believes the truth, and he does not believe the truth because of a mere lucky guess. He did *something* right—and it seems to me that we can, and should, credit him for this. Accordingly, I think that Greco's response is selling Henry short. I reply, secondly, that given Greco's solution to the fake barn objection it remains mysterious *why* Henry believes the truth. Greco cannot really account for this. Putting the previous two points together, I think that the fake barn case presents us with the challenge to acknowledge that Henry exhibits a cognitive achievement whilst at the same time allowing that this cognitive achievement is not sufficient for Henry to *know* that there is a barn in front of him.

Let's agree with Greco that the relevant cognitive ability in this case is the ability to discriminate between real barns and fake barns.[6] The first step towards responding to the fake barn objection whilst taking up the challenge described above is to realize that the ability to discriminate is a contrastive ability. One might be able to discriminate p from q_1, q_2, q_3 and q_4, but unable to discriminate p from q_5 and q_6. For instance, one might be able to discriminate between a canary and a raven, but not be able to discriminate between a canary

---

[6] The fake barn example is due to Carl Ginet, but was introduced in the literature by Alvin Goldman (1976). Indeed, Goldman takes the inability to discriminate fake barns from real barns as essential to this case—as the title of his paper indicates.

©2008 THE ARISTOTELIAN SOCIETY
Proceedings of the Aristotelian Society Supplementary Volume LXXXII
doi: 10.1111/j.1467-8349.2008.00161.x

and a goldfinch (see Schaffer 2005). Given that discrimination is an inherently contrastive ability, we should realize that one's being unable to discriminate *p* from *all* alternatives will not imply that the discriminations one *can* make are epistemically useless. If you can discriminate between a canary and a raven, you have done something right and you deserve credit for this—even if you are unable to discriminate between a canary and a goldfinch.

Turning back to the fake barn case, by accepting that discrimination is a contrastive ability, we are now in a position to coherently say that Henry indeed exhibits an achievement. Henry can discriminate between barns and a variety of other objects, such as houses, hotels and horses. Accordingly, he deserves credit for this. However, Henry is unable to discriminate between real barns and fake barns. And since he is in fake barn county, where the alternative of fake barns is particularly relevant, we will in this case be inclined to deny that Henry knows that there is a barn in front of him. Even though Henry has a solid epistemic position based on his discriminatory abilities, this epistemic position is not solid enough to support knowledge in this case. Put differently, in the fake barn case there is a cognitive achievement; it is just not the cognitive achievement relevant to knowledge.

So, putting all this together, the solution to the fake barn objection I propose is that we should refine what the relevant ability in question is—in this case, the ability to discriminate between fake barns and real barns. Knowledge is success from the *relevant* ability. But even if it is not the relevant ability that leads one to true belief, but another set of abilities, one can still exhibit a cognitive achievement. The cognitive achievement just is not knowledge-supporting. My proposed solution to the fake barn objection is preferable to Greco's solution in that (i) we can accommodate the intuition that Henry exhibits an epistemic achievement, and (ii) we can explain why Henry believes the truth. And so I conclude that the first objection to the virtue-theoretic explanation of the value intuition that Pritchard has introduced can be answered.

III

Testimony and Achievements. Moving on to the second objection, here the idea is that achievements are not even necessary for knowledge. One can know *without* exhibiting a cognitive achievement. In

©2008 The Aristotelian Society
Proceedings of the Aristotelian Society Supplementary Volume LXXXII
doi: 10.1111/j.1467-8349.2008.00161.x

trying to respond to this objection, it might be instructive to formulate an analogous version of this objection in terms of archery. So
consider the following case.

> *Archie Receives Help.* Archie has never handled a bow or an
> arrow before in his life, yet he has always aspired to become an
> archer. He goes to the local archery club and signs up for a les-
> son. The master archer explains to Archie the ins and outs of
> archery, shows him how to handle the bow and the arrows,
> and explains to him in detail how to take a shot at the target so
> that he will hit the bull's-eye. After a couple of hours of inten-
> sive training, Archie is ready to take his first shot. He does ex-
> actly as he was told by his instructor—and hits the bull's-eye.

Question: Can we coherently say that Archie exhibits an achievement?

I intuit that Archie indeed exhibits an achievement. His proud parents would certainly agree, and so would his instructor, the master
archer. Now it seems to me that this case is structurally analogous to
the testimony case Pritchard uses to argue against the achievement
thesis. In both cases, the abilities of someone else help us to succeed
in what we try to do: in the one case, these abilities are the cognitive
abilities of the testifier that help us reach our destination; in the other
case, the abilities are the archery abilities of the master archer that
help us hit the bull's-eye. And if the cases really are structurally analogous, then if we are willing to say in *Archie Receives Help* that
there is an achievement, we should also be willing to say in the testimony case that there is an achievement. Thus, we can answer the testimony objection by *denying* that it is a case without an achievement.

As a second reply to the testimony objection, it seems to me that
asking for directions in an unfamiliar city is a paradigm example of inquiry. We want to obtain a piece of information, and we find a means
to obtain the information we are after. Now obviously, there are many
potential means available to obtain the information we are after. We
can consult a map, we can go to the nearest tourist information desk,
and we can ask a passer-by for directions. When one settles for the last
option, I think that the typical way to approach this task is *not* to halt
the first passer-by one meets. In typical cases, I think, one observes a
few passers-by and approaches the person that looks most reliable
and most likely to give correct information. Now suppose that this
person is indeed reliable and gives you the correct information. In that

©2008 THE ARISTOTELIAN SOCIETY
Proceedings of the Aristotelian Society Supplementary Volume LXXXII
doi: 10.1111/j.1467-8349.2008.00161.x

case, I would think there is a genuine cognitive achievement: you have isolated the most solid piece of evidence you could find.

Asking people for directions in the way Pritchard envisages, however, would be similar to Holmes trying to find the murderer and taking the very first fingerprint he finds at the crime scene as pointing towards the murderer. Indeed, even if this fingerprint points to the murderer, and even if Holmes forms a true belief accordingly, I would be strongly inclined to deny that Holmes *knows* that this particular person is the murderer. So I would reply to the testimony objection by simply denying that the subject knows: she picked up a random piece of evidence without having a clue as to whether the evidence pointed her in the right direction.

Now, to this one might object by introducing the following cases in which one is not deliberating over which potential testifier to approach, but rather just asks the first person one meets—cases, that is, which seem closely aligned to the Lackey testimony case as used by Pritchard. For instance, during a violin lesson one might just ask one's violin-teacher out of the blue, 'In which city did Stradivarius work?' Or one might ask one's parents, 'Where was my grandfather born?' Unlike the testimony case, in these cases if one acquires a true belief it seems highly intuitive to say that one knows. But in these cases there has been no cognitive achievement that involves actively seeking out a reliable testifier at all.

In response, I would deny that these cases are structurally similar to the testimony case, in that in these cases you are familiar with the persons you are interrogating, whereas that is not so in the testimony case. More specifically, you already know that the persons you interrogate are reliable testifiers on the subject of interrogation. So in these cases, there *is* a cognitive achievement present: the cognitive achievement of knowing that these testifiers are reliable. And so I conclude that I don't think that cases of this sort indicate that achievements are not necessary for knowledge.

By way of concluding the previous two sections, I have tried to defend the virtue-theoretic explanation of the value intuition from two objections Pritchard has introduced against them. Pritchard concludes from his two objections that we should separate knowledge from cognitive achievement, thereby also denying the virtue-theoretic explanation of the value intuition. I think that Pritchard has not convincingly shown that we should indeed sever the connection between knowledge and cognitive achievement. And so I con-

©2008 The Aristotelian Society
Proceedings of the Aristotelian Society Supplementary Volume LXXXII
doi: 10.1111/j.1467-8349.2008.00161.x

clude that the virtue-theoretic explanation of the value intuition so far remains unchallenged.

IV

The Question-Relative Treatment of Knowledge. It might be the case that my treatment of Pritchard's two objections is misguided. So in this section I will argue that even if it is misguided, there is another explanation of the value intuition available: the question-relative treatment of knowledge as recently defended by Jonathan Schaffer.[7] By way of briefly explaining this view, consider the following three elements that are crucial to it.

In the first place, Schaffer argues that knowledge attributions certify that the subject is able to answer the question that is relevant in the context of the knowledge attribution. In this way, knowledge attributions serve to score the progress of inquiry. In the second place, Schaffer argues that a question is a set of mutually exclusive options. Every question is a multiple-choice question. The options one can choose from are mutually exclusive and jointly exhaustive in that particular context. Finally, to be able to answer a question is to have an epistemic ability to choose the correct answer from the options the question denotes in that particular context. To know is to be able to answer the question.

A direct consequence of these three assumptions is that knowledge is a ternary relation between a subject s, a proposition p, and a set of contrastive propositions Q. Whenever one knows a proposition (e.g. knows the answer to a question), then one knows this proposition against the background of a set of contrastive propositions (e.g. against the background of the multiple choices the question evokes). One could be a contrastivist about knowledge, however, without also endorsing the question-relative treatment of knowledge.[8]

Now how can the question-relative treatment of knowledge explain the value intuition? Here, an explanation similar to the virtue-theoretic explanation can be put forward. In the first place, let us

---

[7] See, for instance, Schaffer (2004, 2005, 2007, forthcoming).

[8] Contrastivism *without* the question-relative treatment of 'knows' has been defended by Morton and Karjalainen (2003), Johnsen (2001), Sinnott-Armstrong (2006), and Blaauw (2005, forthcoming a). For critical discussion of the various versions of contrastivism, see Blaauw (forthcoming b, forthcoming c), Pritchard (forthcoming a), and Neta (forthcoming).

©2008 The Aristotelian Society
Proceedings of the Aristotelian Society Supplementary Volume LXXXII
doi: 10.1111/j.1467-8349.2008.00161.x

suppose that knowledge is indeed the ability to answer a question (call this the *knowledge question thesis*). Add to this, in the second place, that the ability to answer a question is finally valuable (the *final value of answering questions thesis*). Combining these two theses will result in the conclusion that knowledge is itself finally valuable—and will thus result in an explanation of the value intuition. I'm quite sympathetic to the question-relative treatment of knowledge, and to the contrastive view of knowledge in particular, but I lack the space to engage in a full-blown defence of the knowledge question thesis here.[9] In what follows, then, my sole purpose is to show that *if* the question-relative treatment of knowledge is correct, it can explain the value intuition.[10]

What can be said in defence of the final value of answering questions thesis? Why think that the epistemic ability to answer questions is finally valuable? We should realize, first, that a lucky guess would not qualify as being able to answer a question. As Schaffer points out, the ability to answer a question is an 'epistemic capacity': 'It is epistemic in that one may guess rightly without having the requisite ability (just as a blind throw may find the target)' (Schaffer 2005, p. 236). So the ability to answer a question is grounded in one's epistemic position.

Now without a doubt, being able to answer a question is *instrumentally* valuable. But it is not hard to see that being able to answer a question is *finally* valuable as well. Suppose that in one case one successfully answers a question on the basis of a lucky guess, whereas in another case one successfully answers a question on the basis of one's epistemic capacities. Only in the second case, therefore, is one 'able to answer the question' in Schaffer's sense. Further suppose that in both cases the practical benefits—and thus the instrumental value—are exactly the same. I would think that in such a case, one would still prefer to be 'able to answer the question' rather than answer the question with a lucky guess. And this seems to indicate that being able to answer a question is finally valuable. We not only value the ability to answer a question for its practical consequences, but also because it is something good in itself. And so I

---

[9] I defend epistemological contrastivism in a book manuscript—tentatively entitled *Knowledge in Contrast*—that I am currently working on.

[10] Schaffer himself has recently argued that his version of contrastivism can explain the intuition that knowledge is valuable, but the intuition he explains is slightly different from the intuition I am concerned with in this paper. See Schaffer (2006).

©2008 The Aristotelian Society
Proceedings of the Aristotelian Society Supplementary Volume LXXXII
doi: 10.1111/j.1467-8349.2008.00161.x

conclude that Schaffer's question-relative treatment of knowledge is able to explain the value intuition, an explanation that is at least as intuitive as the virtue-theoretic explanation discussed above.

V

Scepticism. Let me close this paper by briefly considering the ramifications from the previous discussion for the problem of radical scepticism. Pritchard takes his two arguments against the virtue-theoretic explanation of the value intuition to indicate that—pending other explanations of the value intuition—knowledge *simpliciter* is not finally valuable, although knowledge where a cognitive achievement is involved (what Pritchard calls 'knowledge *plus*') *is* finally valuable. Unfortunately, however, when it comes to answering the radical sceptic we can only solve the problem of radical scepticism when it is framed in terms of knowledge *simpliciter* and not when it is framed in terms of knowledge *plus* (or so Pritchard argues at any rate). We have to concede to the sceptic that we cannot possess the more demanding type of knowledge. And so we are not able to rescue from the sceptic the type of knowledge that is really valuable—and for Pritchard, this is 'something that should concern us' (Pritchard 2008, p. 39).

I would first like to point out that this concern is something that is also raised by other standard solutions to the radical sceptical problem. Take semantic contextualism, for instance. Key to this view is the distinction between two types of knowledge: high-standards knowledge and low-standards knowledge.[11] In responding to radical scepticism, the contextualist idea is that we can only rescue low-standards knowledge from the sceptic, *not* high-standards knowledge. And if we assume that knowledge-high is valued more than knowledge-low, it appears that we can only rescue from the sceptic something that is not all that valuable. Now the question-relative treatment of knowledge is in a dialectical position stronger than both Pritchard's own view in terms of knowledge *simpliciter* and knowledge *plus* and the semantic contextualist view in terms of knowledge-high and knowledge-low.

The question-relative treatment of the sceptical argument will say

---

[11] For an explanation and defence of this view, see DeRose (1992, 1995, 1999a, 2002). Cohen (1988, 1999) holds a different view on which justification comes in degrees.

©2008 THE ARISTOTELIAN SOCIETY
Proceedings of the Aristotelian Society Supplementary Volume LXXXII
doi: 10.1111/j.1467-8349.2008.00161.x

that we can know that we have hands rather than stumps, although we cannot know that we have hands rather than brain-in-a-vat images of hands. That is to say, the solution is that we are able to answer the question 'Hands or stumps?' but *not* the question 'Hands or brain-in-a-vat-images of hands?' Now the question-relative treatment of knowledge seems to concede to the sceptic that knowledge out of a more demanding contrast class (involving brain-in-a-vat images of hands) is not possible. But crucially, from this it does not follow that the knowledge we *do* possess has *no* final value. We are still able to answer the question 'Hands or stumps?' by saying 'Hands!'—and our ability to answer this question is finally valuable. Indeed, we would prefer it to be able to really answer this question rather than to answer it by guessing, even if the practical consequences were identical. So it seems to me that the question-relative solution to the problem of radical scepticism is preferable to Pritchard's way of dealing with this problem.

VI

Envoi. Bring the preceding points together, I have argued that the two objections to the virtue-theoretic explanation of the value intuition that Pritchard has introduced are tractable. I have furthermore argued that even if these two objections could not be answered, there is an alternative explanation of the value intuition available: the question-relative treatment of knowledge. I have finally indicated that on the question-relative treatment of knowledge, we can maintain that the knowledge we possess in the face of radical scepticism indeed has final value—unlike the pluralistic account of knowledge that Pritchard sees as flowing from the demise of the virtue-theoretic explanation of knowledge.

So is there reason for concern? I say there is not.

Department of Philosophy
Vrije Universiteit Amsterdam
De Boelelaan 1105
1081 HV Amsterdam
The Netherlands
m.j.blaauw@mac.com

©2008 THE ARISTOTELIAN SOCIETY
Proceedings of the Aristotelian Society Supplementary Volume LXXXII
doi: 10.1111/j.1467-8349.2008.00161.x

REFERENCES

Baehr, Jason forthcoming: 'Is there a Value Problem?' In Adrian Haddock, Alan Millar and Duncan Pritchard (eds.), *The Value of Knowledge*. Oxford: Oxford University Press.

Blaauw, Martijn 2005: 'Contesting Contextualism'. *Grazer Philosophische Studien*, 69, pp. 127–146.

——forthcoming *a*: 'Subject Sensitive Invariantism: In Memoriam'. *Philosophical Quarterly*.

——forthcoming *b*: 'Some Problems for Pyrrhonian Contrastivism'. *Philosophical Quarterly*.

——forthcoming *c*: 'Assertions, Contrasts, Questions'. *Philosophical Issues*.

Cohen, Stewart 1988: 'How to be a Fallibilist'. *Philosophical Perspectives*, 2, pp. 91–123.

——1999: 'Contextualism, Scepticism, and the Structure of Reasons'. In James E. Tomberlin (ed.), *Philosophical Perspectives*, *13*: *Epistemology*, pp. 57–89.

DeRose, Keith 1992: 'Contextualism and Knowledge Attributions'. *Philosophy and Phenomenological Research*, 52, pp. 913–29.

——1995: 'Solving the Sceptical Problem'. *Philosophical Review*, 104, pp. 1–52.

——1999*a*: 'Contextualism: An Explanation and Defense'. In John Greco and Ernest Sosa (eds.), *The Blackwell Guide to Epistemology*, pp. 187–206. Oxford: Blackwell.

——1999*b*: 'Responding to Skepticism'. In Keith DeRose and Ted Warfield (eds.), *Skepticism: A Contemporary Reader*, pp. 1–26. Oxford: Oxford University Press.

——2002: 'Assertion, Knowledge, and Context'. *Philosophical Review*, 111, pp. 167–203.

Goldman, Alvin 1976: 'Discrimination and Perceptual Knowledge'. *Journal of Philosophy*, 73, pp. 771–91.

Greco, John 2000: *Putting Skeptics in Their Place: The Nature of Skeptical Arguments and Their Role in Philosophical Inquiry*. Cambridge: Cambridge University Press.

——2002: 'Knowledge as Credit for True Belief'. In Michael DePaul and Linda Zagzebski (eds.), *Intellectual Virtue: Perspectives from Ethics and Epistemology*. Oxford: Oxford University Press.

——2007*a*: 'The Nature of Ability and the Purpose of Knowledge' (typescript).

——2007*b*: 'Comments on Riggs, Pritchard, Kvanvig' (typescript).

——forthcoming *a*: 'The Value Problem'. In Adrian Haddock, Alan Millar and Duncan Pritchard (eds.), *The Value of Knowledge*. Oxford: Oxford University Press.

©2008 THE ARISTOTELIAN SOCIETY
Proceedings of the Aristotelian Society Supplementary Volume LXXXII
doi: 10.1111/j.1467-8349.2008.00161.x

——forthcoming *b*: 'What's Wrong With Contextualism?' *Philosophical Quarterly.*

Johnsen, Bredo 2001: 'Contextualist Swords, Sceptical Plowshares'. *Philosophy and Phenomenological Research*, 62, pp. 385–406.

Karjalainen, Antti and Adam Morton 2003: 'Contrastive Knowledge'. *Philosophical Explorations*, 6, pp. 74–89.

Lackey, Jennifer 2007: 'Why We Don't Deserve Credit for Everything We Know'. *Synthese*, 158(3), pp. 345–61.

Neta, Ram forthcoming: 'Undermining the Case for Contrastivism'. *Social Epistemology.*

Pritchard, Duncan 2002: 'Recent Work on Radical Skepticism'. *American Philosophical Quarterly*, 39, pp. 215–57.

——2007*a*: 'Knowledge, the Value of'. *Stanford Encyclopaedia of Philosophy*, ed. E. Zalta, at <http://plato.stanford.edu/entries/knowledge-value/>.

——2007*b*: 'Recent Work on Epistemic Value'. *American Philosophical Quarterly*, 44, pp. 85–110.

——2008: 'Radical Scepticism, Epistemic Luck, and Epistemic Value'. *Proceedings of the Aristotelian Society Supplementary Volume* 82, pp. 19–41.

——forthcoming: 'Contrastivism, Evidence and Scepticism'. *Social Epistemology*, 21.

Rieber, Steven 1998: 'Scepticism and Contrastive Explanation'. *Noûs*, 32, pp. 189–204.

Schaffer, Jonathan 2004: 'From Contextualism to Contrastivism in Epistemology'. *Philosophical Studies*, 119, pp. 73–103.

——2005: 'Contrastive Knowledge'. In Tamar Szabó Gendler and John Hawthorne (eds.), *Oxford Studies in Epistemology*, Volume 1. Oxford: Oxford University Press.

——2006: 'The Irrelevance of the Subject: Against Subject-Sensitive Invariantism'. *Philosophical Studies*, 127, pp. 87–107.

——2007: 'Knowing the Answer'. *Philosophy and Phenomenological Research*, 75, pp. 383–403.

——forthcoming: 'The Contrast-Sensitivity of Knowledge Ascriptions'. *Social Epistemology.*

Sinnott-Armstrong, Walter 2006: *Moral Skepticisms*. Oxford: Oxford University Press.

Sosa, Ernest 1991: *Knowledge in Perspective: Selected Essays in Epistemology.* Cambridge: Cambridge University Press.

——1999: 'How to Defeat Opposition to Moore'. *Philosophical Perspectives*, 13, pp. 141–54.

——2007: *A Virtue Epistemology: Apt Belief and Reflective Knowledge.* Oxford: Oxford University Press.

©2008 THE ARISTOTELIAN SOCIETY
Proceedings of the Aristotelian Society Supplementary Volume LXXXII
doi: 10.1111/j.1467-8349.2008.00161.x

KIERKEGAARD'S *FEAR AND TREMBLING*
MICHELLE KOSCH AND JOHN LIPPITT

I — MICHELLE KOSCH

WHAT ABRAHAM COULDN'T SAY

The explicit topic of *Fear and Trembling*'s third Problema (the longest single section, accounting for a third of the book's total length), the theme of Abraham's silence stands not far in the background in every other section, and its importance is flagged by the pseudonym—Johannes *de silentio*—under which Kierkegaard had the book published. Here I aim to defend an interpretation of the meaning of the third Problema's central claim—that Abraham cannot explain himself, 'cannot speak'—and to argue on its basis for an interpretation of the work as a whole.

Fear and Trembling is Kierkegaard's most read, and most elusive, work. It is far from obvious how its various threads are to be drawn together into a coherent picture of the work as a whole.[1] The difficulty of the text is compounded by the fact that Kierkegaard published it under a pseudonym, and with an epigraph suggesting that its intended message to the reader is distinct from its manifest content, something his 'messenger' (the pseudonymous author, perhaps) does not understand.

What seems to be the most common way of reading the book is both philosophically weak and poorly grounded in the text. On this interpretation, it aims to defend the superiority of a religious over an ethical outlook (or over some specific ethical outlook), using the example of Abraham both to point up the difference between these and to identify the limits of ethics (or ethics on a particular account). Abraham's willingness to sacrifice Isaac at God's command must be justified in some sense, if Abraham is the sort of exemplary figure he is taken to be. Yet it is indefensible on available accounts of ethical duties (as well as on the basis of Abraham's presumed desires). Therefore either (a) the traditional or going interpretation of ethics is

---

[1] The most prominent recent interpretations concede from the start that there is no single meaning or picture, no single (or single most important) thing that the work aims to do. See Green (1998), Lippitt (2003).

©2008 THE ARISTOTELIAN SOCIETY
Proceedings of the Aristotelian Society Supplementary Volume LXXXII
doi: 10.1111/j.1467-8349.2008.00162.x

inadequate and must be revised so that it accommodates Abraham's
case, or (b) ethics must be 'teleologically suspended' altogether in favour of a religious account of normativity. There are variations on
both alternatives. (a1) Ethics on the wrong account focuses on the
moral quality of actions or outcomes and ignores the importance of
virtues of character (trust, commitment, courage), and Abraham can
show us why that is a mistake.[2] (a2) Ethics on the wrong account focuses on universal rules, whereas in fact many ethically relevant features of any situation will be unique to it (e.g. the personal
relationships in which the agent is involved or the particular commitments he has taken up).[3] (b1) Ethics on *any* non-religious account is
deficient because of its inability to make sense of individualized duties, without which our practical lives can be neither coherent nor
satisfying, and which only a divine source of norms would make
possible.[4] (b2) A religious standpoint is superior because it can offer,
in addition to normative guidance, both divine assistance and forgiveness of past mistakes, and no secular ethical outlook can make
sense of the possibility of (one or both of) these things.[5]

   On any such reading, if the book is to avoid assuming what it sets
out to prove it must provide an alternative (non-ethical, or non-
standard ethical, but also non-religious) justification of Abraham's
conduct. But no such justification is ever offered.[6] Abraham's right-

---

[2] See Evans (1981, pp. 145ff.), Cross (1999, 2003).

[3] See Evans (1981, pp. 148ff.).

[4] Adams (1987, p. 448) argues that the individual is in danger of being 'morally fragmented,
crushed or immobilized' in cases in which general ethical principles plus non-normative facts
about his situation fail 'to write [his] name legibly on any particular task', and that this is a
major concern of Kierkegaard's and a major impetus behind his endorsement of religious as
opposed to philosophical ethics. Adams acknowledges, though, that the instances of overriding religious duties Kierkegaard discusses (including Abraham's) are cases in which 'uni-
versalist' ethics has indeed written the individual's name perfectly legibly on a particular task
(e.g. refraining from murdering one's son) and that it is a religious commitment that excuses
the individual from what would otherwise unambiguously be required of him.

[5] Quinn (1998, pp. 349–50) invokes R. M. Hare's 'moral gap' ('the gap between the moral
demand on us and our natural capacities to live by it') as the motive behind what he sees as
Kierkegaard's criticism of secular ethics (in *Fear and Trembling* as well as other works).
Arendt (1989, pp. 236–43) argues that in the absence of any possibility of absolution—
which ethics on its own cannot provide—guilt for past wrongdoing must become a debili-
tating psychological burden, leading to a sort of ethical paralysis. For readings along similar
lines (some focusing on *Fear and Trembling*, some on other works, but all assuming a uni-
tary account of the limitations of the ethical in Kierkegaard's works), see also Fahrenbach
(1968, 1979), Hannay (1982), and Whittaker (1988).

[6] In addition to fitting poorly with the text, all require us to read the book as being almost
comically unsuccessful at what it attempts. For a discussion of how such an argument inevitably fails, see Kosch (2006a, pp. 156–60).

©2008 THE ARISTOTELIAN SOCIETY
Proceedings of the Aristotelian Society Supplementary Volume LXXXII
doi: 10.1111/j.1467-8349.2008.00162.x

eousness is not even categorically asserted; instead we are told that *if* there is no teleological suspension of the ethical, no absolute duty to God, etc., *then* Abraham is lost, we must give him up as an example, must regard him as an ordinary murderer, etc. (Kierkegaard 1901–06, III: 115–16, 165, and *passim*; 1997–, 4: 159, 207, and *passim*).[7]

Taken literally, that conditional states only what a religious believer would have to commit himself to *in order* to take Abraham as a model. This suggests that the intended audience consists of people who already embrace a religious point of view and are already tacitly committed to regarding conduct like Abraham's as religiously justified. It suggests an interpretation on which the book's aim is to show exactly how terrifying the situation of someone who believes he has overriding individual obligations to God can be. The price of faith is renunciation of one's most deeply held desires, violation of moral duty, alienation from family and society, inability to explain oneself to others. The opening passages of the preface and the epilogue support this way of looking at the project. The preface opens with the observation that the present age is one in which, in the world of ideas as in the business world, everything is being sold at 'a bargain price' (Kierkegaard 1901–06, III: 57; 1997–, 4: 101). The epilogue opens with a story in which Dutch spice merchants sink a few cargoes in order to drive up the price of their wares and then asks 'Do we need something similar in the world of the spirit?' (Kierkegaard 1901–06, III: 166; 1997–, 4: 208). The aim of driving up the price of faith—convincing Sunday morning Christians who believe that a religious life is compatible with the bourgeois values they otherwise endorse that faith is not to be had as cheaply as that—is certainly in line with one of Kierkegaard's most urgent and continuing concerns.

I am not alone in thinking that the manifest content of *Fear and Trembling* is essentially this.[8] But that cannot be the whole story, as we can see if we ask why Kierkegaard's audience ought to *accept* that this is what they sign on for when they sign on for a religious life. There are alternative accounts to be found in Kant,[9] Schleiermacher,

---

[7] In quoting Kierkegaard's works I usually follow the Hong translation (sometimes with minor changes); translations of quotations from journals and papers are my own.

[8] Green (1998, pp. 258ff.) takes this to be the most plausible preliminary reading; see also Evans (1981, p. 143).

[9] Kant, for instance, judged Abraham's action to be irreligious because immoral. See *Conflict of the Faculties* (Kant 1968, 7: 63, 7: 63n.) and *Religion within the Limits of Reason Alone* (Kant 1968, 6: 87).

©2008 THE ARISTOTELIAN SOCIETY
Proceedings of the Aristotelian Society Supplementary Volume LXXXII
doi: 10.1111/j.1467-8349.2008.00162.x

Hegel,[10] and the many other Enlightenment and post-Enlightenment theologians current in the Copenhagen of the time, accounts on which Abraham's sacrifice is *not* a good indicator of the price of faith, but instead an aberration.[11] The account in *Fear and Trembling* is as much an argument for this alternative as its opposite, and so as likely to drive the bourgeois Christian into the arms of Kant et al. as to succeed in driving up the price of faith. In the absence of an overriding antecedent commitment to taking Abraham (indeed, Abraham on this rather idiosyncratic portrayal) as a model of faith, the reader cannot be convinced in this way that its price is higher than he thought.

The epigraph, of course, suggests that whatever the message to the reader is meant to be, it will not be explicit in the book's manifest content, but only suggested by it. In this paper I will offer, as a clue to understanding the underlying message, an interpretation of one of the book's most puzzling claims—that Abraham cannot explain himself, 'cannot speak'. The explicit topic of the third Problema (which is the longest single section, accounting for a third of the book's total length), the theme of Abraham's silence stands not far in the background in every other section, and its importance is flagged by the pseudonym—Johannes *de silentio*—under which the book was published. The importance of this theme has not been overlooked, though the third Problema has received less attention than the first two. In §I, I will reject two candidate interpretations of Abraham's silence; in §II, I will propose and defend a third interpretation. This will provide the basis for an argument, given in §III, that the hidden message is that we must indeed give up Abraham—though not for the reasons that Kant, Hegel, or the typical enlightened Copenhagener would offer.

---

[10] Hegel argued for limitations on the rights of religious conscience in his *Philosophy of Right* (Hegel 1986, 7:418), suggested in *The Spirit of Christianity and its Fate* that Abraham's near-sacrifice of Isaac was motivated by a desire to prove to himself the limits of his love for Isaac (Hegel 1986, 1:279), and claimed in the Berlin introduction to his *Lectures on the History of Philosophy* that the command to sacrifice Isaac cannot be understood by us as the possible command of anything we would recognize as God (Hegel 1986, 20:503). For further discussion of Kant's and Hegel's views on Abraham and their relevance for *Fear and Trembling*, see Kosch (2006b).

[11] Johannes's apparent answer to this challenge—that life would be despair if there were no heroes to admire and no poets to celebrate them—is so bad that it is perhaps uncharitable to take it as intended to provide an answer (Kierkegaard 1901–06, III:68–9; 1997–, 4:112–13).

©2008 The Aristotelian Society
Proceedings of the Aristotelian Society Supplementary Volume LXXXII
doi: 10.1111/j.1467-8349.2008.00162.x

I

Silence.

> The knight of faith is assigned solely to himself; he feels the pain of being unable to make himself understandable to others ... (Kierkegaard 1901–06, III:128; 1997–, 4:171)

> Abraham remains silent—but he cannot speak. Therein lies the distress and anxiety. Even though I go on talking night and day without interruption, if I cannot make myself understood when I speak, then I am not speaking. This is the case with Abraham. (Kierkegaard 1901–06, III:159; 1997–, 4:201)

> Speak he cannot; he speaks no human language ... he speaks a divine language, he speaks in tongues. (Kierkegaard 1901–06, III:160; 1997–, 4:202)

> Abraham cannot speak, because he cannot say that which would explain everything (that is, so it is understandable) ... (Kierkegaard 1901–06, III:160; 1997–, 4:202)

Johannes *de silentio* is gripped by the thought that there is something that Abraham cannot say—that there is something determinate that would be an adequate characterization of Abraham's situation, that is specific to his situation (or a very narrow range of situations), that would play some role in justifying his behaviour to others, and that he nonetheless cannot convey. What are we to make of this claim? Two broad lines of interpretation have suggested themselves: either what Abraham cannot say is unsayable by anyone, or it is sayable in principle, but not by him.[12]

On the first interpretation, appeal is made to:

(1) *The inexpressibility of Abraham's situation.* There is something that would make his situation understandable to oth-

---

[12] I put aside here a third possible line of interpretation, suggested in Taylor (1981, pp. 183 ff.). Although it occurs alongside suggestions that Abraham cannot speak because his personal relation to God is literally inarticulable (an interpretation I will consider—and reject—below), which leaves me uncertain about whether I am correct in attributing it to him, Taylor seems to suggest that explaining himself would be a defilement of the privacy of Abraham's relation with God. In this case it would be strictly untrue that Abraham *cannot* explain himself (i.e., Johannes's characterization would be false), and I do not see any textual evidence for such an interpretation, in *Fear and Trembling* or in the Genesis account (though the Adler manuscript does suggest that the recipient of a revelation might have an ethical (but *not* religious) obligation to keep silent). For these reasons I set this possible interpretation aside.

©2008 THE ARISTOTELIAN SOCIETY
Proceedings of the Aristotelian Society Supplementary Volume LXXXII
doi: 10.1111/j.1467-8349.2008.00162.x

ers that Abraham cannot communicate because it is not
linguistically expressible.

Taking this first option would appear to have brought an interpreter
to the end of his task, since if what Abraham cannot say is unsayable, then the interpreter cannot say it either. This is true even if the
unsayable thing is some feeling or some practical attitude. These are
either in principle describable or they are not. If they are, then Abraham has something to say after all; and if they are not, then the interpreter must remain as mute with respect to them as Abraham
himself. (More than that, if what Abraham cannot say is unsayable,
then there *can be* nothing—nothing *determinate*—that he cannot
say; successfully individuating the specific thing he cannot say
would amount to saying it.[13]) In this, its only consistent form, the
first alternative has not been popular—though more loquacious
forms have been.

The temptation to say what it is that Abraham could not has been
quite strong. Curiously, Johannes *de silentio* himself succumbs to it;
some of the passages in the third Problema that describe Abraham's
inability to convey his situation end with a concise description of
that very situation: that it is an ordeal, an ordeal in which both his
love for Isaac and his sense of his ethical duty toward Isaac act as
temptations to fail in a divinely set task.

> He can say everything, but one thing he cannot say, and if he cannot
> say that—that is, say it in such a way that the other understands it—
> then he is not speaking. ... Abraham can describe his love for Isaac in
> the most beautiful words to be found in any language. But this is not
> what is on his mind; it is something deeper, that he is going to sacrifice
> him because it is an ordeal. No one can understand the latter, and thus
> everyone can only misunderstand the former. (Kierkegaard 1901–06,
> III:159; 1997–, 4:201)

> Abraham cannot speak, because he cannot say that which would ex-
> plain everything (that is, so it is understandable): that it is an ordeal
> such that, please note, the ethical is the temptation. (Kierkegaard
> 1901–06, III:160; 1997–, 4:202)

---

[13] Some interpreters have claimed that there is some content that cannot be said but can be
shown and that this showing is the aim of Kierkegaard's 'indirect communication'. Conant
(1989, 1993) has argued (convincingly, in my view) that the distinction they rely on
between 'deep' nonsense and ordinary nonsense cannot be maintained.

©2008 THE ARISTOTELIAN SOCIETY
Proceedings of the Aristotelian Society Supplementary Volume LXXXII
doi: 10.1111/j.1467-8349.2008.00162.x

Nor does Johannes stop with this brief description. His Abraham is surrounded by a set of meticulously drawn characters meant to mark out the boundaries between faith and resignation (Kierkegaard 1901–06, III:89–100; 1997–, 4:133–45), between faith and aesthetic and ethical heroism (Kierkegaard 1901–06, III:107–11, 123–9, 158–65; 1997–, 4:151–5, 166–71, 200–7), between faith and sin (Kierkegaard 1901–06, III:145–6, 158; 1997–, 4:187–9, 200), between the 'second' immediacy of faith and the 'first' or aesthetic immediacy (Kierkegaard 1901–06, III:130; 1997–, 4:172). Abraham is a knight of faith rather than resignation because in renouncing what is most important to him he simultaneously retains his original desire for it, and can receive it back light-heartedly should he have the opportunity. He makes the movement of faith, in which he expects at the same time to get Isaac back, 'by virtue of the absurd' (Kierkegaard 1901–06, III:161; 1997–, 4:203). He is a knight of faith rather than a tragic hero because his willingness to sacrifice Isaac is motivated not by a higher ethical demand (e.g. a publicly recognizable collective good), but rather by a purely personal commitment. His silence is that of a knight of faith rather than that of a sinner because it is not motivated by any desire to make things easier on himself or others, nor by pride, contempt, or fear of blame (Kierkegaard 1901–06, III:134–5, 146, 151–7, 158; 1997–, 4:176–7, 188, 193–9, 200). It is not the silence of aesthetic immediacy but that of a higher or 'later' immediacy,[14] since Abraham has passed through the ethical stage and so is, presumably, committed to acting for reflectively endorsable reasons.

Johannes displays sufficient confidence in his insight into the structure of Abraham's beliefs and motivations that he is even able to translate them into a sketch of a modern-day version of the knight of faith (Kierkegaard 1901–06, III:89–91; 1997–, 4:133–5). He confesses that in years of looking he has 'not found a single authentic instance' of a knight of faith, though for all he knows 'every second person may be such an instance'. But he is able to *imagine* one, and the imagined knight of faith is indistinguishable from the

---

[14] An 'immediate' individual, for Kierkegaard, is one who fails to order his desires according to (sufficiently) higher-order principles. (Either he does not reflect on which of his desires he would like to be moved by and which he would prefer to suppress, but acts on the strongest occurrent desire, or else he orders his desires according to norms that are taken up unreflectively from his surroundings or his sensible nature.) In claiming that the knight of faith must exemplify a sort of immediacy other than aesthetic immediacy, Johannes claims at least that he has taken on a commitment to acting for reasons he can reflectively endorse.

©2008 THE ARISTOTELIAN SOCIETY
Proceedings of the Aristotelian Society Supplementary Volume LXXXII
doi: 10.1111/j.1467-8349.2008.00162.x

crowd both in his external appearance and in his desires for worldly
things. His figure betrays no 'crack through which the infinite
would peek'; he 'belongs entirely to finitude'. He finds pleasure in
everything, takes part in everything with an assiduity to be expected
in a worldly man who is attached to such things. What distinguishes
him is nothing beyond a certain irrationality in the structure of his
expectations: he writes nothing off as impossible, and when some
desired outcome fails to materialize, he is unperturbed. Like the
knight of resignation, he has made the 'movement of infinity' and
renounced all finite goods—but then he has 'grasped everything
again by virtue of the absurd'.

    This account of the inner life of the knight of faith leaves much
unclarified, but it does not leave the basics unsaid. Johannes de-
clares himself at several points perfectly able to describe the 'movements' of the knight of faith, simply unable to make them
(Kierkegaard 1901–06, III:87–9; 1997–, 4:131–3). So it seems that
if Abraham cannot explain himself, that is not because he cannot *be*
explained. This suggests that the second line of interpretation—on
which what Abraham cannot say is sayable in principle, just not by
him—is the one worth pursuing. Note that this second line requires
an account of why Johannes (and the interpreter) can say what Abraham could not. There seem to be two ways such an account could
go. Appeal could be made to:

> (2) *Abraham's privileged knowledge.* Abraham understands
> something about his situation that he cannot communicate
> to his contemporaries (Sarah et al.) because *they* would not
> be able to understand it (though Johannes, and therefore
> the reader, can).

Or appeal could be made to:

> (3) *Abraham's ignorance.* There is something about Abraham's
> situation that Abraham *himself* cannot understand and so
> cannot explain (though Johannes, and therefore the reader,
> can).

In both, there is something that we (readers/interpreters) are in a position to understand, but that nevertheless cannot be communicated
to those around him by Abraham himself.

    Many passages suggest option (2). Abraham knows that his situa-

©2008 THE ARISTOTELIAN SOCIETY
Proceedings of the Aristotelian Society Supplementary Volume LXXXII
doi: 10.1111/j.1467-8349.2008.00162.x

tion is an ordeal, and that the ethical is a temptation. He has reason
to sacrifice Isaac, and he has reason to believe he will get Isaac back,
but the force of these reasons is not communicable to those around
him. Care must be taken to construe this second option in a way
that makes it a genuine alternative to the first. This means that a
plausible account must be given of why Abraham's reasons, *while
genuine*, are not shared by those around him.

One strategy that will not work involves an appeal to reasons he
might have that would be intrinsically private. If something is a reason for an agent with given antecedent beliefs (or beliefs and desires)
in given circumstances, then it is a reason for any other agent rele-
vantly similarly situated; any intelligible account of Abraham's reasons must admit this. This is not the only constraint on such an
account. By 'reason' what we must have in mind is a justifying reason. We may assume that (for the agent at issue) a justifying reason
is also a *pro tanto* motivating reason,[15] but a merely motivating (and
not justifying) reason presumably will not do, for then Abraham's
actions would be, from the standpoint of the reader, indistinguishable from those of a sinner or a lunatic. We must also assume that
commands from God provide justifying reasons that override or always outweigh other reasons for acting—a large assumption, not
one Kierkegaard or Johannes anywhere in fact defends, but one that
is apparently made, and in any case one that is needed to fill out this
interpretation.[16] What we would need, then, is something recognizable by Abraham and by us, but not by Sarah et al., as a reason to
think he had in fact received a command from God.

---

[15] Kierkegaard's account of religious motivation can be spelled out in ways that put it on
either side of the internalism debate. I am inclined to read him as an externalist (receipt of
the 'condition' leaves the motivational question open without leaving the normative question open for an individual), but no part of the argument in this paper hangs on that. We
need assume only the disjunction of internalism and externalism coupled with the assumption that the agent at issue is motivated to act in accordance with the justifying reasons he
has.

[16] How they provide them is not an issue on which an explicit stand seems to me to affect
the outcome here, so I will leave the assumption in that very preliminary formulation.
Actually, the assumption in this strong form is not strictly required; we could begin instead
from the weaker assumption that divine commands provide only *pro tanto* reasons. This
would complicate the story, but not in any interesting way. Abraham would in that case
need to have sufficient reasons both for thinking he had in fact received a command from
God and for taking such commands to outweigh or override other practical reasons (at
least in this case). But since one or the other of these (sets of) reasons would then have to
be mysterious to those around him in just the way I describe his reason for believing the
command to come from God as being, the more complicated account would not introduce
any new considerations.

©2008 The Aristotelian Society
Proceedings of the Aristotelian Society Supplementary Volume LXXXII
doi: 10.1111/j.1467-8349.2008.00162.x

There seem to be two options. Abraham might have long experience with similar apparently divine communications, and be convinced on the basis of this experience of the veridicality of this one (or at least of the prudence of obeying it).[17] This would be an inductively-based confidence that certain types of event (viz., apparent divine communications) are reason-giving, a confidence that others without the relevant background beliefs might not share. Alternatively, there might be something about the phenomenology of revelation that seems to provide a direct justification for action, but whose precise character cannot be conveyed except to those who have had similar experiences. In both scenarios, Abraham is left not with nothing to say, but instead with something that would be fully comprehensible only to a limited number of individuals, perhaps to no one in his immediate environment (in fact perhaps to no one at all—though this would be a contingent rather than, as in option (1) above, a necessary fact).

Note that the experiences in question are not such that Abraham cannot convey to others their approximate content or their place in his motivational structure. Rather, they are such that they cannot pass muster *as reasons* for anyone else around him. Since what Abraham needs in order to make himself understood is not a mere statement of his actual motivation but something that approximates a justification of his action—at least, something that makes his having the motivation he does comprehensible—either of these would constitute a description of a scenario in which Abraham cannot explain himself.

Would an Abraham so situated have *reasons* to begin with? We might suspect that their unacceptability to others would itself cast doubt on their legitimacy as reasons for Abraham. What is more, Abraham himself might suspect this. That Abraham is uncertain of his own justification is suggested at several points in the text. An Abraham fully confident in his religious justification would not be unable to sleep (Kierkegaard 1901–06, III:126; 1997–, 4:169), unable to reassure himself that he is legitimate (Kierkegaard 1901–06, III:112ff.; 1997–, 4:155ff.), and while he might find his love for Isaac or his own self-interest a source of temptation, it is difficult to see how he would find *the ethical* a temptation (Kierkegaard 1901–06, III:109, 119–20, 160; 1997–, 4:153, 162–3, 202)—unless it pro-

---

[17] Evans (1981) advances a view something like this—and concludes (correctly, as I will argue) that on it there is nothing Abraham cannot say.

©2008 The Aristotelian Society
Proceedings of the Aristotelian Society Supplementary Volume LXXXII
doi: 10.1111/j.1467-8349.2008.00162.x

vided some normative security his religious justification lacked. This is precisely the basis for Johannes's contrast between the knight of faith and the tragic hero:

> The tragic hero is soon finished ... The knight of faith, however, is kept in a state of sleeplessness, for he is constantly being tested, and at every moment there is the possibility of his returning penitently to the universal, and this possibility may be a spiritual trial as well as the truth. He cannot get any information on that from any man ... (Kierkegaard 1901–06, III:126; 1997–, 4:169)

Not even another knight of faith could reassure him, Johannes tells us (Kierkegaard 1901–06, III:120; 1997–, 4:163). These passages suggest that Abraham's inability to make himself understandable to others is itself a source of uncertainty for him.

That is as it should be. In fact both sorts of reason—inductive and phenomenological—for believing that one has received a command from God are dismissed by Kierkegaard himself in other works, on the basis of familiar philosophical arguments. Kierkegaard seems to have agreed with Kant that there can be no immediately recognizable marks of divinity or divine manifestation.[18] This emerges most clearly in the discussion in chapter five of *Philosophical Fragments* of the follower at second hand, in which we are told that historical contemporaneity is no advantage to the believer, since 'divinity is not an immediate qualification' and even the miraculousness of a divine individual's acts '*is* not immediately but is only for faith, inasmuch as the person who does not believe does not see' (Kierkegaard 1901–06, IV:256; 1997–, 4:290–1).[19] He also seems to have agreed with Hume that no inductive case for religious belief can be mounted—since even were one to admit that certain sorts of events (miracles, prodigies) might constitute evidence for a revelation, one could have no convincing evidence for the actual occurrence of such events. (Hume focuses on the evidence of testimony to miracles, arguing that since miracles are, by their nature, maximally improbable, any report of a miracle is intrinsically incredible. But an analogous argument applies, *mutatis mutandis*, to evidence of the senses. Experi-

---

[18] See Kant (1968, 7:63, 6:87).

[19] We may confidently attribute the view in *Fragments* to Kierkegaard rather than solely to his pseudonym Johannes Climacus. Its occurrence in a book intended until the last moment to be published under Kierkegaard's own name suffices for that, but we find it elsewhere— e.g. in the journals and the Adler manuscript—as well.

©2008 THE ARISTOTELIAN SOCIETY
Proceedings of the Aristotelian Society Supplementary Volume LXXXII
doi: 10.1111/j.1467-8349.2008.00162.x

ence of anything seeming to be a miracle is, because of the intrinsic improbability of miracles, far more likely to have been a sensory hallucination.) Again this emerges most clearly in *Fragments*, with the ridicule of the project of giving a 'probability proof' of the correctness of religious belief (in terms remarkably similar to Hume's): 'wanting to link a probability proof to the improbable (in order to demonstrate: that it is probable?—but then the concept is changed; or in order to demonstrate: that it is improbable?—but to use probability for that is a contradiction)...' (Kierkegaard 1901–06, IV:257n.; 1997–, 4:292n.).[20]

If neither type of experience counts as a reason for believing that something is a command from God, then *a fortiori* neither provides a reason for his actions that Abraham could have but be unable to convey. Unless we can come up with another strategy for filling it out, then, alternative (2) is in trouble as well.

II

Hume, Hamann, and Religious Justification in Philosophical Fragments. *Fragments* offers what looks to be what today would be called an externalist account of the justification of religious belief: if the belief has the right sort of aetiology (having its source in a granting by a god of a 'condition'), then it is justified; if not, then it isn't.[21] On this view, a believer can be justified in his belief without himself having access to the grounds of his justification. The account differs from other forms of epistemological externalism in that these grounds of justification are never accessible to anyone else either; whether or not a belief has its source in an encounter with the divine is not transparent to human inspection. Thus having a religious justification for one's actions is in practice indistinguishable from having no justification at all. (There is in fact a distinction, but

---

[20] In Hume's words, 'Upon the whole, then, it appears, that no testimony for any kind of miracle has ever amounted to a probability, much less to a proof; and that, even supposing it amounted to a proof, it would be opposed by another proof; derived from the very nature of the fact, which it would endeavour to establish' (Hume 1999, p. 183).

[21] 'Only the person who personally receives the condition from the god ... only that person believes' (Kierkegaard 1901–06, IV:265; 1997–, 4:299); 'How, then, does the learner become a believer or a follower? When the understanding is discharged and he receives the condition' (Kierkegaard 1901–06, IV:228; 1997–, 4:265). See also Kierkegaard (1901–06, IV:228, 265; 1997–, 4:265, 299).

©2008 The Aristotelian Society
Proceedings of the Aristotelian Society Supplementary Volume LXXXII
doi: 10.1111/j.1467-8349.2008.00162.x

it is one only God is in a position to draw.)

The account of the justification of non-religious belief in the Interlude of *Fragments* relies transparently on Hume.[22] The division of knowledge claims into matters-of-fact claims and relations-of-ideas claims (Kierkegaard 1901–06, IV:227; 1997–, 4:263–4); the restriction in the scope of the latter sort of claim and the rejection of most of traditional metaphysics (e.g. denial that the existence of God can be proved a priori: Kierkegaard 1901–06, IV:207–11, 236–9; 1997–, 4:245–9, 273–5, denial that a past sequence of events can be understood as having occurred of necessity: Kierkegaard 1901–06, IV:239–47; 1997–, 4:275–83); the endorsement of epistemic scepticism (most of our beliefs about matters of fact cannot be rationally justified, because most of them rely on forms of inference that themselves rely on the unjustifiable assumptions that nature is uniform or that causal necessitation is detectable: Kierkegaard 1901–06, IV:247–8; 1997–, 4:283); and finally, the rejection of the idea that this epistemic scepticism should have some direct practical consequences (we go on holding all sorts of beliefs that cannot be rationally justified, we could not get on without doing so, and we should not feel particularly bad about that: Kierkegaard 1901–06, IV:247–8; 1997–, 4:283)—all echo similar themes in Hume.

Hume's account of specifically religious beliefs stands in the background of the *Fragments* account as well. Although all of our rationally unjustifiable beliefs are produced by mechanisms not under our direct control, Hume thought, not all of the mechanisms are equal. Some are more rather than less likely to produce beliefs that keep us safe and happy—'beliefs in accordance with custom and experience' or 'natural' or 'inevitable' beliefs. Religious beliefs do not belong in that category; instead, Hume seems to have thought them produced by psychological mechanisms we are foolish to rely on.[23] This is what he had in mind when he concluded the chapter on miracles in the *Enquiry* with this observation:

[W]e may conclude, that the Christian Religion not only was at first attended with miracles, but even at this day cannot be believed by any rea-

---

[22] For a more comprehensive treatment of the role of Hume in the Climacus works, see Popkin (1951).

[23] Kierkegaard follows him in drawing a distinction between the sort of ungroundedness beliefs about matters of fact have and the sort of ungroundedness religious beliefs have, in the Appendix to the Interlude. See Kierkegaard (1901–06, IV:250; 1997–, 4:285).

©2008 THE ARISTOTELIAN SOCIETY
Proceedings of the Aristotelian Society Supplementary Volume LXXXII
doi: 10.1111/j.1467-8349.2008.00162.x

sonable person without one. Mere reason is insufficient to convince us
of its veracity: And whoever is moved by *Faith* to assent to it, is con-
scious of a continued miracle in his own person, which subverts all the
principles of his understanding, and gives him a determination to believe
what is most contrary to custom and experience. (Hume 1999, p. 186)

Kierkegaard's acquaintance with Hume seems to have been entirely
second-hand.[24] He found these lines while reading Hamann,[25] who remarks that while Hume intends it as criticism, in fact what he says is
just orthodoxy, the truth from the mouth of one of its enemies. Kierkegaard cites that remark with apparent approval in a journal entry
of 10 September 1836, commenting: 'One sees the complete misunderstanding between the Christian and the non-Christian in the fact
that Hamann responds to Hume's objection: "Yes, that's just the way
it is"' (Kierkegaard 1909–78, IA:100; 1997–, AA:14.1).[26] In a journal
entry of 12 September, he cites another passage from Hamann's correspondence: 'Haven't you often heard me say: incredible but true.
Lies and novels, hypotheses and fables must be plausible, but not the
truths and fundamental doctrines of our faith' (Kierkegaard 1909–
78, I A 237).[27]

It is uncontroversial that Kierkegaard's view of the relation of
Christianity to reason was definitively shaped by his early encounter
with Hamann.[28] That he took a sustained course in Hamann be-

---

[24] Apart from university lectures, major sources seem to have been J. G. Hamann (whom I
will discuss) and F. H. Jacobi.

[25] The quotation is from a letter to Lindner from July 1759 (Hamann 1821–43, 1:406).

[26] Compare Kierkegaard (1901–06, VI:103; 1997–, 6:101).

[27] The quotation is taken from a letter to Hamann's brother, also of July 1759 (Hamann
1821–43, 1:425). In this 12 September journal entry, Kierkegaard remarks on another passage in the above-cited letter to Lindner of July 1759, 'a very interesting parallel Hamann
draws between the law (of Moses) and reason. He begins from Hume's proposition: "the
observation of human blindness and weakness is the result of all philosophy"—"Our reason," remarks Hamann, "is therefore just what Paul called the law—and reason's prohibition is holy, right and good; but is it given in order to make us wise? Just as little as the law
of the Jews [was given] in order to make them righteous, but instead to convict us of the
opposite, how irrational our reason is, and that our errors are multiplied by it, just as sins
were multiplied by the law"' (quoted in Kierkegaard 1909–78, I A 237). Compare Hamann
(1821–43, 1:405). I have quoted the Hume from *Enquiry*, Part 1, §4 (Hume 1999, p. 112).
Hamann's quotation is an inexact German translation, but this seems to be the passage he
has in mind.

[28] See Lowrie (1938, esp. pp. 164ff.) and Pojman (1983). Lowrie: 'I am inclined to say that
[Hamann] is the only author by whom Kierkegaard was profoundly influenced' (p. 164).
And Pojman (perhaps following Lowrie) tells us that Kierkegaard's decision that Christianity and speculation are opposed was cemented through his reading of Hamann in the fall of
1836.

©2008 The Aristotelian Society
Proceedings of the Aristotelian Society Supplementary Volume LXXXII
doi: 10.1111/j.1467-8349.2008.00162.x

tween September 1836 and May 1839 is suggested both by his journals from that period (which show him reading through Hamann's
collected works, volume by volume, in order[29]) and by a later
(1848) remark about a passage from his 1839 journal that it dated
'from the Hamann-reading time' (Kierkegaard 1909–78, IX B 33.3)
—as if reading Hamann partially defined a period of his life.[30] Following Hamann, Kierkegaard took the Humean story about religious belief literally rather than with Hume's intended irony: the
only way for a believer to explain his belief is as a miracle, a 'wonder' (Kierkegaard 1901–06, IV:230; 1997–, 4:267). Part of his reason for accepting it has to be that he found it to conform to the
phenomenological facts of religious belief—not only the epistemic
inadequacy of the reasons that can be offered for holding it, but also
the moral tenuousness of the situation of a believer who has every
reason to think the 'condition' a delusion.

These are the themes of *Fear and Trembling*, because this is precisely Abraham's situation.[31] Interpreters interested in providing an
account of Abraham's justification have typically sought a reason to
which Abraham would have access. If we apply the view of religious
justification offered by *Fragments* to Abraham's case, however, we
can see that his justification would be one to which he could *not* in
principle have access. He would believe (at least to some degree)

---

[29] In September 1836 one sees several citations from the first volume (Kierkegaard 1909–78,
I A 100, I A 233; 1997–, AA:14.1). One sees some undated entries in 1837 from the second
volume (Kierkegaard 1909–78, II A 12, p. 15, II A 75, II A 78, II A 102; 1997–, BB:37,
DD:3, DD:6, DD:18); then in July 1837 some from the third volume (Kierkegaard 1909–78,
II A 118; 1997–, DD:28, 28.a). Sometime in 1836–7 he writes the long entry on Hamann
(Kierkegaard 1909–78, I A 340; 1997–, CC: 25). Later in 1837 (Kierkegaard 1909–78, II A
139; 1997–, DD:37a), he is quoting from the fifth volume, and by May of 1839 from the
sixth volume (Kierkegaard 1909–78, II A 438; 1997–, EE:78.a). In fact there are numerous
entries about Hamann from May 1839. The later volumes of Hamann's collected works
came out after Kierkegaard's period of greatest Hamann-infatuation, but he still purchased
them and read them promptly. For instance, the eighth and final volume came out in 1843,
Kierkegaard bought it (the second part) at Philipsen on 12.2.1843, and there is an 1843
journal entry on that eighth volume (Kierkegaard 1909–78, IV A 39; 1997–, JJ:50).

[30] Compare Kierkegaard (1909–78, II A 420; 1997–, EE:64).

[31] It is also Adler's, and we could further fill out the account here by taking a cue from obvious parallels between *Fear and Trembling* and the Adler manuscript. In fact, the language
used to describe Adler's situation seems calculated to call Abraham to the reader's mind.
The extraordinary individual must be vigilant 'in fear and trembling' lest anyone be harmed
by exposure to his extraordinariness (Kierkegaard 1909–78, VIII, 2 B 13, p. 62); he must 'in
fear and trembling' prevent his example from leading others astray, in part by making his
position as repugnant as possible to them (Kierkegaard 1909–78, VII, 2 B 235, p. 54); he
must keep silent, in so far as this is compatible with exercising authority, in order to mini-
mize the damage to the established order; etc.

©2008 THE ARISTOTELIAN SOCIETY
Proceedings of the Aristotelian Society Supplementary Volume LXXXII
doi: 10.1111/j.1467-8349.2008.00162.x

that he has received a command from God,[32] but he would not be
able to say why he believes that, or to say anything to distinguish his
situation from the obvious contrast case (namely, the one in which
he is in the grip of a delusion). As Johannes describes it, the individual occupying a higher immediacy would have to combine the characteristics of acting for objectively sufficient reasons and acting for
reasons that he clearly sees to be insufficient by every measure he is
in a position to apply. Again, this would not mean that he has no
justification in thinking what he does—only that he is not in a position to *appeal* to that justification. In other words, (3) above would
be the correct interpretation of Abraham's silence: Johannes knows
(and so we readers also know) that Abraham has a command from
God and is therefore justified—but Abraham himself does not.

III

The Messenger and the Message. The obvious question at this point
is, how does *Johannes* know? If the account I have given of the reason for Abraham's ignorance is correct, the same account applies to
us readers as well, and to Johannes himself. It is no accident that for
all he knows he has never encountered 'a single authentic instance'
of a knight of faith, even though 'every second person may be such
an instance' (Kierkegaard 1901–06, III:89; 1997–, 4:133). The aetiology of the knight of faith's belief is not something any human being is in a position to inspect, from which it follows that being a
knight of faith—rather than a lunatic—is no more discernible to
others than it is to the individual.

On what grounds can Johannes assume what, on his own account, he cannot see? Johannes knows that the Abraham he describes is a knight of faith because, and only because, that Abraham
is as much a work of his imagination as the knight of faith who

---

[32] Cross (2003) argues that Abraham does not even *believe* he has received a command of
God—that he believes the opposite. What makes Abraham a paradigm of faith is rather his
trust in God, which is to be taken as a 'practical' rather than a cognitive attitude. Like others who emphasize the importance of Abraham's trust over the propositional content of his
beliefs, Cross fails to notice that this description of Abraham's conduct relies on the
assumption that it is God (and not, for example, his own mental illness) that Abraham is
trusting—and that is impossible in the absence of a belief on Abraham's part that the command comes from God. Of course an account of (the virtue of) Abraham's trust as a practical attitude becomes possible once one has an account of (the reason for) Abraham's
belief—but it cannot *replace* such an account, as Cross contends.

©2008 The Aristotelian Society
Proceedings of the Aristotelian Society Supplementary Volume LXXXII
doi: 10.1111/j.1467-8349.2008.00162.x

'looks just like a tax collector'. *Fear and Trembling* is a poetic construction, and one of the ways in which the poetic constructor's standpoint is privileged is that it allows him to stipulate of Abraham what it is impossible for any human being to know or even to reasonably believe: that it was a command from God, that it was an ordeal in which the ethical was a temptation, that Abraham was a knight of faith. Likewise, we readers know that the Abraham of *Fear and Trembling* is a knight of faith because, and only because, his creator has told us so.

This interpretation of Abraham's silence, and the recognition it requires that the Abraham at issue is a fictional character, throws up an obvious obstacle to the success of what we have taken to be Johannes's project.[33] How can the portrayal of a fictional character, a 'poetic construction', drive up the price of faith? It can do so only if, and to the extent that, the character is identified with the historical Abraham of the biblical account—the Abraham to whose exemplary status believers are at least tacitly committed. But note that this identification is illegitimate, precisely because about *that* Abraham, Johannes is in no position to stipulate anything, and *a fortiori* in no position to stipulate that he was a knight of faith. The identification must fail at precisely the critical point. The biblical Abraham cannot serve an example of faith because we can have such examples only in fiction.[34]

Let me return to the question of what we are to make of the epigraph, a quotation from Hamann: 'What Tarquinius Superbus said in his garden [by striking off] the heads of the poppies, his son understood but the messenger did not' (Kierkegaard 1901–06, III:56; 1997, 4:100). What Tarquin's message conveyed was that his son should eliminate the leading citizens of Gabii as a way of consolidating his power in the city. The reference is to a story found in Livy among other classical sources, a story with which Kierkegaard would have been acquainted already as a schoolboy. If there was a reason to quote Hamann in particular, it did not lie in the aesthetic

---

[33] Readings on which the project is to argue for a religious over a secular ethical standpoint face the same obstacle, by the way. See Kosch (2006a, pp. 156–60).

[34] Just in case we missed this, Kierkegaard tells us in *Concluding Unscientific Postscript* that *Fear and Trembling*'s portrayal of the knight of faith was 'only a rash anticipation', that 'the beginning was made by ignoring the contradiction—how an observer could become at all *aware* of him in such a way that he could place himself, admiring, outside and admire that there is nothing, nothing whatever, to *notice* ...' (Kierkegaard 1901–06, VII:435n.; 1997-, 7:453n.).

©2008 The Aristotelian Society
Proceedings of the Aristotelian Society Supplementary Volume LXXXII
doi: 10.1111/j.1467-8349.2008.00162.x

quality of Hamann's prose, which is here unexceptional. It must rather have had to do either with the context from which the quotation is taken (it appears in one of Hamann's letters as part of a reflection on his own style of communication[35]) or with something else Kierkegaard thought he owed Hamann.

The epigraph in the penultimate draft of *Fear and Trembling* was considerably more complicated. Before sending the manuscript to the printer, Kierkegaard deleted three other passages.[36] The first of these, which he labels 'an old saying' (Kierkegaard 1909–78, III A 203), he had copied from Herder into his journal in 1842.[37] ('Write'—'For whom?'—'Write for the dead, for those in the past, whom you love'—'Will they read me?'—'Yes, for they will return as posterity.') The second, 'an old saying, slightly altered', is the same passage with the final response changed ('Yes, for they will return as posterity' becomes 'No!'). The third, like the Tarquin reference, comes from a passage in Hamann's correspondence in which he reflects on his own style of communication. It is an extract ('matters of fact and first principles all mixed up') from a longer passage which, in this same penultimate draft of *Fear and Trembling*, was to serve as the epigraph of the Problemata section, but which was also deleted from the version sent to the printer:

> A layman and an unbeliever must declare my style of writing nothing but nonsense, for I express myself with many tongues, speak the language of sophists, of wordplay, of Cretes and Arabs, Whites and Moors and Creoles, babble criticism, mythology, matters of fact and first principles all mixed up, and argue now $\kappa\alpha\tau'$ $\overset{\text{'}}{\alpha}\nu\theta\rho\omega\pi\text{o}\nu$, now $\kappa\alpha\tau'$ $\overset{\text{'}}{\epsilon}\xi\text{o}\chi\grave{\eta}\nu$. (Kierkegaard 1909–78, IV B 96 IC 4)[38]

All these passages deal with communication—its aim and strategies for achieving it—but the last has to do with the specific problem of communication of religious content to non-believers. Recall Kierkegaard's journal entry of 10 September 1836, on the encounter between Hamann and Hume and the 'complete misunderstanding between the Christian and the non-Christian'—and recall that this

---

[35] Compare Hamann (1821–43, 3:190), from a letter to Lindner, March 1763—Hamann quoting from a letter he has composed or is composing to his publisher Nicolai.

[36] See Kierkegaard (1909–78, IV B 96, 1a–1c).

[37] Kierkegaard's citation is to *Herder zur Litteratur und Kunst* (XVI:114). A source more readily available is Herder (1985, 7:530), from the 7th fragment of the 8th collection of the *Briefe zur Beförderung der Humanität*—on the topic of 'Schrift und Buchdrückerei'.

[38] Compare Hamann (1821–43, 1:467)—from a letter to Lindner, August 1759.

©2008 The Aristotelian Society
Proceedings of the Aristotelian Society Supplementary Volume LXXXII
doi: 10.1111/j.1467-8349.2008.00162.x

misunderstanding is premised on the very account of religious belief that Hamann and Hume share. The epigraph tells us to look for a hidden message; it also tells us *where* to look: to Hamann. What the account of the source of religious belief that Kierkegaard will give in *Philosophical Fragments* entails, that faith cannot be learned from another human being (Kierkegaard 1901–06, IV:189, 230, 264; 1997–, 4:227–8, 267, 298), is just the conclusion that Johannes fails to draw from his own account: that taking the biblical Abraham as a model of faith is impossible in principle. Abraham is taken to be faith's most eminent representative, and Johannes has (unwittingly) conveyed the message that in order to survive in the terrain of faith the reader must eliminate him, along with every other example.

Sage School of Philosophy
218 *Goldwin Smith Hall*
Cornell University
Ithaca, NY 14853
USA
mak229@cornell.edu

REFERENCES

Adams, Robert M. 1987: 'Vocation'. *Faith and Philosophy*, 4(4), pp. 448–62.

Arendt, Hannah 1989: *The Human Condition*. Chicago: University of Chicago Press.

Conant, James 1989: 'Must We Show What We Cannot Say?' In Richard Fleming and Michael Payne (eds.), *The Senses of Stanley Cavell*. Lewisburg, PA: Bucknell University Press.

——1993: 'Kierkegaard, Wittgenstein and Nonsense'. In his *Pursuits of Reason*. Lubbock, TX: Texas Tech.

Cross, Andrew 1999: '*Fear and Trembling*'s Unorthodox Ideal'. *Philosophical Topics*, 27(2), pp. 227–54.

——2003: 'Faith and Suspension of the Ethical in Fear and Trembling'. *Inquiry*, 46, pp. 1–27.

Evans, C. Stephen 1981: 'Is the Concept of Absolute Duty to God Unintelligible?' In Robert Perkins (ed.), *Kierkegaard's* Fear and Trembling: *Critical Appraisals*. University, AL: University of Alabama Press.

Fahrenbach, Helmut 1968: *Kierkegaards Existenzdialektische Ethik*. Frankfurt: Klostermann.

——1979: 'Kierkegaards Ethische Existenzanalyse (als "Korrektiv" der

©2008 THE ARISTOTELIAN SOCIETY
Proceedings of the Aristotelian Society Supplementary Volume LXXXII
doi: 10.1111/j.1467-8349.2008.00162.x

Kantisch-idealistischen Moralphilosophie)'. In Michael Theunissen and Walter Greve (eds.), *Materialien zur Philosophie Søren Kierkegaards*. Frankfurt: Suhrkamp.

Green, Ronald M. 1998: '"Developing" Fear and Trembling'. In Alastair Hannay and Gordon D. Marino (eds.), *The Cambridge Companion to Kierkegaard*. Cambridge: Cambridge University Press.

Hamann, Johann Georg 1821–43: *Schriften*, ed. F. Roth. Berlin: Reimer.

Hannay, Alastair 1982: *Kierkegaard*. Boston, MA: Routledge & Kegan Paul.

Hegel, Georg Wilhelm Friedrich 1986: *Werke*. Frankfurt: Suhrkamp.

Herder, Johann Gottfriied 1985: *Werke in Zehn Bänden*, ed. M. Bollacher et al. Frankfurt: Deutsche Klassiker.

Hume, David 1999: *An Enquiry Concerning Human Understanding*. Oxford: Oxford University Press.

Kant, Immanuel 1968: *Werke*, ed. Königlich Preussische Akademie der Wissenschaften. Berlin: Akademie Verlag.

Kierkegaard, Søren 1901–06: *Samlede Værker*, ed. A. B. Drachmann, J. L. Heiberg and H. O. Lange. Copenhagen: Gyldendal.

——1909–78: *Papirer*, ed. N. Thulstrup. Copenhagen: Gyldendal.

——1997–: *Skrifter*, ed. N. J. Cappelørn, J. Garff, J. Knudsen, J. Kondrup and A. McKinnon. Copenhagen: Gad.

Kosch, Michelle 2006a: *Freedom and Reason in Kant, Schelling, and Kierkegaard*. Oxford: Oxford University Press.

——2006b: 'Kierkegaard's Ethicist: Fichte's Role in Kierkegaard's Construction of the Ethical Standpoint'. *Archiv für Geschichte der Philosophie*, 88, pp. 261–95.

Lippitt, John 2003: *Kierkegaard and* Fear and Trembling. New York: Routledge.

Lowrie, Walter 1938: *Kierkegaard*. Oxford: Oxford University Press.

Pojman, Louis 1983: 'Christianity and Philosophy in Kierkegaard's Early Papers'. *Journal of the History of Ideas*, 44 (1).

Popkin, Richard H. 1951: 'Hume and Kierkegaard'. *Journal of Religion*, 31 (4).

Quinn, Philip L. 1998: 'Kierkegaard's Christian Ethics'. In Alastair Hannay and Gordon D. Marino (eds.), *The Cambridge Companion to Kierkegaard*. Cambridge: Cambridge University Press.

Taylor, Mark C. 1981: 'Sounds of Silence'. In Robert Perkins (ed.), *Kierkegaard's* Fear and Trembling: *Critical Appraisals*. University, AL: University of Alabama Press.

Whittaker, John H. 1988: 'Suspension of the Ethical in *Fear and Trembling*'. *Kierkegaardiana*, 14, pp. 101–13.

©2008 THE ARISTOTELIAN SOCIETY
Proceedings of the Aristotelian Society Supplementary Volume LXXXII
doi: 10.1111/j.1467-8349.2008.00162.x

II — JOHN LIPPITT

WHAT NEITHER ABRAHAM NOR JOHANNES DE SILENTIO COULD SAY

Though there are significant points of overlap between Michelle Kosch's
reading of *Fear and Trembling* and my own, this paper focuses primarily
on a significant difference: the legitimacy or otherwise of looking to para-
digmatic exemplars of faith in order to understand faith. I argue that
Kosch's reading threatens to underplay the importance of exemplarity in
Kierkegaard's thought, and that there is good reason to resist her use of
Philosophical Fragments as the key to interpreting the 'hidden message' of
Fear and Trembling. Key to both claims is the *Concluding Unscientific
Postscript*. I also briefly sketch an alternative reading of the 'hidden mes-
sage', one in which Kierkegaard's Christian commitments play a notably
different role.

I

Fear and Trembling*'s Secret Message*. The perennial interest in, and
range of interpretations of, *Fear and Trembling* is remarkable. It
shows Kierkegaard's prediction in his journals that 'once I am dead,
Fear and Trembling alone will be enough for an imperishable name
as an author' (Kierkegaard 1967–78, 6:6491).[1] to have been prophetic indeed. For good or ill, *Fear and Trembling* is probably the
text most commonly associated with his name, although—*pace*
Michelle Kosch—I think there is serious competition for the title of
Kierkegaard's 'most elusive' work. Yet as Kosch rightly notes, the
mystery trailed by the epigraph—that *Fear and Trembling* might
have a 'hidden message', and if so, what that message might be—
has long since fascinated commentators. Kosch and I will disagree

---

[1] For references to Kierkegaard's published works, I cite the first edition of the *Samlede
Vaerker*, the volume numbers and pagination of which is preserved in the margins of *Kierkegaard's Writings*, the standard English-language translations by the Hongs. For quotations
from the journals, I use the seven-volume Hong translation of the *Journals and Papers*: references are given by volume and entry number.

©2008 THE ARISTOTELIAN SOCIETY
Proceedings of the Aristotelian Society Supplementary Volume LXXXII
doi: 10.1111/j.1467-8349.2008.00163.x

on what that message is, but before getting down to the points of disagreement, let me outline some central issues on which we do agree. First, and most important, we both think it implausibly simplistic to read *Fear and Trembling* as arguing straightforwardly for the superiority of 'the religious' to 'the ethical'. Second, we both agree that it is important to note how the pseudonymous author Johannes de Silentio makes clear that a key part of his aim is to prevent faith being sold off too cheaply, at a bargain price. To this end, Kosch draws attention, as have numerous other commentators, to the economic imagery with which the book begins and ends. Third, and relatedly, I agree that 'the intended audience consists of people who already embrace a religious point of view and are already tacitly committed to regarding conduct like Abraham's as religiously justified' (Kosch 2008, p. 61). But Kosch would presumably balk at the way I would describe this: that the book properly aims at clarifying what is involved in taking Abraham as a paradigmatic exemplar of faith. This point—on the legitimacy or otherwise of the attempt to understand faith through the use of paradigmatic examples or exemplars—turns out to be probably the main point of disagreement between us.

Kosch claims that the entailed message of *Philosophical Fragments* is that 'faith cannot be learned from another human being' and that this is the hidden message of *Fear and Trembling*: 'taking the biblical Abraham as a model of faith is impossible in principle … in order to survive in the terrain of faith the reader must eliminate him, along with every other example' (Kosch 2008, p. 77). (Hereafter, I shall refer to this as 'Kosch's conclusion'.) I think this is problematic on a number of levels.

Kosch's critique of the legitimacy of discussing faith through the use of exemplars thereof is interesting because the use of exemplars is, it seems to me, quite central to Kierkegaard's methodology. Vital to his authorship are pseudonyms—Johannes de Silentio, Johannes Climacus, Anti-Climacus, and so on—each of whom represents a distinct existential standpoint. Similarly, characters such as Judge William, the spokesman for 'the ethical' in *Either/Or*, both argue for and in various ways embody the position they represent. Moreover, a number of texts, such as *Either/Or* and *Stages on Life's Way*, present us with *multiple* authors and manifestations of the various existence-spheres. (To understand 'the aesthetic', for instance, requires us to get to grips with Don Giovanni, 'A' and Johannes the

©2008 The Aristotelian Society
Proceedings of the Aristotelian Society Supplementary Volume LXXXII
doi: 10.1111/j.1467-8349.2008.00163.x

Seducer in *Either/Or* and the various speech-makers of 'In Vino Veritas' in *Stages*.) I take this practice to show Kierkegaard's commitment to the following two ideas. First, that the concrete embodiment of abstract ideas in examples and exemplars aids a reader's subjective understanding. Second, with specific reference to ethical and religious notions, that Kierkegaard tacitly endorses a broadly Aristotelian idea: that we learn the good through direct reference to exemplars. This is particularly clear in the case of the imitation of Christ: the ultimate instance, for Kierkegaard, of the idea that human moral growth and education involves imitating the paradigmatically wise and good. To suppose that concrete exemplars of faith play no legitimate role in a Kierkegaardian understanding of it would therefore be a very surprising conclusion.

As I shall argue in what follows, there are ambiguities in Kosch's conclusion that Kierkegaard's view, and *Fear and Trembling*'s hidden message, is that 'faith cannot be learned from another human being' (Kosch 2008, p. 77). I shall here make two preliminary assumptions as to what she means. First, since Abraham is an Old Testament figure, I shall assume that when Kosch talks about 'faith' she does not (despite the reference to *Fragments*, but in common with Johannes de Silentio) mean specifically *Christian* faith. But second, given what is for Kierkegaard the 'special case' of Christ, I assume that Kosch means her claim to exclude that human being who, according to the Christian orthodoxy to which Kierkegaard subscribed, was also God. It is very clear that Christ plays a pivotal role for Kierkegaard as an exemplar of faith; as the 'prototype' to be followed and imitated. (See especially *Practice in Christianity*.) Nevertheless, the follower does not do this under their own steam:

> It must be firmly maintained that Christ has not come to the world only to set an example [*Exempel*] for us. ... He comes to save us and to present the example. This very example should humble us, teach us how infinitely far away we are from resembling the ideal. When we humble ourselves, then Christ is pure compassion. And in our striving to approach the prototype [*Forbilledet*], the prototype itself is again our very help. It alternates; when we are striving, then he is the prototype; and when we stumble, lose courage, etc., then he is the love which helps us up, and then he is the prototype again. (Kierkegaard 1967–78, 1:334)

In view of the centrality of Christ as the prototype or pattern to be imitated, both in Kierkegaard's thought and in the wider Chris-

tian context, therefore, I shall assume that Kosch is taking it as a
given that within this tradition Christ's divine status makes him an
exception to her rule. To put this in the language of *Fragments*
(more of which imminently), it is, for Kierkegaard, because Christ is
'the god' who provides 'the condition' that he is 'the prototype'.

II

Philosophical Fragments: *'The Condition' and Examples*. In assessing Kosch's conclusion, then, let us turn to the aspect of *Philosophical Fragments* on which she bases her argument as to *Fear and
Trembling*'s hidden message. In the *Fragments*, Johannes Climacus
certainly argues that no human being can provide 'the condition'
(Kierkegaard 1901–06, IV:184) for understanding the truth necessary for salvation; that the teacher is 'the god' who gives both the
condition and the truth (Kierkegaard 1901–06, IV:185). But this
leaves open a range of possible views of exactly what 'the condition'
involves. For orthodox Christian belief, scripture is part of what is
'given' in 'the condition'. It is clear both that Kierkegaard takes seriously the question of what constitutes religious authority[2] and that
he takes scripture to be authoritative.[3] For instance, in *For Self-Ex-
amination*, we read:

> God's Word is given in order that you shall act according to it ... If
> you do not read God's Word in such a way that you consider that the
> least little bit you do understand instantly binds you to do accordingly,
> then you are not reading God's Word. (Kierkegaard 1901–06, XII:
> 318–19)

And in *Without Authority*—in stark contrast to Kant, for
instance—we get this:

> It is not by evaluating the content of the doctrine esthetically or philo-
> sophically that I will or can arrive at the conclusion: ergo the one who
> has delivered this doctrine is called by a revelation, ergo he is an apos-

---

[2] On this point, as well as Kierkegaard's manuscript on Adler to which Kosch refers, see
Evans (2000).

[3] For an account of Kierkegaard that puts his acceptance of the authoritative role of the
Bible in Christian life and identity at the heart of his enterprise, see Polk (1997). On the
importance of Biblical quotations in the pseudonymous authorship specifically, see Pons
(2004).

©2008 THE ARISTOTELIAN SOCIETY
Proceedings of the Aristotelian Society Supplementary Volume LXXXII
doi: 10.1111/j.1467-8349.2008.00163.x

tle. The relationship is just the reverse: the one called by a revelation, to whom a doctrine is entrusted, argues on the basis that it is a revelation, on the basis that he has authority. I am not to listen to Paul because he is brilliant or matchlessly brilliant, but I am to submit to Paul because he has divine authority ... (Kierkegaard 1901–06, XI:98)[4]

Naturally, this will (as Kierkegaard predicted) offend many a secular philosopher, but the point for our purposes is to note that this puts Johannes de Silentio, grappling with Abraham, in a rather different position to someone grappling with an example generated at random from his own imagination. The scriptures clearly do give examples of faith—including Abraham—from whom the reader is expected to learn. Hebrews 11, for example, offers its readers a litany of examples from history of what faith does as encouragement towards perseverance, Abraham being a central such example.[5] And in Romans 4:3–5, Paul famously offers Abraham as a classic example of justification by faith rather than works:

> For what saith the scripture? 'Abraham believed God, and it was counted unto him for righteousness.' Now to him that worketh is the reward not reckoned of grace, but of debt. But to him that worketh not, but believeth on him that justifieth the ungodly, his faith is counted for righteousness.

What does this use of exemplars of faith in the New Testament suggest about the Kierkegaardian view of their legitimacy? I propose the following line of interpretation, consistent with the central argument of the *Fragments* which Kosch mentions. It does not follow that we need to eliminate all examples, either when 'the condition' is met or when it is not. (I shall return to the latter case in §IV.) Sure, for Kierkegaard (and Climacus), the biblical Abraham, not being divine, does not provide 'the condition' for faith. But it does not follow from this that he cannot provide an important example of faith for those who possess 'the condition': and this is presumably what the writers of Romans 4 and Hebrews 11 intend. Indeed, in her impressive book, Kosch (2006, pp. 156–7) recognizes the possibility of an argument from scriptural authority. What I am suggesting here seems perfectly consistent with what she (rightly, I believe) argues there: that rather than read *Fear and Trembling* as an argument in-

---

[4] I am grateful to Kyle Roberts for reminding me of this passage.
[5] See especially Hebrews 11:8–19.

©2008 THE ARISTOTELIAN SOCIETY
Proceedings of the Aristotelian Society Supplementary Volume LXXXII
doi: 10.1111/j.1467-8349.2008.00163.x

tended to take a reader from the ethical to the religious, it should be read as 'aimed primarily at articulating the constraints imposed by a life of faith, and so presupposing, rather than arguing for, a religious standpoint' (Kosch 2006, p. 160).

In her book, Kosch dismisses the argument from scriptural authority as question-begging. Indeed it is, if we suppose that what Kierkegaard is about is trying to argue the non-Christian into Christianity. But as the above quote shows, this is not what Kosch supposes him to be doing. I wonder, then, whether—to allude to the Hume passage she quotes—we could say of Kosch here something akin to what Hamann said of Hume? That while she intends this 'question-begging' charge as criticism, in fact the claim in question—that a commitment to scriptural authority is part of (Christian) faith—is just orthodoxy?[6] Kosch worries that *Fear and Trembling*'s verdict on Abraham—that *if* there is no teleological suspension of the ethical or absolute duty to God, then Abraham is 'lost', just a common murderer—is 'as likely to drive the bourgeois Christian into the arms of Kant et al. as to succeed in driving up the price of faith' (Kosch 2008, p. 62). What we need, she argues, is an *antecedent* commitment to taking Abraham as a model of faith. But for Kierkegaard, I submit, that antecedent commitment is simply biblical authority.[7]

Exactly what is Kosch's charge against Johannes de Silentio? One line of objection to Johannes found in the secondary literature is that his grappling with the Abraham story causes him to play too fast and loose with the biblical Abraham. That is, his attempted imaginative identification with Abraham means that the figure who emerges from his reflections is not in fact the biblical figure, but one of his own invention. There does seem to be *something* in such a charge— though in §IV below I shall offer a partial defence of Johannes from

---

[6] In her discussion, Kosch mentions Kant's rejection of the Abraham story, on the grounds that 'apparent direct manifestations of the will of God can never be action guiding, because they either tell us to do something in conformity with the moral law (in which case they are redundant ...), or they tell us to do something in contravention of the moral law (in which case we are obliged to ignore them, because our certainty of the dictates of the moral law is total, whereas our certainty that something is a divine command can never be)' (Kosch 2006, p. 157). But Kierkegaard is far more sceptical about what we can know about the moral law than is Kant, in significant part because he is more sceptical about what unaided human reason can achieve. Relatedly, special revelation plays a role in his thought that is at odds with Kant's views on the matter.

[7] Kosch (2008, p. 60–1) claims that in *Fear and Trembling*, 'Abraham's righteousness is not even categorically asserted'. Yet in Problema III, Johannes asserts that Abraham 'did not become the single individual by way of sin—on the contrary, he was a righteous man, God's chosen one' (Kierkegaard 1901–06, III:146).

©2008 THE ARISTOTELIAN SOCIETY
Proceedings of the Aristotelian Society Supplementary Volume LXXXII
doi: 10.1111/j.1467-8349.2008.00163.x

it. But Kosch's charge seems stronger than this. True, she does claim that the Abraham of *Fear and Trembling* is 'rather idiosyncratic' (Kosch 2008, p. 62) and Johannes's own fictional creation. But she also concludes that taking even 'the biblical Abraham as a model of faith is impossible in principle' (Kosch 2008, p. 77). This is because of Abraham's inaccessible interiority: 'While the actions of the knight of faith are visible, his being a knight of faith (rather than a lunatic) is not' (Kosch 2006, p. 158). But once we have noted Kierkegaard's commitment to scriptural authority, the answer to the question 'What are the grounds for supposing that Abraham is an exemplary instance of faith?' is clear: 'Because the scriptures tell us so.' While this may strike many as philosophically disappointing, it does seem to fit quite squarely with Kierkegaard's overall religious position on biblical authority, and also the view, which we have seen that Kosch herself endorses, that *Fear and Trembling* is about articulating what a life of faith may involve, rather than arguing from first principles for 'the religious'.[8] In other words, we do not need to conclude that Kierkegaard's ultimate intention is that we see the Abraham of *Fear and Trembling* as no more than Johannes's 'poetic construction'; a purely fictional artifice. But we can recognize—as does Kierkegaard, on Kosch's account (and here I have no desire to quarrel)—that this reliance on biblical authority provides no reasons for holding it that are epistemically acceptable to a sceptic. That is as it should be, for this uncertainty—'out on 70,000 fathoms', as Climacus famously puts it (Kierkegaard 1901–06, VII:195)—is part of the very nature of Kierkegaardian faith.

We should not lose sight of the first objection raised against Johannes de Silentio in the paragraph above, and I shall return to this in §IV. But first, given the importance of Climacus's *Fragments* to Kosch's conclusion, let me propose two reasons to doubt that Kosch's conclusion is in fact Climacus's ultimate view.

III

Climacus as a Key to Interpreting Fear and Trembling: *From the* Fragments *to the* Postscript. First, note that in the *Postscript* to the *Fragments*, Climacus himself uses exemplars to illustrate faith.

---

[8] Keep in mind also Kierkegaard's determination, *contra* Hegel, not to subordinate religious to philosophical categories.

There is a sense in which arguably that text's central character, Socrates, himself illustrates some essential points about faith. Second, also in the *Postscript*, Climacus draws an important distinction between understanding what Christianity *is* and understanding what it is to *be* a Christian. Applying this distinction to faith more generally (so as to encompass the Abraham case), a question for Kosch is what exactly it is that exemplars of faith are supposed to be unable to teach us: what faith *is*, or what it is like to *have* faith? Could they do the former, even if not the latter? Let me flesh out these points in turn.

A. *Socrates and Faith.* The *Postscript* makes considerable use of exemplars to make its points, none more so than Socrates. I have argued elsewhere (Lippitt 2000) that we can look to Socrates as presented in the *Postscript* for illumination on what it is to be both an ironist and a humorist (irony and humour being two crucial 'boundary zones' between the aesthetic, ethical and religious existence-spheres). But this is so because of a more fundamental role that Socrates plays in the *Postscript*: as Climacus's paradigm exemplar of the 'subjective thinker' and indirect communicator.[9] As Jacob Howland (2006, p. 192) notes, in emphasizing this aspect of Socrates in the *Postscript*, Climacus 'correct[s] the misleading impression of Socrates left by the *Fragments*'. What matters most for our current purposes is that Socrates *qua* subjective thinker embodies a certain sort of faith—which causes a difficulty for Kosch's conclusion.

How so? The *Postscript* describes faith as 'the highest passion of subjectivity' (Kierkegaard 1901–06, VII:107). Obviously, Socrates does not embody the *Postscript*'s ostensible central topic: specifically *Christian* faith. But as every reader of the *Postscript* notes, Climacus's explicit treatment of Christian faith arrives rather late on the scene of that text, prefigured by a much lengthier discussion of 'subjective thinking' and Religiousness A that Climacus treats as an essential prerequisite to his comparatively brief discussion of Religiousness B (Christianity).[10] As noted, Socrates is central to the discussion of subjective thinking. Howland (2006, p. 198) observes

---

[9] Though the *Postscript* discusses other 'subjective thinkers' (Lessing, for instance), it has been noted that even in the chapter ostensibly devoted to Lessing, Climacus refers more often to Socrates. See Rubenstein (2001, p. 442, cited in Howland 2006, p. 193).

[10] Religiousness A is, in brief, a worldview characterized by resignation, suffering and guilt in which nevertheless the 'absolute paradox' of the incarnation plays no role.

how Climacus argues that 'the Socratic or philosophical appropria-
tion of the truth—like Socrates' ascent to the truth, which could not
proceed without the help of the god—involves a kind of faith'. Let
us elaborate on this claim.

In a famous passage, Climacus claims that there is 'more truth' in
the person who prays 'with all the passion of infinity' to an idol
than in the person who 'prays in untruth' (that is, half-heartedly, in-
sincerely or 'objectively') in 'the house of the true God' (Kierkegaard 1901–06, VII:168). This valorizing of the inner subjective
state of the worshipper over and above 'objectively' correct doctrine
is immediately followed by a discussion of Socrates, specifically his
attitude towards the immortality of the soul. Climacus's point is
that although Socrates 'poses the question objectively', what matters
is that 'He stakes his whole life on this "if"; he dares to die, and
with the passion of the infinite he has so ordered his whole life that
it might be acceptable—*if* there is an immortality' (Kierkegaard
1901–06, VII: 168). In other words, Socrates lives his life on the basis of his *faith* that the soul is immortal.

In his *Postscript* discussion, then, Climacus seems to be doing
precisely what Kosch infers from the *Fragments* as illegitimate: illus-
trating faith by the example of one who possessed it. Of course, this
is not Christian faith—but then neither is Abraham's. The question
then is this: why should we take the *Fragments* as key to determin-
ing *Fear and Trembling*'s message when its *Postscript* does not practice what Kosch takes the *Fragments* (and, indirectly, *Fear and
Trembling*) to preach?

B. *There's Understanding and There's Understanding.* Second, let us
turn to Climacus's distinction between understanding 'what Christianity is' and understanding 'what it is to be a Christian' (Kierkegaard 1901–06, VII:322). Climacus raises this in the context of his
concern about the dangers of turning Christianity into 'a kind of
philosophical theory' (Kierkegaard 1901–06, VII:321). Since Christianity is an 'existence-communication' (Kierkegaard 1901–06,
VII:322n.) and '*becoming* a Christian is what is difficult' (Kierkegaard 1901–06, VII:322, my emphasis) then (beyond a certain point)
'wanting to understand it is a cunning evasion that wants to shirk
the task' (Kierkegaard 1901–06, VII:322n.). The context makes
clear that the kind of understanding Climacus is here criticizing is the
kind of detached intellectual reflection in which the thinker, rather

than relating the 'existence-communication' to his own life, endlessly
defers and thus evades the demand Christianity makes on him. But
Climacus is quite clear that one can understand 'what Christianity is'
on an intellectual level ('the objective question about the truth of
Christianity' (Kierkegaard 1901–06, VII:321)) without being exis-
tentially committed to its claims: indeed, Kierkegaard's repeated
contrast between faith and 'offence' would only seem to make sense
on the assumption that one must be able to have some understanding
of what Christianity claims in order to be able to reject it. Hence Climacus's conclusion that 'one can know what Christianity is without
being a Christian' but that one cannot 'know what it is to be a Christian without being one' (Kierkegaard 1901–06, VII:322).

What is said here of Christianity in particular, I suggest, applies
also to faith in general. Here we clearly see another sense in which
Kosch's claim (2008, p. 77) that 'faith cannot be learned from another human being' is ambiguous. Is she claiming that 'what faith is'
cannot be learned from another human being, or that 'what it is to
have faith' cannot be so learned? The distinction in *Postscript* suggests that a person could gain a provisional, outsider's understanding of faith (perhaps, after the fashion of Hegelianism, on a
conceptual level) while yet falling short of understanding on a phenomenological level what it is to have faith. In the Preface to *Fear
and Trembling*, Johannes claims: 'Even if someone were able to
transpose the whole content of faith into conceptual form, it does
not follow that he has comprehended faith, comprehended how he
entered into it or how it entered into him' (Kierkegaard 1901–06,
III:59). What then is Johannes ultimately claiming when he says
that he cannot 'understand' Abraham? There seems good reason to
read him as denying just the phenomenological understanding: his
repeated attempts to think himself inside Abraham's head seem ultimately to end up in a failure to grasp the phenomenology of Abraham's specific position. Yet this failure is not inconsistent with the
relative confidence he seems to have in drawing such conceptual distinctions as that between faith and infinite resignation; faith and
tragic heroism; and so on. Once we consider Climacus's distinction
between these two levels of understanding, we can see that there is
no performative contradiction here.

When we pay attention to his *Postscript* as well as his *Fragments*,
then, we see that Climacus is committed to a view according to
which there are limits to the degree of understanding of a 'higher'

©2008 The Aristotelian Society
Proceedings of the Aristotelian Society Supplementary Volume LXXXII
doi: 10.1111/j.1467-8349.2008.00163.x

existence-sphere possible from outside it. And Johannes de Silentio, as every reader notes, claims to be 'outside' faith. But exemplars or examples of faith can still have a distinct, legitimate purpose even to such a person: a person who lacks 'the condition' but who is conscientiously trying to understand faith. According to Martha Nussbaum and others, imaginative engagement with literary characters can play a distinctive role in a person's ethical development.[11] For someone like Johannes, a similar role is played by imaginative engagement with figures, such as Abraham, in biblical narratives. I shall elaborate on this claim in the next section.

IV

Exemplars Without 'The Condition': A Partial Defence of Johannes de Silentio. At the end of §II above, I noted a tradition of interpretation (with which Kosch's overlaps) in which Johannes is accused of misrepresenting the biblical Abraham, of creating a fictional character of his own invention some way removed from the biblical figure. Several critics have suggested that it is in this respect that we are supposed to find Johannes an unreliable narrator; that his fixation upon Abraham's inaccessible interiority, in Daniel Conway's words, 'diverts our attention (and his own) from the pressing question of *his own* interiority' (Conway 2002, p. 101). In other words, Johannes embodies with respect to faith precisely the kind of evasion discussed in §III.B above. I have argued elsewhere (Lippitt 2003, ch. 7) that this charge against him is unfair. Since Kosch too seems to consider Johannes's confusion to be crucial to the hidden message of *Fear and Trembling*, let me briefly outline that argument here.

One of the most forceful statements of this charge is made by Andrew Cross (1994), who draws on a distinction made by Anti-Climacus in *Practice in Christianity* concerning the difference between ethically impotent 'admiration' of an exemplar (think of 'hero-worship' that does not issue in action) and the mode of 'imitation' in which the exemplar is 'assimilated into' one or taken 'as one takes medicine' (Kierkegaard 1901–06, XII:222). On Anti-Climacus's view, it seems that anything less than immediate emulation of an exemplar should be condemned as merely ethically impotent 'ad-

---

[11] See especially Nussbaum (1990).

©2008 The Aristotelian Society
Proceedings of the Aristotelian Society Supplementary Volume LXXXII
doi: 10.1111/j.1467-8349.2008.00163.x

miration'. And Cross (1994, p. 211) charges Johannes with embod-
ying precisely this sort of impotent admiration.

But this charge is unfair. In his continual telling and retelling of
the Abraham story in order better to understand his paradigmatic
exemplar of faith, Johannes is not merely a detached admirer, but a
highly *engaged* observer, who has what Kierkegaard himself describes and commends as a 'passionate concentration' (Kierkegaard
1967–78, 3:3130). I suggest that it is crucial to note that there is an
important middle ground between admiration and imitation: something like the Aristotelian 'perception' and attention discussed by
Nussbaum in her work on the ethical salience of literature. If Nussbaum is right that an essential element of ethics is developing the
right kind of highly attuned perception available to us through sustained attention to great literature, then (transferring this thought to
a religious context) the kind of imaginative engagement with a biblical narrative in which Johannes engages can have an ethical and religious value even if it falls short of direct 'imitation'. Note that this
exercise of imagination can legitimately take the form that Johannes's investigation takes: detailed attention to the particularities of
Abraham's situation. A significant aspect of Johannes's method
throughout *Fear and Trembling* involves contrasting Abraham's apparently forthcoming loss of his son with superficially similar instances of such loss (for instance, the fact that Abraham is—unlike
Agamemnon, for example—called upon to make the sacrifice himself) (Kierkegaard 1901–06, III:74). This results from Johannes's
commitment to the idea that it is rare to find someone who 'can tell
what happened as it deserves to be told' (Kierkegaard 1901–06,
III:74). 'Telling it as it deserves to be told', I take it, includes not
conflating it with superficially similar stories. This 'attention to the
particular' continues throughout the book, and underpins
Johannes's repeated attempts to get closer to understanding
Abraham by comparisons with figures who might at first sight be
analogous, but according to Johannes turn out on closer inspection
not to be: the knight of infinite resignation; the tragic hero; and the
instances of aesthetic rather than religious concealment. We might
even suggest that, on Kierkegaard's view, Johannes's exercise of the
imagination brings one as close as one can get to understanding
faith without 'the condition'.

What supports this view? Jamie Ferreira's much admired work on
imagination and will in Kierkegaardian faith offers a clue, I suggest,

as to what useful work Johannes's grappling with Abraham might be doing. Ferreira (1991, pp. 35–6) argues that though Kierkegaard does not believe that religious beliefs can be directly willed, the will does play an important role in his thought; Kierkegaard's is not a position according to which 'the condition' is given by an utterly mysterious, 'magical' grace. Ferreira presents religious transitions on the model of *Gestalt* shifts, but she compares such transitions to an explosive which does not explode gradually by degrees, but only once a critical threshold has been reached. Though the explosion then occurs suddenly, this is only because of the gradual increase of heat. Similarly, on Ferreira's view, the qualitative shift of a person's 'transforming vision' (such as a religious conversion) may come about as a result of years of reflection, deliberation, prayer, etc. The point here is that the kind of imaginative engagement with a paradigmatic exemplar of faith in which Johannes engages is a perfectly legitimate part of such reflection.

However, that reflection need not take the immediately 'self-concentrated' form of Anti-Climacan 'imitation', in which I 'think about myself, simply and solely … think about myself' (Kierkegaard 1901–06, XII: 221). It is significant for Nussbaum that the engagement of our emotional and imaginative faculties with great narratives takes place outside our practical engagement in our own lives. This is significant because such practical engagement can give rise to certain major 'sources of distortion that frequently impede our personal jealousies or angers or … the sometimes blinding violence of our loves' (Nussbaum 1990, p. 48). Such sources of distortion are 'obstacles to correct vision' (Nussbaum 1990, p. 162). Engagement with great literature enables us to avoid them, and thus we find and experience 'love without possessiveness, attention without bias, involvement without panic' (Nussbaum 1990, p. 162). And this, for Nussbaum, is itself an ethically valuable form of experience.

Note that Kierkegaard himself expresses a similar view in *Two Ages*. For literary 'persuasion' to be possible, he claims, we need 'the inviting intimacy of the cosy inner sanctum from which heated emotions and critical, dangerous decisions and extreme exertions are excluded' (Kierkegaard 1901–06, VIII: 18). David Gouwens (1982, pp. 358–9), citing Martin Thust (1931), glosses this as follows: 'Kierkegaard understands the virtue of literature to be that it operates first to lead one away from oneself: the aesthetic distancing functions positively as a mirror of possibilities … And this objectivity is preparatory to a possible return to concrete actuality in subjective passion.' In other words, for Kierkegaard, not all engaged reflection short of immediate 'imitation' is culpable evasion.

Johannes's ultimate failure fully to 'understand' Abraham shows that the will alone cannot provide 'the condition': cannot bring about faith. But this does not show that reflection on exemplars of faith of the kind in which Johannes engages is either illegitimate or totally fruitless.

V

Fear and Trembling's *Hidden Christianity.* Yet what justifies taking Abraham in particular as exemplary? Kosch (2008, p. 61) questions why Kierkegaard's audience ought to accept that commitment to a religious (she presumably here means Christian-religious) life commits them to taking faith as more demanding than 'Sunday morning Christians' take it to be in the light of the alternative accounts of Kant, Hegel, Schleiermacher, and so on, according to which Abraham's willingness to sacrifice Isaac is 'an aberration'. This, I have argued, is less of a puzzle than she makes it. If Kierkegaard's project is to explicate what Climacus calls 'old-fashioned orthodoxy in its rightful severity' Kierkegaard (1901–06, VII:234n.), then Johannes is taking Abraham as exemplary simply because this is what scripture, which he takes to be authoritative, does. This assumption generates precisely the puzzle that Johannes faces up to: *given* that Abraham is an exemplar of faith, what does Abraham show us about that faith? And what he shows us is, *prima facie*, far more troubling that the 'Sunday morning Christians' like to admit to themselves. Unless, that is, the Abraham story has a different message entirely. What, then, is the book's hidden message, if it is not the one for which Kosch has argued?

In the book already cited (Lippitt 2003, especially ch. 6), I have offered an overview of various alternative attempts to explain the 'hidden message' of the text. In the space that remains, let me give a brief account of what strikes me as the most likely intended meaning of this message, given the Pauline and Lutheran tradition to which Kierkegaard belonged. As noted, Abraham holds a special status within the Christian tradition as the paradigm of righteousness as well as faith. Allied with Kierkegaard's own Christian com-

mitments, it is therefore no surprise that several commentators—
amongst them Louis Mackey (1972), Ronald M. Green (1998) and
Stephen Mulhall (2001)—have seen in *Fear and Trembling* a distinctly Christian message. On this view, the book is really about
Christian teachings on sin, grace, forgiveness and salvation. This
claim, which is made in slightly different ways and in very varying
degrees of detail by different commentators, belongs within the ana-
gogical tradition of seeing the Old Testament as foreshadowing
themes in the New. It takes seriously the explicit use of the phrase
'fear and trembling' in the context of a discussion of Christian salvation in Philippians 2:12–13. In terms of Kosch's divisions, such a
reading could be classified as:

> (3b) *Abraham's and Johannes's ignorance.* There is something
> about Abraham's situation that Abraham *himself* cannot
> understand and so cannot explain. Neither can Johannes,
> but the reader sufficiently clued into the anagogical tradi-
> tion of reading (and to Kierkegaardian devices of indirect
> communication) can.[12]

(Note that on this reading, the problem of Kosch's §III—how does
Johannes know what Abraham doesn't?—does not emerge.)

Though there is no space to go into the full details of such readings here, we can draw out certain key features.[13] The first and most
obvious point on this reading is the significance of the fact that Isaac
is Abraham's *son*. This foreshadows the Christian atonement, in
which God the Father is prepared to sacrifice God the Son to redeem humanity. Hence according to this reading the central indirect
message of *Fear and Trembling* is as follows. God transcends the ordinary standards of the ethical—what, as sinners, we *deserve*—and
through making both a 'teleological suspension of the ethical' and a
sacrifice of God the Son, redeems humanity. A 'natural' sense of justice would suggest that, if humanity is in a state of sin, then we do
not *deserve* redemption. But just as on a more straightforward reading Abraham teleologically suspends the ethical, so by this analogy
God can teleologically suspend a natural sense of justice (read: 'the

---

[12] Not all commentators in this interpretative tradition would endorse this claim. Stephen
Mulhall, for instance, holds that Johannes is in on the game. Notwithstanding my use of
Mulhall in what follows below, I am unconvinced on this point: for the disagreement, see
Lippitt (2003, pp. 202–5).

[13] The following paragraphs draw on my earlier discussion of this in Lippitt (2003).

©2008 THE ARISTOTELIAN SOCIETY
Proceedings of the Aristotelian Society Supplementary Volume LXXXII
doi: 10.1111/j.1467-8349.2008.00163.x

ethical') in service of a higher *telos*: his love for humanity.

Note that on such an interpretation, the teleological suspension of the ethical that troubles Johannes and most readers—Abraham's willingness to sacrifice Isaac—is not the teleological suspension of the ethical that really matters. This is the 'hidden message' that Johannes misses.

The above has an important implication for the believer's relation to the demands of the ethical, since living up to the demands of the moral law is no longer the primary criterion for self-acceptance. C. Stephen Evans (1993, p. 26) describes this as 'morality in a new key', in which one is motivated by 'grateful expression of a self that has been received as a gift'. (In this sense, it fits with a central theme in *Fear and Trembling*, that of 'getting Isaac back' under a new mode of valuation.) One obvious objection might be that on such a reading the 'anguish' of Abraham that Johannes repeatedly stresses drops out of the picture. But this is too hasty. If Abraham stands for God the Father, yet Abraham's anguish is central to the story, this actually highlights a second key feature of the Christian reading. Abraham's (read: God the Father's) anguish draws attention to the Christian claim that God the Father *suffers* along with his creation: a view thought by many to be part of any adequate answer to the problem of evil.

Proponents of a Christian reading of *Fear and Trembling* have also made much of the gnomic mention of sin in Problema III's discussion of Agnete and the merman (Kierkegaard 1901–06, III: 145–6). Such commentators take this—rather than the question of 'what Abraham couldn't say'—as the key to the riddle of the text. Kosch doesn't discuss this, and though she mentions one of Climacus's criticisms of *Fear and Trembling* in the *Postscript*, she does not add the following important aspect of Climacus's review of the earlier text:

> The teleological suspension of the ethical must have an even more definite religious expression. The ethical is then present at every moment with its infinite requirement, but the individual is not capable of fulfilling it. This powerlessness of the individual must not be seen as an imperfection in the continued endeavour to attain an ideal, for in that case the suspension is no more postulated than the man who administers his office in an ordinary way is suspended. The suspension consists in the individual's finding himself in a state exactly opposite to what the ethical requires. (Kierkegaard 1901–06, VII: 226)

The echoes of the Christian reading's focus are clear. This 'state exactly opposite to what the ethical requires' is sin, which Climacus claims to be 'the crucial point of departure for the religious existence' (Kierkegaard 1901–06, VII: 227). Moreover, sin 'is not a factor within another order of things, but is itself the beginning of the religious order of things' (Kierkegaard 1901–06, VII: 227). This echoes the central Kierkegaardian idea that an ethic with sin (and forgiveness) at its heart is a radical break with ethics as otherwise conceived.

Stephen Mulhall (2001, pp. 354–88) provides a particularly intriguing case for a Christian reading. Mulhall argues that Abraham's words, when he says 'God will provide a lamb for the burnt offering', have 'a prophetic dimension ... of which he is oblivious' Mulhall 2001, p. 379). Since God actually provides a ram rather than a lamb, Abraham's prediction turns out to be literally false, but prophetically true, since on the Christian reading, God eventually provides Christ, the 'Lamb of God' (John 1:29). Relatedly,

> Isaac's unquestioning submission to his father's will (his carrying of the wood of his own immolation to the place of sacrifice) prefigures Christ's submission to his own Father. In this sense, Isaac's receptive passivity represents the maturation of Abraham's activist conception of faith—a transition from an understanding of God as demanding the sacrifice of what is ours to an understanding of God as demanding the sacrifice of the self. (Mulhall 2001, pp. 379–80)[14]

Mulhall also has an interesting gloss on how the Christian reading affects the question of what the 'teleological suspension of the ethical' means:

> If the allegorical or analogical reading of Abraham's ordeal as a prefiguration of Christ's Atonement is correct, then we must reject the idea that God could conceivably require a form of worship that involves murder; for the maturation of faith that the ordeal symbolizes is precisely a shift towards a conception of God as willing to shed his own blood rather than eager to spill the blood of others—as concerned not only to transcend the primitive idea of human sacrifice by substituting a ram for Isaac, but also to transcend the idea of sacrificing one's possessions to God in favour of an idea of sacrificing oneself

---

[14] Tertullian makes this point about the significance of Isaac's carrying the wood: 'Isaac when delivered up by his father for sacrifice, himself carried the wood ... and did at that early date set forth the death of Christ, who when surrendered as a victim by his Father carried the wood of his own passion' (Tertullian 1972, 3.18, p. 225, cited in Lee 2000, p. 383).

©2008 THE ARISTOTELIAN SOCIETY
Proceedings of the Aristotelian Society Supplementary Volume LXXXII
doi: 10.1111/j.1467-8349.2008.00163.x

(the act and attitude by means of which one incarnates God by imitating his essential self-sacrificial nature). (Mulhall 2001, p. 383)

Thus faith requires not so much the *violation* of ethical duty but —
as we have been suggesting—its *transformation*. Mulhall roots this
in the text by noting Johannes's remarks on the importance of the
claim that Abraham *loves* Isaac 'with his whole soul'. Johannes
claims that if at the point of sacrifice Abraham hates Isaac, then

> he can rest assured that God does not demand this of him; for Cain
> and Abraham are not identical. He must love Isaac with his whole
> soul. Since God claims Isaac, he [Abraham] must if possible love him
> even more, and only then can he *sacrifice* him. (Kierkegaard 1901–06,
> III:122)

That is, he can only genuinely give Isaac up—sacrifice him—if he
genuinely considers him to be the most terrible loss. Mulhall (2001,
p. 384) reads this passage as saying that 'a voice in one's head incit-
ing one to kill one's son can only be the voice of God if one's love
for one's son is perfect'. Any impurity in 'one's attachment to the
Isaac in one's life' make one a Cain rather than an Abraham, 're-
vealing the voice in one's head as an evil demon'. All this means that
if Isaac represents the demands of the ethical, then 'only an ethically
perfect being ... could ever be in a position to judge that an impulse
to suspend the demands of the ethical might be the manifestation of
a divine command' (Mulhall 2001, pp. 384–5). But who meets this
criterion? This question leads Mulhall into his own discussion of
Agnete and the merman and the sin passage, in which he points out
that if we think of ourselves in terms of sin, then 'the idea of ethical
perfection is utterly lost': repentance for our sin cannot 'entirely
eradicat[e] the stain of past wrongdoing because even the smallest
past misdemeanour reveals our absolute difference from Absolute
Goodness, and hence our inability to save ourselves by our own
powers' (Mulhall 2001, p. 386). For salvation to be possible at all,
then, divine grace is necessary. And the 'ethically perfect being' who
alone is able to suspend the ethical is God himself.

So we see here in more detail how, on this reading, the real 'hidden message' of the teleological suspension of the ethical is to make
space for a conception of the ethical that includes grace:

> Acknowledging our sinfulness means acknowledging our inability to
> live up to the demands of the ethical realm; acknowledging Christ

©2008 THE ARISTOTELIAN SOCIETY
Proceedings of the Aristotelian Society Supplementary Volume LXXXII
doi: 10.1111/j.1467-8349.2008.00163.x

means acknowledging that those demands must nevertheless be met, with help from a power greater than our own. (Mulhall 2001, p. 386)

Finally, note one especially important feature of Mulhall's version of the Christian reading. One criticism of readings of *Fear and Trembling* that see it simply as endorsing a divine command ethics is that if what matters is that God's word should take precedence over 'the ethical', there seems no obvious reason why Abraham should not have to go through with sacrificing Isaac. In other words, such readings leave mysterious the significance of God's substituting the ram and 'calling off' the sacrifice. But Mulhall's version of the Christian reading (unlike some others) clearly explains the significance of this. As we saw, Mulhall claims that essential to the Christian vision is a move away from one picture of sacrifice and towards an alternative. Gone is the idea that one could legitimately view another human being as a possession that one could sacrifice to God. And this is replaced with the idea that the sacrifice God requires is a sacrifice of one's self: the idea of 'dying to the self' that plays so central a role in Kierkegaard's religious thought.[15] The 'calling off' of the 'blood' sacrifice of Isaac, allied to Abraham's realization that he 'gets Isaac back' under a new mode of valuation—not as his property, but as a 'gift' that is not to be viewed as a possession—is meant, on this view, to draw the astute reader's attention to this crucial shift. The 'hidden message' of *Fear and Trembling* is another manifestation of the 'old-fashioned orthodoxy' so close to Kierkegaard's heart.

Philosophy, School of Humanities
University of Hertfordshire
de Havilland Campus
Hatfield
Hertfordshire ALIO 9AB
UK
j.a.lippitt@herts.ac.uk

---

[15] Consider, for example, the centrality of the notion of 'self-denial' in Kierkegaard's religious writings. For a detailed recent treatment of this part of the authorship, see Walsh (2004).

©2008 THE ARISTOTELIAN SOCIETY
Proceedings of the Aristotelian Society Supplementary Volume LXXXII
doi: 10.1111/j.1467-8349.2008.00163.x

REFERENCES

Conway, Daniel W. 2002: 'The Confessional Drama of *Fear and Trembling*'. In Daniel W. Conway (ed.), *Søren Kierkegaard: Critical Assessments*, vol. III. London: Routledge.

Cross, Andrew 1994: *Moral Exemplars and Commitment in Kierkegaard's Fear and Trembling*. Ph.D. thesis, University of California, Berkeley.

Evans, C. Stephen 1993: 'Faith as the *telos* of Morality: A Reading of *Fear and Trembling*'. In Robert L. Perkins (ed.), *International Kierkegaard Commentary: Fear and Trembling and Repetition*. Macon, GA: Mercer University Press.

——2000: 'Kierkegaard on Religious Authority: The Problem of the Criterion'. *Faith and Philosophy*, 17 (1), pp. 48–67.

Ferreira, M. Jaime 1991: *Transforming Vision: Imagination and Will in Kierkegaardian Faith*. Oxford: Clarendon Press.

Gouwens, David J. 1982: *Kierkegaard's Dialectic of the Imagination*. Ph.D. thesis, Yale University.

Green, Ronald M. 1998: '"Developing" *Fear and Trembling*'. In Alastair Hannay and Gordon D. Marino (eds.), *The Cambridge Companion to Kierkegaard*. Cambridge: Cambridge University Press.

Howland, Jacob 2006: *Kierkegaard and Socrates: a Study in Philosophy and Faith*. Cambridge: Cambridge University Press.

Kierkegaard, Søren 1901–06: *Samlede Vaerker*, ed. A. B. Drachmann, J. L. Heiberg and H. O. Lange. Copenhagen: Gyldendal.

——1967–78: *Søren Kierkegaard's Journals and Papers*, ed. and trans. Howard V. and Edna H. Hong, 7 vols. Bloomington and Indianapolis: Indiana University Press.

——1978–2000: *Kierkegaard's Writings*, ed. and trans. Howard V. and Edna H. Hong et al., 26 volumes. Princeton, NJ: Princeton University Press.

Kosch, Michelle 2006: *Freedom and Reason in Kant, Schelling and Kierkegaard*. Oxford: Oxford University Press.

——2008: 'What Abraham Couldn't Say'. *Proceedings of the Aristotelian Society Supplementary Volume* 82, pp. 59–78.

Lee, Jung H. 2000: 'Abraham in a Different Voice: Rereading *Fear and Trembling* with Care'. *Religious Studies*, 36, pp. 377–400.

Lippitt, John 2000: *Humour and Irony in Kierkegaard's Thought*. Basingstoke: Macmillan.

——2003: *Kierkegaard and Fear and Trembling*. London: Routledge.

Mackey, Louis 1972: 'The View from Pisgah: A Reading of *Fear and Trembling*'. In Josiah Thompson (ed.), *Kierkegaard: a Collection of Critical Essays*. Garden City, NY: Doubleday.

Mulhall, Stephen 2001: *Inheritance and Originality: Wittgenstein,*

©2008 THE ARISTOTELIAN SOCIETY
Proceedings of the Aristotelian Society Supplementary Volume LXXXII
doi: 10.1111/j.1467-8349.2008.00163.x

Heidegger, Kierkegaard. Oxford: Oxford University Press.

Nussbaum, Martha C. 1990: *Love's Knowledge: Essays on Philosophy and Literature.* Oxford: Oxford University Press.

Polk, Timothy Houston 1997: *The Biblical Kierkegaard: Reading by the Rule of Faith.* Macon, GA: Mercer University Press.

Pons, Jolita 2004: *Stealing a Gift: Kierkegaard's Pseudonyms and the Bible.* New York: Fordham University Press.

Rubenstein, Mary-Jane 2001: 'Kierkegaard's Socrates: A Venture in Evolutionary Theory'. *Modern Theology,* 17 (4), pp. 441–73.

Tertullian 1972: *Adversus Marcionem,* ed. and trans. Ernest Evans. Oxford: Clarendon Press.

Thust Martin 1931: *Søren Kierkegaard: Der Dichter des Religioesen.* Munich: CH Beckshe Verlagsbuchhandlung.

Walsh, Sylvia 2004: *Living Christianly: Kierkegaard's Dialectic of Christian Existence.* University Park, PA: Pennsylvania State University Press.

©2008 THE ARISTOTELIAN SOCIETY
Proceedings of the Aristotelian Society Supplementary Volume LXXXII
doi: 10.1111/j.1467-8349.2008.00163.x

MATERIAL COINCIDENCE
KIT FINE AND JOHN DIVERS

I — KIT FINE

COINCIDENCE AND FORM

How can a statue and a piece of alloy be coincident at any time at which they exist and yet differ in their modal properties? I argue that this question demands an answer and that the only plausible answer is one that posits a difference in the form of the two objects.

Many philosophers are pluralists about material things. They believe that distinct material things may coincide at a time, i.e. that they may occupy the very same spatial region and be constituted by the very same matter at that time. A familiar example is that of an alloy statue and the piece of alloy from which it is made. They are clearly coincident, and they would also appear to be distinct, given that the piece of alloy may exist before the statue is created or after it has been destroyed.

A number of these philosophers also believe that two distinct material things may coincide *in a world*, i.e. that they may exist at the same times in the world and coincide at each time at which they exist. Again, a familiar example is one in which, through a freak in circumstances, an alloy statue and its constituting alloy happen to be created and destroyed at the very same time. It seems clear that the statue and the piece of alloy are coincident throughout the period during which they exist, and they would also appear to be distinct, given that the piece of alloy is possibly spherical in shape while the statue is not.

Pluralism—at least in its second, stronger form—faces a problem. For the modal difference between the piece of alloy and the statue—with the one being possibly spherical and the other not—would appear to stand in need of explanation. It cannot simply be accepted as a brute fact that the one is possibly the way it is while the other not. There must therefore be an underlying non-modal difference between them, one in virtue of which there is the modal dif-

©2008 THE ARISTOTELIAN SOCIETY
Proceedings of the Aristotelian Society Supplementary Volume LXXXII
doi: 10.1111/j.1467-8349.2008.00164.x

ference.[1] But how can there be a non-modal difference between them without a worldly difference, i.e. without a difference in how they 'are' in the world in question? And how can there be a worldly difference given that they coincide in the world, i.e. exist at the same times and coincide at each time at which they exist? Or, to put the argument in summary form: there can be no modal difference without an underlying non-modal difference, no non-modal difference without a worldly difference, and no worldly difference if the objects are worldly coincidents.[2]

This is a problem for the pluralist, at least if he accepts that there is a modal difference between the statue and the piece of alloy (and I know of no pluralist who does not accept this). It may also be a problem with the intuitive evidence for the pluralist position. For pluralists often argue for the distinctness of the statue and the piece of alloy on the grounds that, even though they are coincident, it is possible for the piece of alloy to be spherical and yet not possible for the statue to be spherical. But this piece of intuitive evidence is put under suspicion if there is something incoherent in the idea that worldly coincidents might differ in their modal properties. In any case, the force of the present considerations has led a number of philosophers to abandon the pluralist position even though they might have been initially willing to admit that there was some intuitive evidence in its favour.

There are various deflationary responses to the problem which we would do well to explore before considering those responses that take the problem more seriously. The deflationary responses all reject the demand for explanation. So while conceding that there may be a modal difference between the statue and the piece of alloy, they do not allow that there must therefore be an underlying non-modal difference.

One response of this sort is to deny that there is a *genuine* modal difference between the statue and the piece of alloy. It is true to say that the piece of alloy is possibly spherical and that the statue is not, but that is because the modal attributions are relative to how the object is being described; as a *piece of alloy* it is possibly spherical, while as a *statue* it is not. Thus what accounts for the modal differ-

---

[1] Of course, the explanation of the modal difference might be another modal difference, but that too then requires explanation, and so, if the demand for explanation is fully to be met, the sequence of explanations should eventually terminate in a non-modal difference.

[2] This problem has gone under the names of the *grounding problem* and the *indiscernibility problem*; and it has been considered, in one form or another, by Bennett (2004), Burke (1980, 1992), Heller (1990, pp. 30–2), Levey (1997), Sider (1999, p. 929), Sosa (1987, pp. 78–82), van Inwagen (1990, p. 290, n.45), and Zimmerman (1995).

©2008 The Aristotelian Society
Proceedings of the Aristotelian Society Supplementary Volume LXXXII
doi: 10.1111/j.1467-8349.2008.00164.x

ence is not a non-modal difference in the objects of reference, for there is only one such object, but a difference (presumably non-modal) in how the object is to be described. Whatever the merits of this view might be, my interest is in philosophers who take there to be a genuine modal difference between the two objects and for whom such a response is therefore inappropriate.[3]

Another reason for being sceptical of the explanatory demand is that one cannot reasonably expect there to be a *scientific* explanation of the modal difference between the statue and the piece of alloy. A scientist may explain the malleability of some alloy in terms of its chemical composition. But it is clear that we cannot expect to find a similar explanation of the malleability of the *piece* of the alloy or of the lack of malleability of the statue. It is not as if further scientific investigation of the piece of alloy—as opposed to the alloy itself—might reveal it to be malleable or that further scientific investigation of the statue might reveal it not to be malleable.

But even though there may be no reasonable demand for a scientific explanation of the modal difference between the two objects, it may still be reasonably required that the difference between them be explained. Let it be granted that the alloy is malleable. Our problem is then to explain why the piece of alloy is malleable (able to survive great deformations) while the statue is not. What enables the one to ride on the malleability of the alloy, so to speak, and not the other? Surely there must be some difference between them in virtue of which this is so—even if it is not a difference that might be discovered or even acknowledged by science.

A better paradigm of the kind of explanation we are after concerns the modal status of propositions. Consider the proposition that Socrates is a carpenter and contrast it with the proposition that Socrates is a carpenter and not a carpenter. The first proposition is possibly true while the second is not. But what accounts for this difference in their modal status? An answer might go as follows. Each proposition has a certain structure, with the first being the result of predicating the predicate-constituent *carpenter* of the subject-constituent *Socrates* and with the second being the result of predicating the conjunction of *carpenter* and its negation of *Socrates*. In virtue of their structure, it is necessarily the case that the first proposition is true just in case Socrates is a carpenter and that the second proposition is true just in case

---

[3] Some objections to the 'opacity' view are given in Fine (2003, 2006).

Socrates is a carpenter and not a carpenter. But it is possible that Socrates is a carpenter yet not possible that Socrates is a carpenter and
not a carpenter, and hence possible that the first proposition is true yet
not possible that the second proposition is true.

We have here an explanation of the modal difference between the
two propositions; and it is even an explanation in terms of an underlying structural difference, just as it is with many scientific explanations. But we do not have a scientific explanation, since the relevant
structure and its connection with the behaviour of the objects are
discovered by a priori means rather than through scientific investigation. And it is very plausible that if there is an explanation of the modal difference in the case of coincidents, then it will be along the lines
of the philosophical rather than the scientific model of how such explanations might proceed.

A third reason to be sceptical of the explanatory demand concerns the perceived analogy between modality and time. Let us suppose, by way of illustration, that when two particles collide, they
interpenetrate (perhaps as indicated by a doubling of mass in their
joint location) and subsequently proceed on their respective ways.
There will then be a difference in their temporal profiles—in where
and how they are at each moment at which they exist. But we do
not think that there must be some explanation of this difference—it
could just be a brute fact that each particle has the temporal profile
that it does; and even if we think that there is an explanation of the
difference, we will not necessarily think it must be in terms of a difference in how the particles are at the moment of interpenetration.

But then why believe it is not the same in the modal case? Here we
have a difference in the modal profiles (of how the particles are in each
world in which they exist) rather than a difference in the temporal
profiles, and coincidence within a world rather than coincidence at a
time. But just as there need be nothing that accounts for the difference
in the temporal profiles, and certainly nothing at the time of coincidence, why should there be anything—at the world of coincidence or
at all—that accounts for the difference in the modal profiles?

I am generally suspicious of arguments that 'dimensionalize' modality and treat it in the same way as space or time, and the general
suspicion would appear to be justified in the present case. For the
temporal profile of a particle is a contingent matter, and we seem
prepared to concede that its temporal profile might be a brute con-
tingency or, at least, something that does not turn on how the parti-

©2008 The Aristotelian Society
Proceedings of the Aristotelian Society Supplementary Volume LXXXII
doi: 10.1111/j.1467-8349.2008.00164.x

cle is at any given time. But a particle's modal profile is a necessary matter, and we seem much less willing to concede that it might be a brute necessity or something that does not turn on how the particle *is*. I do not wish to deny that there are brute necessities, but it seems especially troubling to suppose that there might be a difference in the possibilities for the statue and the piece of alloy which does not turn upon some underlying difference in the objects themselves. The way of the world might account, so to speak, for the difference in temporal profile, but it seems that there must be something about the objects themselves that accounts for the difference in modal profile.

There is a strong intuitive case for thinking that the modal difference between the statue and the piece of alloy stands in need of explanation, should there be such a difference, and I know of no reason, apart from the difficulty of actually finding an explanation, for thinking that it does not. Indeed, it seems to me that the explanatory demand posed by the case of coincident objects is more extensive and stringent than is commonly supposed.

For one thing, there are other differences between the statue and the piece of alloy which also appear to stand in need of explanation and for which it is not clear what the explanation might be.[4] The most obvious difference, in this regard, is the difference in *sort*. The statue is a *statue* though not a *piece of alloy* while the piece of alloy is a *piece of alloy* though not a *statue*. Of course, no monist would recognize these differences in sort but the philosophers of interest to us, who recognize a genuine modal difference, are also likely to acknowledge a sortal difference.

Moreover, the sortal differences plausibly stand in need of explanation. It is perhaps not always true that sortal differences stand in need of explanation. It might be thought, for example, that the difference in the behaviour of certain particles is to be explained in terms of their belonging to different basic sorts or kinds, even though there is no explanation of what the difference in kind consists in. But the difference between the sorts *statue* and *piece of alloy* are not plausibly regarded as basic in this way. Surely, one wants to say, there must be some account of what is involved in being a statue or a piece of clay, from which it should then be apparent why a given object is the one rather than the other.

Many philosophers have been reluctant to accept that there is an

---

[4] Bennett (2004, §1) and Olson (2001, p. 339) make related points.

©2008 THE ARISTOTELIAN SOCIETY
Proceedings of the Aristotelian Society Supplementary Volume LXXXII
doi: 10.1111/j.1467-8349.2008.00164.x

independent sortal difference. They have supposed that to be of a certain sort is simply a matter of having a certain modal profile (or of conforming to certain 'identity conditions') so that any sortal difference is, *ipso facto*, a modal difference. But, common as the view may be, it runs counter to our intuitions about what is most naturally explained in terms of what. For if we ask how it is possible for the piece of alloy to survive being moulded into the shape of a sphere but not possible for the statue, then the answer which most naturally suggests itself is that it is *because* the one is a piece of alloy and the other is a statue of Goliath that they enjoy the capacities or incapacities for variation in shape that they do. But this explanation would lose its explanatory force if being a statue or being a piece of alloy were simply a matter of having a certain modal profile.

If the modal difference in these cases is to be explained in terms of the sortal difference, then this would suggest that the fundamental problem is to account for the sortal difference; and indeed there may well be other differences that are also to be explained in terms of a difference in sort. If, for example, a person is able to think while his body does not, then this must presumably be (in part) because the one object is a person and the other is not. It is therefore worth noting that there may be modal differences which do not turn upon a difference in sort, and that there may even be differences standing in need of explanation which turn neither on a difference in sort nor on a modal difference. I have argued, in Fine (2000), for example, that two letters could coincide in a world even though they differ in writer, content, and addressee. Since one of these letters could exist without the other, we will have the case of a modal difference without any sortal difference. I have also argued in the same paper that two letters might necessarily coincide even though they are addressed to different people. Here there is no difference of sort or modal difference. Yet surely there should be some explanation of the difference in addressee, of what it is about the letters that makes it true that the one letter is addressed to one person and the other letter to another person. A full solution to the explanatory challenge should somehow take all of these various differences into account.

Another way in which focus on the problem may have been unduly narrow concerns the question of *difference*. I have talked of explaining various differences between the coincident objects—be they modal or sortal or of some other kind. But the more fundamental problem is to explain the corresponding intrinsic features of the objects. We need to explain why the objects have the modal profiles that they do, or why they are of the sorts that they are, or why each letter, say, is addressed to a given person. Indeed, if the modal profile were not in need of explanation, then the modal difference would not stand in need of explanation either, and, of course, once we have explained the modal profile of each object we will thereby have explained the modal differences between them; and similarly for the other kinds of difference that might be in question.

From this point of view, the emphasis on differences merely serves the purpose of making graphic a desideratum to which an adequate explanation of the corresponding features should conform. For if I use the fact that a given object ϕ's, for example, to explain why it has the modal profile that it does, then I had better be sure that a coincident object with a different modal profile does not also satisfy ϕ.

An explanation of an object's features may appeal to two kinds of circumstance: *how* the object is; and *what* it is. The first is a matter of the object's *accidental* features, of how it happens to be, while the second is a matter of its *essential* features, of what it is by its very nature. These features may require explanation in their turn. Thus what we will reach, at the terminus of explanation, are accidental or essential features that the object simply has. It is a brute fact, requiring no further explanation, that this is what or how the object is.

Now the accidental features of the object are relatively unimportant in the present context; for it is clear what they are, and the question of how, if at all, they might be further explained is irrelevant to the problem at hand. Thus the critical question concerns the essential features of the object. What we need is an account of what the object fundamentally is from which it will be evident, in the light of the particular circumstances, that the object will have the various features that it does. Nothing less—and nothing more—is required if the explanatory challenge is fully to be met.

A third, perhaps more significant, way in which focus on the problem may have been unduly narrow concerns the question of coincidence. It has been thought that the pluralist faces a *special* problem in accounting for the modal differences between objects. For he must explain the modal difference between objects that are worldly coincidents; and given that they are worldly coincidents, it is hard to see what the underlying non-modal difference between them might be. The monist, by contrast, need only explain the modal difference between objects that are not worldly coincidents; and, given that they fail to be worldly coincidents, there will be a non-modal difference between them in terms of which the modal difference might then be explained.

It is true that for the monist there will always be a non-modal difference between the objects and hence no problem in principle of coming up with an explanation of the modal difference. But that is not to say that there is no problem, for the non-modal difference between the objects may not be *relevant* to the modal difference, i.e. it may not serve to account for the modal difference. Whether or not this is so will depend upon what sort of object is in question. Suppose the monist believes only in quantities of matter—of gold, say, or water. Then he may presumably provide the standard scientific explanation for the modal profile of such objects. It is because gold has the atomic structure that it has or because water has the molecular structure that it does that each will be capable of behaving in the way that it does. Or again, suppose that the monist believes only in point-particles and in sums of such particles. He might then with some plausibility claim that it is because something is a point-particle that it is incapable of being composed of other point-particles and that it is because something is composed of particular point-particles that it is incapable of not being so composed; and similarly for the other aspects of their behaviour.

But suppose now that the monist believes in some of the things we ordinarily take to exist—pieces of alloy, statues, or the like—and takes them to have the kind of modal profile that we ordinarily take them to have. Thus he supposes that pieces of alloy are capable of varying their shape as long as they remain in one piece, but that statues are generally incapable of any great variation in shape. How then is he to account for the modal profile of these objects or for the modal difference between them? How is he, for example, to account for the possibility that a piece of alloy might be spherical, or for the necessity that a given statue not be spherical?

He may provide us with the worldly profile of each of the objects in question. Perhaps the piece of alloy is always in some odd jagged shape and perhaps the statue, through wear and tear, is sometimes a perfect image of Goliath and sometimes a not-so-perfect image. What then in these worldly profiles is capable of explaining how the piece of alloy is capable of having a very different shape from one that it had, even though the statue is not? There seems to be nothing for him to say. Perhaps the piece of alloy has always had the same

©2008 The Aristotelian Society
Proceedings of the Aristotelian Society Supplementary Volume LXXXII
doi: 10.1111/j.1467-8349.2008.00164.x

odd jagged shape, while the statue of Goliath has slowly altered its
shape. But how might this, or any other factors to which he might
appeal, explain how great variation in shape is possible in the one
case and yet not in the other? There would appear to be no explanatory route in these cases that might plausibly take us from how the
object is to how it might or must be.

If this is right, then the explanatory challenge that monists have
posed for the pluralist is as much of a challenge for the more plausible forms of monism. For any monist who accepts ordinary things
and takes them to have the modal profiles they are ordinarily taken
to have will face a similar difficulty.[5] He might appear to have an
advantage over the pluralist in that he is able to appeal to the non-
modal differences that will obtain between objects that do not coincide. But since these non-modal differences do not appear to be relevant to the modal differences, it is not clear that he is any better off.

Indeed, he may be worse off. For as we shall see, the means by
which the modal differences or features are to be explained might
lead irresistibly to a pluralist position and might therefore only be
available to the pluralist. So ironically, the great explanatory challenge—upon which the whole position of pluralism has been thought
to founder—may turn out to be more of a problem for the monist.[6]

It has seemed to many philosophers that the explanatory challenge
cannot be met. And one can understand why. For if two objects are
worldly coincidents, then any difference between them will stand in
need of explanation. We will need to know how, in the face of the coincidence, they could be different. But then no satisfactory explanation of the difference between them can be given, since it will always

---

[5] He faces another difficulty, of course. For he must provide a description, compatible with
his monism, as to how things are in putative cases of coincidence. He might suppose in the
statue/alloy case, for example, that there is a single object there that is just a statue, or just a
piece of alloy, or just some alloy, or perhaps both a statue and a piece of alloy, but with a
modal profile somehow appropriate to both. But whatever stand he takes on these questions will be largely independent of the present issue.

[6] One is reminded of Kripke's (1979) description of the dialectical situation in the debate
between the Fregean and referentialist on the semantics of names. Fregeans have raised sub-
stitution-style counterexamples to the referentialist position on names and Kripke has
argued that the kinds of case they raise do not essentially depend upon referentialist
assumptions and hence pose as much of a problem for the Fregean as they do for the referentialist. I have gone on to argue (Fine 2007, pp. 117–19) that such cases actually present
more of a problem for the Fregean, since his position, in contrast to that of the referentialist,
will deprive him of any suitable means by which they might be resolved. In my view, the
general dialectical situation in the current debate between the monist and the pluralist is
much the same.

rest on some other difference that stands in need of explanation.

However, it seems to me that, in looking for an underlying differ-ence, these philosophers have been looking in the wrong place. They have focused on the ordinary empirical features of an object (its lo-cation, colour, weight, etc.), when they should have been attending to its composition. The statue and the piece of alloy are both com-posed of, or constituted by, some alloy. This therefore suggests that the difference between them might turn on *how* they are respectively composed of the alloy. The statue will be composed of the alloy in one way and the piece of alloy, given that it is distinct from the stat-ue, will be composed of the alloy in some other way; and it is in this difference in how each is composed of the alloy that the account of the other differences is to be sought.

But what, it might be objected, could this difference in the man-ner of composition be? We have one thing, the alloy, and two fur-ther things composed of the alloy—one in one way and the other in another way. Yet how is it possible for even one further thing to be composed of the alloy? How could there be room, so to speak, for a further thing unless it were composed of additional material?

Before responding to this difficulty, let us make a simplifying as-sumption. We shall suppose that we are dealing with a coincident al-loy *sphere* rather than a coincident alloy *statue* and that, in order for the sphere or for the piece of alloy to continue to exist, their matter must remain exactly the same. Once we have considered this special case, we shall consider how the solution might be extended to cover the more general case in which the matter is capable of variation.

Our problem is to explain the distinctive manner in which the al-loy sphere or in which the piece of alloy is composed of the alloy, one which will render them distinct from one another and distinct from the alloy itself. I believe that a clue to this distinctive manner of composition can be found by considering the natural response to the question 'What *is* the alloy sphere?' 'The alloy sphere', we are inclined to say, 'is the alloy in the shape of a sphere.' The phrase 'the alloy in the shape of a sphere' contains two singular terms, 'the al-loy' and 'the shape of a sphere', and the preposition 'in'. The term 'the alloy' signifies a certain parcel of alloy. The term 'the shape of a sphere' signifies a certain shape, the shape of a sphere; and presum-ably this is the shape of some particular sphere—one that is six inches in diameter, say, rather than the shape of a sphere in general. The preposition 'in' signifies some way in which the two come together. Thus the phrase as a whole signifies the result of somehow bringing together the alloy and the shape.

We already have a rudimentary account of what the sphere is. There is a method of composing wholes from parts, signified by the preposition 'in', and the alloy sphere is the result of applying this method of composition to the alloy and the spherical shape. If Σ is the manner of composition, s the sphere, a the alloy and S the shape, the account will take the form of the following identity: $s = \Sigma(a,S)$. Similarly, the piece of alloy may be taken to be the alloy in the shape of a piece. So where p is the piece of alloy and P is the shape of a piece (not now a particular piece but of a piece in general), the account will be of the form: $p = \Sigma(a,P)$.

With this rudimentary account on the table, we can now see why there might be 'room' for the sphere and the piece of alloy in addition to the alloy. The previous objector was correct in thinking that the sphere and the piece of alloy must be composed of some further component if they are to be something in addition to the alloy. But he was mistaken in thinking that this further component must be some additional material. Rather than being material, it is formal— something in the nature of the shapes S and P rather than something in the nature of the particular alloy a.

Any further clarification of the compositional character of the sphere or the piece of alloy will devolve upon the method of composition, Σ, through which they are produced. When we consider what this method might be, it seems clear that it cannot be the standard operation of 'fusion', that pools some given objects $x_1, x_2, x_3, \ldots$ into a mere aggregate or sum $x_1 + x_2 + x_3 + \ldots$ of those objects. For the existence of the aggregate $a + P$ at a given time does not require that the alloy a actually be in the shape P of a piece at that time; it requires, at most, that a and P both exist. But the existence of the alloy sphere at a given time does require that the alloy be in the shape of a sphere at that time.[7] As much is suggested by the use of the preposition 'in'. For the alloy sphere is not the alloy *with* the shape as it would be if it were merely an aggregate of the two. It is the alloy *in* the shape of a

---

[7] This objection only works when p is a universal rather than a 'particularized' property or trope. There are other objections that might be developed against the trope view. But we may note that the trope of *F-ness in x* may plausibly be regarded as the result of applying the very same method of composition Σ to *F-ness*, considered now as the 'matter', and to the property of inhering in x, considered now as the 'form'. We would then face a similar problem in taking the trope to be the mere aggregate of the universal and the property of inhering in the particular.

©2008 The Aristotelian Society
Proceedings of the Aristotelian Society Supplementary Volume LXXXII
doi: 10.1111/j.1467-8349.2008.00164.x

sphere; and this suggests that the alloy must actually be in the shape
of the sphere if the alloy in the shape of a sphere is to exist.

We see that the method of composition of interest to us is not a
form of fusion; and it is plausible that there is no other more basic
method of composition by which it might be defined. We should simply accept that it is a further basic method, in addition to fusion, by
which wholes may be formed from parts. From the intuitive point of
view, we might think of the form F in the matter-form combination
$\Sigma(m,F)$ as a kind of mould to which the matter m is meant to conform. In moulding the matter to the form, we obtain a composite of
which both the mould and the matter will then be parts.

If we wish to elucidate further what the method of composition is,
we can perhaps do no better than to specify the principles by which
it is governed. I have attempted to do this in my paper 'Things and
Their Parts' (Fine 1999).[8] The peculiar composite $\Sigma(m,F)$ is there
called a *rigid embodiment* (of m in F), since its matter m is not allowed to vary, and may be denoted by m/F. Rather than reproduce
all of the principles here, let me state four that will be critical to the
ensuing discussion (we ignore certain subtleties of formulation). The
first provides conditions under which a rigid embodiment will exist;
the second states *when* a rigid embodiment will exist; the third states
where it will be; and the fourth tells us what *parts* it will have:

Existence   The rigid embodiment a/F exists iff a and F exist
                and a has F at some time.

Temporality   The rigid embodiment m/F exists at time t iff m/F
                exists, m exists at t and m has F at t.

Location   The rigid embodiment m/F is located at position p
                at time t iff m/F exists at t and m is located at po-
                sition p at t.

Parthood   The object x is a part of m/F iff $x = m$ or $x = F$ or x
                is a part of m or x is a part of F.

Thus, according to the first principle, a matter/form composite will
exist just in case the matter exists, the form exists, and the matter at
some time has the form. Given that a composite exists, the second
principle tells us that a matter/form composite will exist at those

---

[8] An earlier version of the theory is to be found in Fine (1982), where the composites m/F
are called *qua objects*.

times at which the matter exists and has the form. Given that a composite exists at a particular time, the third principle tells us that a matter/form composite will be located at those places at which the matter is located. And the fourth principle states that the parts of a matter/form composite will be mediated through its matter and its form. It is our intention that all of these principles should hold of necessity and should hold not merely of m and F that actually exist but also of any m and F that might exist.

With this mini-theory of rigid embodiments at hand, we are in a position to meet the previous explanatory challenge.[9] Consider first the question of the modal difference between the sphere and the piece of alloy. We need somehow to account for their respective modal profiles.

To this end, we shall assume that the sphere s is the rigid embodiment a/S of the alloy a in the spherical shape S (and similarly for the piece of alloy). From the Existence Principle, it follows that the sphere s will exist in exactly those worlds in which the alloy has the shape S (granted that the alloy a and the shape S must then also exist); from the Temporality Principle, it follows that at each world in which the sphere exists, it will exist at exactly those times at which the alloy has the shape S; and from the Location Principle, it follows that at each world and time at which the sphere exists, its location will be that of the alloy—and so, given that being of a certain shape is a matter of location, the sphere s will be in the shape S at any time at which it exists. Thus the modal profile of the sphere and the piece of alloy will be essentially determined by these principles; and the sphere will necessarily be spherical whenever it exists while the piece of alloy will not be (given that it is possible for the alloy to be of a piece and yet not be spherical).

It is of course essential to the adequacy of this explanation that the facts about the alloy sphere and the piece of alloy to which we appeal should not themselves be modal. But this does indeed appear to be the case. For they concern the *composition* of the alloy sphere and the piece of sphere (with the one being the appropriate composite of a and S and the other the appropriate composite of a and P). Of course, these

---

[9] Other responses to the challenge are to be found in Sosa (1987), Johnston (1992), Baker (1997, p. 621), Rea (1997a), and Corcoran (1999). Sosa's account is closest to my own; he has something like the notion of a qua object or rigid embodiment, and uses it to explain the modal differences. Kathrin Koslicki has also developed a hylomorphic response to the challenge in her unpublished book 'The Structure of Objects'.

©2008 THE ARISTOTELIAN SOCIETY
Proceedings of the Aristotelian Society Supplementary Volume LXXXII
doi: 10.1111/j.1467-8349.2008.00164.x

compositional facts may have certain modal consequences for the objects in question but the compositional facts are not themselves modal.

Consider now the question of the sortal difference. The alloy sphere s is a *sphere*—indeed, an *alloy sphere*—while the piece of alloy is not. The piece of alloy p, on the other hand, is a *piece*—indeed, an *alloy piece*—while the alloy sphere is not. What accounts for this difference in their sorts or for each being of the sort that it is?

Again, we make use of the assumption that the sphere s is the rigid embodiment a/S of the alloy a in the spherical shape S and that the piece of alloy is the rigid embodiment a/P of the alloy a in the shape of a piece P. We must now say what it is for something to be a *alloy sphere* or, at least, what it is for a rigid embodiment to be an *alloy sphere* and also what it is for something, or a rigid embodiment, to be a *piece of alloy*. It is plausible, once we have the concept of a rigid embodiment, that what it is for a rigid embodiment m/F to be an *alloy sphere* is for m to be some alloy and F to be the shape of a sphere and that what it is for the rigid embodiment m/F to be a *piece of alloy* is for m to be some alloy and for F to be a the shape of a piece.[10]

We can now provide an explanation of the sortal difference between the sphere $s = a/S$ and the piece of alloy $p = a/P$. For it is evident that a is some alloy, that S is the shape of a sphere, and that P is the shape of a piece; and so s will be an alloy sphere and p a piece of alloy. It may also be shown that the sphere $s = a/S$ is not a *piece of alloy* and that the piece of alloy $p = a/P$ is not an *alloy sphere*. For suppose that the sphere $s = a/S$ were a *piece of alloy* (the argument in the case of the piece of alloy p is similar). It would then have to a rigid embodiment of the form b/Q, where b is some alloy and Q is the shape of a piece. Now, there are a number of ways to show within our theory that $s = a/S$ is not identical to $q = b/Q$. One is in terms of their modal properties; for as we have seen s must be in the shape of a sphere while q may not be. Another is in terms of their parts; for s will have the shape of a sphere S as a part. But the only way for S to be a part of q is for it to be identical to or a part of either b or Q; and it is hard to see how either of these could be so.[11]

It is worth noting that we do not provide an account of the sortal difference between the alloy sphere and the piece of alloy in modal

---

[10] There may be some ambiguity here, irrelevant to our purposes, as to what exactly is meant by 'the shape of a sphere' or 'the shape of a piece'.

[11] Any plausible principle of identity for rigid embodiments will also secure the difference between s and q.

©2008 THE ARISTOTELIAN SOCIETY
Proceedings of the Aristotelian Society Supplementary Volume LXXXII
doi: 10.1111/j.1467-8349.2008.00164.x

terms; and, indeed, the explanation of the sortal difference is somewhat different from the explanation of the modal difference. It is also
plausible that the modal difference can be explained in terms of the
sortal difference. For given that the one object is a *sphere* and the other is a *piece*, it will follow that the one must be in the shape of a sphere
while the other need only be in the shape of a piece. Thus our pre-the-
oretic intuitions on the proper order of explanation are vindicated.

Our theory is also able to provide plausible explanations of other
differences between the alloy sphere and the piece of alloy. The alloy
sphere may be misshapen, for example—perhaps through having a
dent at one end—while the piece of alloy is not.[12] Indeed, it is not
even clear that the piece of alloy can properly be said to be misshap-
en or not misshapen. Whence the difference?

An object that has a spherical shape may be a more or less perfect
specimen of that shape and the sphere a/S may, accordingly, be said to
be misshapen if it is a sufficiently imperfect specimen of its form. An
object that has the shape of a piece, by contrast, cannot properly be
said to be a more or less perfect specimen of that shape and, consequently, we cannot properly talk in the same way of the piece of alloy
being misshapen, even though it happens to be in the shape of a
sphere. Trifling as this example may appear to be, I suspect that there
are many significant cases—such as how it is that a person is able to
think while his body is not—that can be explained in a similar way.

I have so far dealt with a rather special case, one in which the objects under consideration have a fixed material constitution. But, of
course, most of the objects of interest to us are not of this sort; their
matter can vary from one moment to the next and from one possible
circumstance to another. How are we to explain the modal, sortal
and other differences in these cases?

I am inclined to think that in these cases too there is a non-modal
account of what the object is, on the basis of which the possession of
the various other features can be explained. The key is the notion of
a *variable embodiment*. Given a principle ϕ for picking out an object
at different times (under actual or counterfactual circumstances),
there will be an object $/\phi/$, the variable embodiment of ϕ, which will
be 'manifested' at different times by the object which the principle ϕ
picks out. So, for example, the principle ϕ might pick out the different rigid embodiments a/S, a'/S, a''/S, a'''/S, …, where S is the partic-

---

[12] Differences of this sort are briefly discussed in Fine (2003, pp. 206–8).

©2008 The Aristotelian Society
Proceedings of the Aristotelian Society Supplementary Volume LXXXII
doi: 10.1111/j.1467-8349.2008.00164.x

ular shape of a sphere as before, and where a, a', a'', a''', ... constitute a maximum 'continuous' succession of parcels of alloy. Change in the underlying matter is allowed as long as it is not too great and as long as the spherical shape S is preserved. We would thereby obtain an object whose susceptibility to material change would correspond more closely to our actual conception of a sphere.[13]

Just as in the case of rigid embodiment, the principles governing variable embodiments can be laid down, and the behaviour of various objects can then be explained in terms of their identity as variable embodiments and the principles by which they are governed. Thus one such principle is that a variable embodiment will be like its manifestations—existing at just those times at which it has a manifestation and, given that it exists at a particular time, being exactly where the manifestation is at that time (for further details, see Fine 1999). If an alloy sphere, more realistically conceived, is taken to be a variable embodiment of rigid embodiments of the form a/S, we can then show how an alloy sphere will necessarily be spherical in shape whenever it exists. We can likewise show how a piece of alloy, more realistically conceived, will necessarily be of a piece—and thereby explain the modal difference between the alloy sphere and the piece of alloy. And similarly, it would seem, for other objects that are susceptible of material change and for other kinds of difference.

The account of an object as a given rigid or variable embodiment may be regarded as a *fundamental* account of what the object is, one that itself stands in need of no further explanation. We may therefore claim, with some plausibility, to have traced the various features and differences of such objects to their source.[14]

Department of Philosophy
New York University
5 Washington Place
New York, NY 10003
USA

---

[13] The exact determination of ϕ will also depend upon resolving various questions concerning transworld identity and interrupted existence.

[14] An earlier version of this paper was given at the Kline Workshop on metaphysics in 2005. I should like to thank the respondents, Berit Brogaard and Mark Moyer, and the other participants for their helpful comments. The central ideas of the paper go back to the account of 'qua objects' in Fine (1982).

©2008 The Aristotelian Society
Proceedings of the Aristotelian Society Supplementary Volume LXXXII
doi: 10.1111/j.1467-8349.2008.00164.x

REFERENCES

Baker, L. 1997: 'Why Constitution is not Identity'. *Journal of Philosophy*, 94, pp. 599–621.

Bennett, K. 2004: 'Spatio-temporal Coincidence and the Grounding Problem'. *Philosophical Studies*, 111:3, pp. 339–71.

Burke, M. 1980: 'Cohabitation, Stuff and Intermittent Existence'. *Mind*, 89, pp. 391–405.

——1992: 'Copper Statues and Pieces of Copper: A Challenge to the Standard Account'. *Analysis*, 52, pp. 12–17.

Corcoran, K. 1999: 'Persons, Bodies and the Constitution Relation'. *Southern Journal of Philosophy*, 37, pp. 1–20.

Fine, Kit 1982: 'Acts, Events and Things'. In *Language and Ontology*, pp. 97–105, as part of the proceedings of the Sixth International Wittgenstein Symposium, 23–30 August 1981, Kirchberg/Wechsel, Austria. Vienna: Holder-Pichler-Tempsky.

——1999: 'Things and Their Parts'. *Midwest Studies* XXIII, ed. Sean French and Howard Wettstein, pp. 61–74.

——2000: 'A Counter-example to Locke's Thesis'. *Monist*, 83(3), pp. 357–61.

——2002: 'The Varieties of Necessity'. In Tamar Szabó Gendler and John Hawthorne (eds.), *Conceivability and Possibility*, pp. 253–82. Oxford: Clarendon Press.

——2003: 'The Non-Identity of a Thing and its Matter'. *Mind*, 112, pp. 195–234.

——2006: 'Arguing for Non-Identity: A Response to King and Frances'. *Mind*, 115, pp. 1059–82.

——2007: *Semantic Relationism*. Oxford: Blackwell.

Heller, Mark 1990: *The Ontology of Physical Objects: Four-Dimensional Hunks of Matter*. Cambridge: Cambridge University Press.

Johnston, Mark 1992: 'Constitution is Not Identity'. *Mind*, 101, pp. 89–105; reprinted in Rea 1997*b*.

Koslicki, Kathrin (unpublished): *The Structure of Objects*.

Kripke, Saul 1979: 'A Puzzle About Belief'. In A. Margalit (ed.), *Meaning and Use*. Dordrecht: Reidel.

Levey, S. 1997: 'Coincidence and Principles of Composition'. *Analysis*, 57, pp. 1–10.

Olson, Eric 2001: 'Material Coincidence and the Indiscernibility Problem'. *Philosophical Quarterly*, 51, pp. 337–55.

Rea, Michael 1997*a*: 'Supervenience and Co-Location'. *American Philosophical Quarterly*, 34, pp. 367–75.

——(ed.) 1997*b*: *Material Constitution: A Reader*. New York: Rowman & Littlefield.

©2008 THE ARISTOTELIAN SOCIETY
Proceedings of the Aristotelian Society Supplementary Volume LXXXII
doi: 10.1111/j.1467-8349.2008.00164.x

Sosa, Ernest 1987: 'Subjects, Among Other Things'. *Philosophical Perspectives, 1: Metaphysics*, ed. James E. Tomberlin. Atascadero, CA: Ridgeview.

Sider, Theodore 1999: 'Global Supervenience and Identity Across Times and Worlds'. *Philosophical and Phenomenonological Research*, 59, pp. 913–37.

van Inwagen, Peter 1990: *Material Beings*. Ithaca, NY: Cornell University Press.

Zimmerman, Dean 1995: 'Theories of Masses and Problems of Constitution'. *Philosophical Review*, 104, pp. 53–110.

Proceedings of the Aristotelian Society Supplementary Volume LXXXII
doi: 10.1111/j.1467-8349.2008.00164.x

II – JOHN DIVERS

COINCIDENCE AND FORM

I compare a Lewisian defence of monism with Kit Fine's defence of pluralism. I argue that the Lewisian defence is, at present, the clearer in its explanatory intent and ontological commitments. I challenge Fine to explain
more fully the nature of the entities that he postulates and the relationship
between continuous material objects and the parts of those rigid embodiments in terms of which he proposes to explain crucial, modal and sortal,
features of those objects.

I

Introduction. Imagine that there is a statue (Statue) which is composed of a piece of alloy (Piece): Statue and Piece exist continuously,
they exist at exactly the same times, they are composed of exactly
the same matter and they exist at exactly the same places. Let us say
that Piece and Statue are, in exactly that sense, worldly coincidents.
Monists say that Piece and Statue are one and the same object
(which has two different names); pluralists say that Piece and Statue
are two different objects. One focal point of dispute between monists and pluralists is a cluster of acknowledged modal differences
which attend the case. To keep the matter neutral—so that it is correct to say that the differences are, indeed, acknowledged—these
are differences in truth-value arising from uniform modal predication. It is true to say (on occasion) of actually and always spherical
Piece that Piece could have been tetrahedral, and it is false to say (on
occasion) of actually and always spherical Statue that Statue could
have been tetrahedral. Some monists think that they have reason to
be monists, and some pluralists think that they have reason to be
pluralists, because each considers herself to be in possession of the
better explanation of such modal differences (and related data). I
am not sure how we are supposed to decide, in such cases, which of
two competing explanations is superior—even once the explana-

©2008 THE ARISTOTELIAN SOCIETY
Proceedings of the Aristotelian Society Supplementary Volume LXXXII
doi: 10.1111/j.1467-8349.2008.00165.x

tions are on the table, and it is clear exactly what is being explained and how it is being explained (what kind of explanation is intended). But it is hardly contentious that for the purpose of deciding such matters we should have, at least, in the case of each position, a clear idea of exactly what is being explained and how it is being explained. In that regard, I think that there are three (potentially) distinct kinds of claims which figure in—figure as—explanations of modal difference (and related data).

There are theses of ontology: theses about what exists and about what is a part, or more broadly, a constituent of what. These include, in particular, claims about differences in constituents.

There are theses of non-ontological metaphysics: theses about how things are which are precisely not about the existence of things or what is a constituent of what. These include, in particular, claims of non-compositional difference.

There are theses of representation: theses about how we represent the world (how we represent the ontological and metaphysical facts). These include, in particular, claims of differences in representation (of one and the same thing) and of differences in semantic values between expressions.

I won't attempt to anticipate or forestall the complaints which this tripartition might provoke, or the qualifications that might be necessary to make it more attractive. For I think it is serviceable enough, as it stands, to promote clarification of the debate between monists and pluralists.

Kit Fine (2008) offers a defence of pluralism which I intend to compare and contrast in its explanatory profile with a Lewisian defence of monism. For the sake of full disclosure, in positioning my own view in relation to this Lewisian defence of monism, I am very sympathetic to monism, but far from being a convinced genuine modal realist. However, I am impressed by the Lewisian defence of monism, precisely because I think it is relatively clear on exactly how it seeks to explain modal difference (and related matters). The Lewisian defence allows us to identify the points at which the explanation is ontological, what its ontological commitments are, where it is more broadly metaphysical, and where it is representational. Thus far, I have not been able to appreciate exactly how various elements of Kit Fine's defence of pluralism are to be understood in relation to these categories of explanation. I intend the present paper as an invitation to Fine to clarify his intentions in this regard: or, per-

©2008 The Aristotelian Society
Proceedings of the Aristotelian Society Supplementary Volume LXXXII
doi: 10.1111/j.1467-8349.2008.00165.x

haps, to show up the limitations of the tripartition of kinds of explanation with which I try to work.

II

The Lewisian Defence of Monism and Its Explanatory Profile. Take the following as a paradigm case of the standard modal argument for pluralism:

> Piece is possibly tetrahedral.
> Statue is not possibly tetrahedral.
> So Piece ≠ Statue.

The monist cannot find this argument sound—save perhaps for some devious moves on what the conclusion really means, which I won't explore here. In defence of monism, there is a Lewisian diagnosis of the unsoundness of the argument which is well-known and long-established.[1]

This Lewisian response to the paradigm modal argument for pluralism is that, for any token instance of such an argument, counterpart-theoretic interpretation shows either that the argument has an invalid form or that it is not the case that both of its premises are true. Two cases are generated since there are two relevant possibilities concerning the counterpart relations that are invoked in the truth conditions ascribed to the premises of the argument. Either one counterpart relation might figure twice in the interpretation or two different counterpart relations might figure.

In the first (univocal) case, we take the same counterpart relation to figure in the interpretation of both premises; thus (for example):

> Piece has an origin-counterpart which is tetrahedral.
> Statue does not have an origin-counterpart which is tetrahedral.
> So Piece ≠ Statue.

In that case, the argument is valid. But it cannot be that both of its premises are true. And there is no opacity, no 'Abelardian' predication, in the interpreting language of counterpart theory which will permit escape from that consequence. If Piece (aka Statue) has an

---

[1] The *locus classicus* of this defence of monism is Lewis (1971). In constructing the Lewisian defence, I will draw broadly on themes from that source and also from Lewis (1970, 1978, 1986).

©2008 The Aristotelian Society
Proceedings of the Aristotelian Society Supplementary Volume LXXXII
doi: 10.1111/j.1467-8349.2008.00165.x

origin-counterpart which is tetrahedral, then only the first premiss is true: if not, then only the second premiss is true. To fill out the picture, we might add that Piece does have an origin-counterpart which is tetrahedral. The following case is sufficient. There is a world, w, the earlier segment of which is a duplicate of the earlier segment of the actual world: a duplicate of the segment which takes us up to the moment at which Piece comes into existence. So in w, there is an object, Piece*, which is not only a duplicate of Piece, but also perfectly similar to actual Piece with respect to features of origin. In subsequent developments in w, the material that composes Piece* is formed into a tetrahedron.

In the second (multivocal) case, we take two different counterpart relations to figure across the interpretation of the premisses—thus (for example):

> Piece has an origin-counterpart which is tetrahedral.
> Statue does not have a career-counterpart which is tetrahedral.
> So Piece ≠ Statue.

In that case the argument is invalid. The underlying, invalidating, principle is that an object—the one object—may (in general) be similar in one respect to something that is F, but dissimilar in some other respect to everything that is F. The counter-possibility, in this particular instance, is given by the existence of one thing—Piece (aka Statue)—which has an origin-counterpart which is tetrahedral (see above) but which has no career-counterpart which is tetrahedral (nothing, in any world, goes on to develop just as Piece does and becomes tetrahedral).

It is a central part of a Lewisian theory of communication that, for typical sentence-types, a wide range of features of their tokens will typically operate to produce significant variation in the semantic values of those sentence tokens (and of their parts).[2] This holds, *a fortiori*, for sentences involving *de re* modal predications, for these predications introduce a distinctive source of variation in semantic value across tokenings: variation in counterpart relations expressed. The core thesis of the inconstancy of *de re* modal predication is, precisely, that there is no unique (*de jure*) correct interpretation of any such sentence-type: no single counterpart relation which is guaranteed to figure in the truth condition of every token of any one sen-

---

[2] For an expanded version of this story see Divers (2007).

tence-type which involves *de re* modal predication.[3] So there is no question of there being one interpretation of the modal argument which is (*de jure*) correct in every relevant context. However, the modal argument for pluralism and its proponents push us towards consideration of those contexts in which both premisses are (heard as) true. In this case, our Lewisian will say that the appropriate interpretation is multivocal: it is appropriate to assign different counterpart relations in interpreting the respective premisses (even if not exactly those that figure in our illustration).

Clearly, then, the Lewisian explanation of the modal difference which is mooted in the argument for pluralism is a representational explanation. It is difference in modal properties expressed, not difference in modal properties possessed. Both premisses can be true because the first premiss expresses Piece/Statue having one modal property and the second premiss expresses Piece/Statue lacking a different modal property. Thus, merely apparent metaphysical difference is explained away by real differences of representation.

The explanation might end there, in so far as the mooted modal difference has been accounted for. But that would be to leave matters in an unsatisfactory state. For in the case of *de re* modal predication (as ever) the truth-value of a sentence is naturally taken to be a product of both representational content (truth conditions) and the reality that is represented. But almost nothing has been said thus far about the non-representational aspect of the defence of monism. Moreover, as Fine persuasively argues in his paper, it is not only modal differences, or even differences *tout court*, that a comprehensive defence of monism (or pluralism) is obliged to explain. And, indeed, further arguments for pluralism, or arguments against monism, will require an exploration of non-representational aspects of the cases. So what is to be said, in completing the Lewisian defence, about the ontology and metaphysics, more generally, of monism?

The first step in this direction is sure. On the Lewisian account, the metaphysical ground of (true) *de re* modal predication—the facts which are semantically relevant to the truth-values of token sentences—are facts about what there is, and about what is similar (in this or that respect) to what. The ontological dimension of the Lewisian story is in one respect familiar and straightforward:

---

[3] Intuitions of constancy are to be accounted for in terms of all tokens turning out *de facto* to merit interpretation in terms of certain counterpart relations. But that need not concern us here. See again Divers (2007).

(L1) There are at least as many individuals as there are possible ways for an individual to be (and any sum of individuals is an individual).

Perhaps, thereafter, there are different ways in which a Lewisian ontology might be developed. But, on the development of the Lewisian story which I favour, there are two further ontological theses.

(L2) There are sets of the individuals, and sets of such sets ... and so on up.

(L3) There is nothing else.

Everything that exists is covered by (L1) and (L2), and the properties are among these—they are sets of individuals (in the monadic case) or sets of sequences of individuals (otherwise).[4] So much for what exists. But what should be said about how those things are, and which would explain—fundamentally—what (*de re*) modal truth consist in once the matters of truth conditions are settled or, at least, held fixed? I will illustrate the network of Lewisian explanations by focusing on the case of modal (and non-modal) properties. The upshot will be this. In matters of ontology: there are modal properties, and each is identical with a non-modal property. In matters of representation: modal properties figure in the explanation of truth conditions (and so truth-values) and of the unsoundness of the modal argument for pluralism. In matters of metaphysics: appeal to modal properties (or any properties) is no part of the fundamental explanation of what modal truth consists in. Moreover, in all of these respects, the case of modal properties is but a particular case of the case of properties in general.[5] The fuller story is as follows.[6]

The property of *being possibly tetrahedral* is, at first go, the property of *having a tetrahedral counterpart*. Let us begin under the simplifying assumption that there is a unique counterpart relation. This counterpart relation then determines a set of individuals: the set of all and only those things x such that, for some y, xCy and y is tetra-

---

[4] I am aware that Lewis sometimes toys with the idea of adding universals to genuine modal realism and that at other times, when he is not pressing his own account of various matters, he works with a more metaphysically substantive conception of properties. But I take these occasions to be digressions from the core view.

[5] I believe that an exactly parallel story is appropriate for modal facts, but I won't rehearse that here.

[6] Here I am, as far as I know, extrapolating from Lewisian themes and do not attribute to Lewis the story offered.

hedral. This set, then, is the property of *being possibly tetrahedral*. Before we consider what to say in face of a multitude of counterpart relations, let us note various features of the one-relation account that will carry over.

Firstly, the ontological claims are that modal properties exist and that they are (identical to) sets of individuals. (By default, I will be concerned with the basic level and monadic case throughout.) Secondly, there is no difference in constitution between modal properties (in general) and non-modal properties (in general): both are sets of individuals. The property of *being possibly tetrahedral* is of the very same ontological kind or category as the property of *being tetrahedral* (or *being a statue*, or *being an elephant*, ...). Thirdly, every modal property will be identical to some non-modal property: if a non-modal property is just any set of possible individuals then every modal property, on the present proposal, will be identical with one of these. Once all the non-modal properties are accounted for, there is nothing else for a modal property *to* be except one of those. How can a property be both modal and non-modal? On this account, that is the case only in the deflationary sense that one property can have both a proper modal description and a proper non-modal description. And of course many properties will have no description at all. In general, on this account, to be a modal property is to be a property (a set of individuals) which is picked out by a modal description. Fourthly, some modal properties will be very natural properties and others will be very unnatural. Whether some set makes for a natural property will be a matter of both the extent and kind of similarity that holds across its membership. If x has a counterpart-in-virtue-of-S which is F and y has a counterpart-in-virtue-of-S which is F, then both x and y will be instances (members) of the property *being possibly F*. But, of course, this does not establish either that x is F or that y is F, far less that both are: in general, there will not be similarity in the respect F across the membership of the property-set. Also, the similarity underpinning the counterpart relation need not be similarity in any very natural respect, or similarity to any great degree. Take similarity in respect of containing metal— any quantity of any metal. The things that have *some* counterpart in that respect are radically heterogeneous; and the requirement that said counterpart be F does not remedy that. Even if the condition F is very natural and very demanding, that does not cut down significantly on the range of things which have *some* weak counterpart

which satisfies that condition. The sun and I and Piece and … all
have such counterparts that are tetrahedral, but the Sun and I and
Piece and … do not make for a natural set. Moreover, we should
dismiss the temptation to think that the possibility-properties contrast neatly with the necessity-properties in this regard. Take the
property of *being necessarily partially metallic*. That is the set of all
and only those things all of whose counterparts (in this respect) are
metallic; but that (also) turns out to be all of the things that contain
any quantity of any metal. Modal properties will be natural properties just in case the underlying counterpart relation (which determines set membership) ensures that x and y will be similar to each
other just by being similar in that respect to third parties.[7] So modal
properties, like properties in general, are heterogeneous: some natural and some non-natural. But, it may be worth adding, nothing
turns on the natural versus non-natural distinction as far as the ontological status of modal properties is concerned. For there is no ontological difference between natural properties and non-natural
properties: properties of each sort are sets and are constituted by the
membership of individuals. Moreover, being non-natural does not
deprive modal (or other) properties from playing a fundamental role
in the metaphysical explanation of predication: no properties play
that role (see below).

What happens, then, when we introduce the multitude of counterpart relations into this account of modal properties? Evidently, if the
property of *being possibly F* is the set of things that have a C-coun-
terpart which is *F*, and there are various ways of filling out 'C', then
various sets are implied: the set of things which have an origin-counterpart which is *F*, the set of things which have a career-counterpart
which is *F*, …. Where now are the modal properties? The answer I
commend is threefold. Firstly, the features of modal properties as
generated under the one-relation hypothesis remain features of all of
the properties (sets) generated by each of the many counterpart relations: swiftly, each is identical to some non-modal property and
many are non-natural. Secondly, the only remaining issue is which of
these properties is to be counted as the relevant modal property in a
given context. Thirdly, the question of what deserves to be counted
as a certain modal property in a context is the question of which set

---

[7] Some of the counterpart relations treated as salient cases by Hazen (1979) have this character.

©2008 The Aristotelian Society
Proceedings of the Aristotelian Society Supplementary Volume LXXXII
doi: 10.1111/j.1467-8349.2008.00165.x

should be taken as the value of a modal predicate. If the use of a predicate like 'possibly tetrahedral' in a context makes salient for the purposes of interpretation the origin-counterpart relation, then it is appropriate to identify, in that context, the property of *being possibly tetrahedral* with the set of things that are origin-counterparts (of the relevant individual) and which are tetrahedral.[8]

Properties so construed sustain the Lewisian defence of monism at two points. Firstly—and this point ought not to be underrated—by admitting properties and including modal properties among them, we have a repudiation of the soundness of the modal argument which admits a straightforward construal and endorsement of Leibniz's Law. Leibniz's Law appears to involve, essentially, quantification over properties, and is typically put to work in the *prima facie* assumption that predicates are genuinely predicative—that they stand for properties. The present acknowledgement of modal properties calls for no re-evaluation of Leibniz's Law and no special pleading over *de re* modal predication in that regard. Secondly, and more obviously, the modal properties so understood are exactly what is required to fill out semantically the diagnosis of semantic inconstancy in *de re* modal predication: different modal properties may feature as values of the same modal predicate on different occurrences of that predicate.

I hope that three features of the foregoing account loom large. Firstly, modal properties and non-modal properties are perfectly congruent ontologically. Both exist and have the same kind of constitution and constituents: the 'mode of constitution' is set membership and the constituents are individuals. Secondly, the case of modal predicates is continuous with that of non-modal predicates with respect to their representational (semantic) function: in each case, interpretation proceeds by inconstant association with proper-

---

[8] We might entertain the idea that the modal property is the union of these sets, and perhaps seek encouragement from the model of determinable and determinate properties. So the union set is like the set of all coloured things and the relevant subsets like the set of all red things, the set of all green things …. But in the present context this invites a conception of the determinable modal properties which is not obviously suited to play any role in explanation. The most obvious kind of property-role that needs to be filled is that of (intended) semantic value of modal predicate-token. And the candidates for these roles are the 'determinate' sets such as the set of things that have an origin-counterpart which is tetrahedral. In this respect, I note, the account is continuous with the standard Lewisian treatment of non-modal predication. There are, for example, many different sets that one might associate with the use of the English predicate, 'is white': many candidates available to play the role of that predicate type's semantic value (the semantic role of the property of *whiteness*) across contexts when we speak of wine, when we speak of skin, when we speak of teeth, etc.

ties, but there is an additional dimension of inconstancy in the modal case. Thirdly, the (modal and non-modal) properties which are endorsed in this representation-driven account of properties will have no role to play in the metaphysical explanation of what truth (or differences in truth-value) consists in. The last point needs elaboration.

Take some fundamental feature, F, of our world and an individual a which is F. We can correctly say that a has the property F, and that a is a member of the set of F things. This much may figure in explaining the representational features of names and predicates (if we have them) and of the sentences in which they feature. But it is no part of the intention that we explain what it is metaphysically for a to be F by pointing to the fact that a is a member of any set. If there is a metaphysical order of things, it looks right to say (in one sense) that a is a member of the set of F things because a is F rather than vice versa. So what is the metaphysical explanation of fundamental predication such as a being F? There is none. Ontologically, there is no place to go: there is no fundamental entity afoot here other than a and, *a fortiori*, no kind of underlying or fundamental relation between a and F (or between a and anything else). Metaphysically, there is nothing more fundamental than that a is F: that is metaphysical bedrock. And what goes for monadic properties goes for relations, and in particular—we might emphasize—for the relation of mereological composition. Facts of the sort a is a part of b are metaphysical bedrock, and insusceptible to any ontological articulation that would yield a metaphysically substantive relation of mereological composition. However, not all relational facts are fundamental relational facts. In particular, facts about similarity are not fundamental. When a is similar in some respect, R, to b, that is explained by more fundamental facts—for example that a is F and that b is F.

In sum, then, and with due attention to the different kinds of explanation involved at each stage, the Lewisian story is this.

What does the truth of 'a is possibly F' consist in (for some basic feature, F)? At the first stage we have claims about representational content: on one occasion, the truth condition is that a has a counterpart-1 that is F, on another occasion, the truth condition is that a has a counterpart-2 which is F, ... What, metaphysically, explains a's having a counterpart-n which is F? It is that there is some thing b which is similar to a in some respect R and which is F. The only entities which are intended to be implicated in this claim are the individuals a and b. But that ontological fact, the existence of these individuals, does not exhaust what is metaphysically fundamental. What is metaphysically fundamental is that (for some appropriate monadic feature, F) a is F and b is F. The metaphysical fundament of true *de re* modal predication is the existence of individuals and their (primitively) having non-modal features.

The details merit scrutiny, and not every complication has been covered. And, I emphasize, I am not ready to endorse the Lewisian explanation. But I think that I understand it, at least in intent. In particular, I think I understand the ontological claims, the representational claims and the metaphysical claims; and I think I understand which is which and where each enters the picture. Thus, I believe that monism lends itself to a defence which is admirably clear in its explanatory intent.

III

The Finean Defence of Pluralism. With Fine, I shift the example of the modal argument for pluralism to a closely related case. Recall that Statue is, by hypothesis, spherical. Fine defends and explains a version of pluralism which discerns a difference even between Piece and Sphere, the sphere, rather than the statue, with which Piece is coincident.[9] Hence the argument:

> Piece is possibly tetrahedral.
> Sphere is not possibly tetrahedral.
> So Piece ≠ Sphere.

The pluralist, I suppose, finds this argument sound. Since she finds these premises both true, she takes these simpler sentences to differ in truth-value:

(1) Piece is possibly tetrahedral.
(2) Sphere is possibly tetrahedral.

The pluralist takes validity to be established via Leibniz's Law (the

---

[9] I suspect that no consistent pluralist can stick at mere dualism in any such case. The ensuing and obvious question is how many different coincident objects there are in any such case. Perhaps there is one for each sort-picking principle that could be applied. But how many are they?

indiscernibility of identicals) conjoined to an interpretation of '_ is possibly tetrahedral' on which it has the same semantic value in both occurrences.

Fine has (here) no objection to the soundness of the modal argument, nor to this orthodox pluralist articulation of it. But the argument does not accord with Fine's conception of what is fundamental, explanatorily and/or in the metaphysical order of things. The direction of explanation implied by the argument—i.e. explanation of the conclusion by the premisses—is wrong: since (in this case, at least) there are non-modal facts which are more fundamental than the modal facts. Differences in modal properties do not fundamentally explain facts about non-identity. For Fine, those non-modal facts which are fundamental are not represented explicitly in the modal argument, but when these facts are produced they will be presented as a common source of explanation of the truth of both premisses and conclusion. The fundamental facts in which modal and other relevant differences between Piece and Sphere consist, are not only non-modal facts, they are presented as facts of ontology— facts about constitution. Sphere has a constituent part which Piece lacks, and vice versa.

It is noteworthy that these (putative) facts about composition will, of course, support a swift and direct argument from Leibniz's Law to the pluralist conclusion: non-identity from difference of parts. So one effect of the thesis of the compositional difference thesis is to downplay, or marginalize, the role of the modal argument in the monist–pluralist dialectic. The argument was unsatisfactory when construed as an explanation of plurality and is now shown to be epistemologically dispensable. For non-modal theses which are among those required to justify the premisses of the modal argument lead more surely, in their own right, to the conclusion. So there is (allegedly) a sound argument for pluralism—difference in objects from difference in parts—which does not immediately involve any modal commitments at all: no commitments concerning the semantics of modal predication, nor any concerning the nature of modal properties or modal facts, nor—a fortiori—the reducibility of modal facts to non-modal facts. However, another effect of the thesis of compositional difference is to vindicate properly the claim that the modal argument is sound. For, Fine suggests, the right to hold true the premisses of the modal argument depends upon the availability of an explanation, in non-modal terms, of the imputed

©2008 The Aristotelian Society
Proceedings of the Aristotelian Society Supplementary Volume LXXXII
doi: 10.1111/j.1467-8349.2008.00165.x

difference in modal properties, and the thesis of compositional difference affords such an explanation.

Before proceeding to the detail of the compositional theory, let us emphasize the basics of what, at least, appears to be the explanatory intent. Firstly, Fine does not intend to explain modal difference as a function of differences at the level of representation. Secondly, the clear suggestion is that the fundamental metaphysical explanation of modal (and other) differences is ontological: Sphere is modally different from Piece because they have different constituent parts.

I should make clear that I have nothing to say here against the proposed explanatory route from the theory of composition to modal and sortal differences. I propose to scrutinize the theory of composition itself concerning its intelligibility, and its precise metaphysical and ontological content. If all of that is in order, I have nothing to say here that would block the explanatory move from the facts about composition to the modal facts.

Fine suggests a two-stage account of the natures of continuous material objects. Many material objects including Piece and Sphere are variable embodiments (Fine 2008, p. 116). (I do not know whether the ambition extends to accounting for all continuous material objects in this way.) The three key elements in the explanation of variable embodiments are principles, rigid embodiments and succession. A principle is a principle for picking out an object at different times under actual and counterfactual circumstances: I take it that the intention is that there is (at least) one such principle for picking out statues and another such principle for picking out pieces of alloy. A rigid embodiment is a non-mereological composite of matter and form: in general, $r = \Sigma(m, F)$. In particular, for our piece of alloy Piece (p) and Sphere (s) we have :

(3) $p = \Sigma(a, P)$
(4) $s = \Sigma(a, S)$

Here, a is 'a certain parcel of alloy' (Fine 2008, p. 110), P is the shape of 'a piece in general' (Fine 2008, p. 111) and S is the 'shape of some particular sphere' (Fine 2008, p. 110). Then, given a (the?) principle, $\phi\text{-}S$, for picking out spheres, the (continuous) Sphere, s, is the variable embodiment $/\phi\text{-}S/$ of a certain succession of rigid embodiments, $a/S, a'/S, a''/S, a'''/S, \dots$, for certain $a, a', a'', a''', \dots$. Extrapolating to the case of Piece (since it is not treated explicitly), given the principle, $\phi\text{-}P$, for picking out pieces, the (continuous)

✳

Piece, p, is the variable embodiment, $/\phi\text{-}S/$, of a certain succession of rigid embodiments, a/P', a'/P'', a''/P''', ..., for certain a, a', a'', a''', ... and P', P'', P''', ...[10]

In seeking to press this account on detail, two kinds of question are salient. What kind of explanation is on offer of variable embodiments? And to exactly what ontology is the (proponent of) the account committed by being committed to rigid embodiments?

The explanation of variable embodiments, if read with maximal ontological intent, would be taken to involve three kinds of entity: principles, succession relations and rigid embodiments. In the case of principles, it is possible to see an entity behind the name. In the case of a principle for picking out statues, one might detect the relation x-is-the-same-statue-as-y. Perhaps Fine would countenance the existence of such a relation, but not as a metaphysical primitive. In any case, it seems that the precise role of principles in Fine's stated account is representational: the principle points us towards rigid embodiments which are of the right kind for the continuous object in question. For, beginning with a rigid matter-form composite which is (somehow) implicated in a sphere, not just any succession of such things will make for a (continuous) sphere.[11] So let us put principles out of the ontological picture, leaving, in a given case, succession and rigid embodiments. The question now is whether what is intended a full-blooded ontological explanation of variable embodiment in terms of rigid embodiments and a succession relation: is the thesis that a variable embodiment consists in some kind of composite of these things?

Either way, more must be said. If the claim is that variable embodiments are composites, then what is the relevant mode/kind of composition? Is a variable embodiment a mereological sum of these parts? Is it composed of these parts in the same non-mereological mode which we find in rigid embodiments? Or is there here a third distinctive mode of composition. Perhaps, on the other hand, variable embodiments are not supposed to be composites. But I am not sure that this route is easily available to Fine. For one thing, if Fine

---

[10] My use of different symbols (P', P'', P''', ...) in the latter case is intended to leave open the question whether these stand for the same form or different forms. This reflects my uncertainty about the nature of such forms (see below).

[11] Perhaps spheres are so indifferent to succession and make an awkward case. The claim that succession is crucial is general is borne out more clearly by consideration of the likes of statues and persons.

©2008 The Aristotelian Society
Proceedings of the Aristotelian Society Supplementary Volume LXXXII
doi: 10.1111/j.1467-8349.2008.00165.x

believes in the existence of both rigid embodiments and metaphysically substantive succession relations then should he not believe that variable embodiments are composites of these—even if only, loosely, on grounds of analogy with his belief that rigid embodiments are composites (of matter and form)? But there is more pressure exerted here than that generated by appeal to loose analogy. If difference in variable embodiments is to be explained by differences of parts (forms) at the level of rigid embodiment, do we not have to add the premiss that the rigid embodiments are parts of the variable embodiment in order that the forms are parts of variable embodiments? Can the parts of the rigid embodiments (matter and form) be parts of the variable embodiments otherwise? And if the parts of the rigid embodiments are not supposed to be parts of the variable embodiments, then what kind of explanation is intended? Moreover, if full-blooded ontological explanation of variable embodiments as composites is the intent, it does not seem a live option for Fine to remove the succession relation from the composite; at least, that is so unless the mode of composition is indifferent to temporal order of parts. Perhaps the case of the sphere is special, since (fortunately) the relevant rigid embodiments, in any ordering, make for a continuous sphere. But surely that will not in general be the case, as, for example, not just any succession of rigid embodiments of a human would make for a (continuous) human. So it will not be easy for Fine to avoid commitment to the claim that variable embodiments are composites, and with that commitment comes the further commitment to state and defend a thesis about their mode of composition.

Even if it is not yet quite clear what the ontological/compositional intention is in the case of variable embodiments, Fine's intentions in this respect are perfectly clear in the case of rigid embodiments. Rigid embodiments exist, and each is a non-mereological composite of matter and form. Fine then contends that 'any further clarification of the compositional character of the sphere or the piece of alloy will devolve upon the method of composition, Σ' (Fine 2008, p. 111), and he goes to work on explaining the features of that method of composition. But the contention is rather too quick. For there is ample scope for clarification concerning the nature of the entities that are supposed to be the parts of the entity so composed. I shall consider here only issues about the nature of these parts, and not about the method of composition.

The natural way, or the familiar way, to construe the elements of a rigid embodiment is to take the matter, *a*, as some particular (individual?) and the forms, *P* and *S*, as properties. If that can be done, then it might be claimed that there are no new ontological categories of entity—nothing beyond particulars and properties—implicated in Fine's account. But is the natural and conservative construal straightforward?

We might begin by asking what kind of particular is the element of matter, *a*—that 'certain parcel of alloy' (Fine 2008, p. 110) which is common to both Piece and Sphere? It is—crucially—not a piece of alloy, or, at least, it is not the same piece as Piece. For, on the account, Piece has *a* as a *proper* part. The question then is whether *a* is a particular of *any sort* at all. If so, of what sort is it, and what principle picks out things of that sort? If not, what are the options? Do we have intimated here an ontology of stuff, or of quantities of stuff, in addition to particulars (and properties)? Or is *a* simply the mereological sum of the material parts of Piece? The last option is of some interest for it implies that the present metaphysical explanation of what it is for Sphere to be a sphere (or Piece to be a piece) involves at least two different kinds of composition: mereological composition of some parts and non-mereological composition of others. And it seems appropriate to emphasize that it is *at least* two modes of composition that are in the offing, in so far as it has not yet been ruled out that a third kind of composition is implicated in the intended relationship between rigid embodiments and variable embodiments. Finally, concerning *a*, it would be helpful to have clarification on the question of whether *it* is the kind of thing that has a form (as a part). Perhaps this is relevant to questions already raised about what sort of thing it is, but it is also of interest in its own right. To be clear, the concern is not that some regress is afoot that would vitiate the explanations that are presently on offer. If *a* has a form (as a part), then we have not yet reached ontological bedrock at *a*. But that doesn't matter, since that would not prevent the differences that have already been identified (Sphere has one form and Piece another) being sufficient to explain the modal and sortal differences between Piece and Statue. However, the question whether *a* is the kind of thing that has a form does bear on the question of what (and where) the ontological primitives of the theory of composition are. And, in particular, whether the appeal to matter introduces some category of entity which is distinct from that of particulars (but which has been presented to us in particular clothing).

©2008 The Aristotelian Society
Proceedings of the Aristotelian Society Supplementary Volume LXXXII
doi: 10.1111/j.1467-8349.2008.00165.x

The second constituent of a rigid embodiment is a form. In this case, my understanding of Fine's intentions (based on Fine 2008, p. 111, n.7) is that forms are nothing new: they are properties. As I read Fine, because such form-properties, as it were, are put to work in fundamental metaphysical explanation, they have to be conceived in *some* metaphysically substantive way: sets of individuals, for example, are not up to the job. So form-properties might be conceived as universals or as tropes, but the account, as it stands, is neutral about *which* substantive choice is made. Thus, I take it, forms are intended to be properties, and properties are ontologically substantive and ontologically primitive—it is an open question whether they are universals or tropes, but either way, they are not composed of entities of any further category.

The first question that arises, then, is whether all properties are forms and, if not, whether anything can be said about which properties are forms—anything other than that they are those properties which are combined with matter in rigid embodiments.[12] On the examples we are given, forms are (related to) shape-properties. But I presume that the intention cannot be that all of the forms are shape-properties—that all forms are geometrical forms. At least that cannot be so if the idea is to arm pluralists about cases other than those of simple inorganic objects and artefacts such as statues and dishpans. For there are those who find sortal and modal difference to sustain their belief that (the likes of) cells, persons, nations and wars are not identical to various things with which they (respectively) coincide, and they are not likely to think that shape has any role to play in the explanation of those differences. However, I leave aside the question of non-geometrical forms and concentrate on the geometrical examples given.

The second question is a request for clarification of the nature of the postulated entity, P—the form of Piece. I take it that these are constraints on the nature of P: (i) P is, or is related to, some kind of shape-property; (ii) P cannot be the same thing as S, the form of s (for otherwise the crucial difference between Rigid-Sphere and Rigid-Piece disappears)—and in this regard, note that S is presented as a familiar sort of shape-property (either *being spherical, being a sphere of diameter n*, or *being the sphericality of s*); (iii) the form, P, of Piece, can-

---

[12] Assuming that some properties are not forms, note that the earlier question of whether a has a form is not equivalent to asking whether a has any properties at all. So denial that a has a form is not so expensive as it might appear in the absence of that distinction.

©2008 The Aristotelian Society
Proceedings of the Aristotelian Society Supplementary Volume LXXXII
doi: 10.1111/j.1467-8349.2008.00165.x

not be also the form of quantity of matter a—Piece is the composite of matter a and form P, so if a is itself a form-involving composite, the form-part of a cannot be P; (iv) P is not the shape-property that all pieces have, for there is no one shape-property that all pieces have; (v) P is not the 'higher-order property' of *being shaped*, or of *having one-or-other shape*, for that is a property that does not differentiate sphere s from piece p—both have it. What Fine (2008, p. 111) says is that P is 'the shape of ... a piece in general'. But I am unable to see what might be intended by this other than interpretations that are ruled out by constraints (i)–(v). So the challenge emerges of clarifying the proposed ontology of forms at a very elementary stage—the first stage at which we are asked to think of a form as anything other than the kind of familiar shape-property which sphere s has.

IV

Summary. The fundamental elements of the Lewisian defence of monism are the following. The fundamental ontology is the individuals. The fundamental metaphysics is ontologically unarticulated facts about individuals: a is F, b is G, c is R to d. The semantic values of predicates are sets of individuals. The explanation of modal difference proceeds from these basics and three hypotheses: (a) difference in truth-values of relevant modal sentences is explained by difference in representational features—difference in semantic values of modal predicates; (b) modal facts (properties) are similarity facts (properties); and (c) similarity facts are metaphysically explained by non-similarity facts—a is similar to b in some respect because, for example, a is F and b is F. The only kind of composition involved (in non-sets) is mereological composition. This claim involves no commitment to a substantive parthood relation; the metaphysical basis of composition is ontologically unarticulated facts such as that a is a part of b. There is no role for metaphysically substantive or ontologically articulated facts in this story, nor for metaphysically substantive properties.

   I find the fundamentals of the Lewisian defence of monism clear. I find the Finean defence of pluralism unclear in respects that have prompted the following questions of clarification. Are rigid embodiments parts of variable embodiments? If not, what kind of explanation is intended of the latter by the former; if so, does this involve a third mode of composition? How does the ontological category of (quantities of) matter relate to that of particulars? How does the ontological category of forms relate to that of properties: in particular, how does it relate to the shape-properties, and can any account of the nature of the postulated non-specific forms satisfy the constraints put on them? When the fundamental ontological and metaphysical commitments of Fine's theory of composition are clarified, we might see whether it will bear the weight of explanation placed upon it.[13]

School of Philosophy
University of Leeds
Leeds LS2 9JT
UK
j.divers@leeds.ac.uk

REFERENCES

Divers, John 2007: 'Quinean Skepticism About De Re Modality After David Lewis'. *European Journal of Philosophy*, 15, pp. 40–62.

Fine, Kit 2008: 'Coincidence and Form'. *Proceedings of the Aristotelian Society Supplementary Volume* 82, pp. 101–18.

Hazen, Allen 1979: 'Counterpart-Theoretic Semantics For Modal Logic'. *Journal of Philosophy*, 76, pp. 319–38.

Lewis, David 1971: 'Counterparts of Persons and Their Bodies'. *Journal of Philosophy*, 68, pp. 203–11.

——1979: 'Scorekeeping in a Language Game'. *Journal of Philosophical Logic*, 8, pp. 339–59.

——1983: 'New Work for a Theory of Universals'. *Australasian Journal of Philosophy*, 61, pp. 343–77.

——1986: *On the Plurality of Worlds*. Oxford: Blackwell.

---

[13] I should also emphasize that I have tried to address here only what is specific in Fine's account. There are, of course, very familiar and difficult issues that attend all accounts of this type—for example, issues of vicious regress that arise from questions about how complex entities are unified by certain relations. It would be, at least, interesting to find out how Fine would deal with these issues arising from an understanding of variable and rigid embodiments as complex entities in which a composition relation is a further element. Lewis avoids these problems by refusing ontological articulation of facts about composition (what is part of what) as complex entities, taking the only entities afoot to be individuals. Fine takes facts about composition to be at least partially ontologically articulated, at least at the level of rigid embodiment, into two sorts of entity: (items of) matter and forms. Perhaps we then hit metaphysical bedrock: it is a fundamental metaphysical fact that matter *m* is in form *F*, and this is not to be further articulated as the existence of a complex entity in which a non-mereological composition relation is a third part. But enough speculation.

©2008 THE ARISTOTELIAN SOCIETY
Proceedings of the Aristotelian Society Supplementary Volume LXXXII
doi: 10.1111/j.1467-8349.2008.00165.x

EQUALITY AND BUREAUCRACY
ELIZABETH ANDERSON AND JOHN SKORUPSKI

I — ELIZABETH ANDERSON

EXPANDING THE EGALITARIAN TOOLBOX: EQUALITY AND BUREAUCRACY

Many problems of inequality in developing countries resist treatment by formal egalitarian policies. To deal with these problems, we must shift from a distributive to a relational conception of equality, founded on opposition to social hierarchy. Yet the production of many goods requires the coordination of wills by means of commands. In these cases, egalitarians must seek to tame rather than abolish hierarchy. I argue that bureaucracy offers important constraints on command hierarchies that help promote the equality of workers in bureaucratic organizations. Bureaucracy thus constitutes a vital if limited egalitarian tool applicable to developing and developed countries alike.

I

Rethinking the Goal of Egalitarianism. A survey of global egalitarian strategies reveals three principal tools: (i) getting states to constitutionalize fundamental human rights, including anti-discrimination principles; (ii) installing the formal apparatus of democracy, including periodic elections and a free press; and (iii) redistributing resources, often through public provision or funding of goods such as education and health care. The selection of these tools is theoretically motivated by a distributive conception of equality. On this view, the egalitarian goal is to equalize the resources or primary goods— rights, political liberties, opportunities, income—at individuals' disposal. This conception of equality as a pattern of distribution is not fundamentally challenged by prominent recent debates concerning the metric of equality—whether just distributions should be measured in terms of primary goods or other resources, or in terms of capabilities or opportunities for welfare.

Rohinton Mistry's *A Fine Balance* (2001), a novel about India from Independence to the Emergency, illustrates some of the practi-

©2008 THE ARISTOTELIAN SOCIETY
Proceedings of the Aristotelian Society Supplementary Volume LXXXII
doi: 10.1111/j.1467-8349.2008.00166.x

cal limitations of these egalitarian strategies. On election day, lower caste villagers are rounded up to cast empty ballots, to be filled in later by the local headman. When one dares to insist on his right to fill in his ballot as he pleases, he is killed. As members of the untouchable Chamaar (tanner) caste, his family is banned from the local school. His son and brother leave the village to make their way as tailors in a big city. The only available housing is a foul squatter settlement lacking sewers and running water for most of the day. When the government bulldozes the settlement, they lose all their possessions and must pay a night-watchman for the privilege of sleeping on the sidewalk next to an all-night pharmacy. Police round them up as vagrants, deaf to their protests that they have regular employment, and sell them to a business that puts them to a regime of forced labour that nearly kills them. Desperate to escape, they resort to the help of 'Beggarmaster', who buys them out of slavery in return for a huge share of their future wages. Beggarmaster controls the beggars in the city, offering them protection from abuse at the hands of police and private parties in return for the lion's share of their takings. The hapless tailors then get arrested by police during the Emergency's forced sterilization campaign. Civil servants bid to have the captives credited to their sterilization quota. One tailor loses his legs to post-surgical infection; the other is castrated at the orders of the village headman, in revenge for his defiance of the headman's rule and of the caste order, which dictated that he remain a lowly, untouchable tanner rather than aspire to the higher state of a (still impoverished) tailor. Their disabilities reduce them to begging, now wholly under the control of Beggarmaster.

Consider the standard egalitarian strategies in light of these events. The formal apparatus of democracy cannot deliver on its promises to the poor majority if they are effectively subject to the rule of upper-caste headmen who can determine their votes and inflict violence with impunity on those who defy them. The constitutionalization of human rights has little effect in a state riddled with corruption, where civil servants treat the discretionary powers of their office as private property, violating the rights of the poor for pay by private parties who themselves operate in collusion with a state determined to establish 'order' by destroying the homes of squatters, putting them to forced labour, and forcibly constraining their reproduction. Redistributive policies formally designed to open up opportunities to the poor have little effect when actual delivery is stymied by a caste system that keeps lower-caste children from attending school.

My point is not the trivial one, that bad actors often prevent justice from being achieved. It is a naïve mistake to blame the failure of these egalitarian policies on individual bad actors. The failures here are *systematic*. 'Booth capturing' and intimidation of lower-caste voters are long-standing problems (Narula 1991, p. 7). On any given day, only half of employed teachers in India are actually teaching, and one quarter do not bother to show up, with absentee rates concentrated in schools for the poor (Kremer et al. 2005). Public sector corruption is taken for granted.[1] Until the economic liberalization of 1991, the notorious 'Licence Raj' terrorized the lives of poor microentrepreneurs, as civil servants used their discretionary power to shut down unlicensed enterprises as a tool for extorting a steady stream of bribes from the meagre incomes of the self-employed. Even today, the poor cannot count on the police or courts enforcing their rights in disputes with the rich or higher caste individuals. All this goes on notwithstanding the formal abolition of caste in India's constitution.

These failures are systematic because they conform to reigning norms rather than deviating from them. The situation in India, as in many other countries in the developing world, consists in a formal apparatus of democracy and human rights overlain on feudal, caste, and other hierarchical social relations, the constitutive norms of which deeply contradict the official legal norms. In this light, the intimidation of lower-caste voters amounts to an exercise of the traditional 'rights' of landlords and local leaders to exercise political authority over their tenants and subordinates; denial of education to lower-caste children, a legitimate enforcement of the cosmic order that would be threatened by people aspiring to rise above their rank; corruption, a fulfilment of what are viewed as overriding obligations to family members, patrons, and clients.[2]

This diagnosis of the practical limitations of standard egalitarian strategies traces their difficulties to underlying inequalities in social relations. Recognizing this point should, in turn, lead us to recon-

---

[1] In 2007, Transparency International rated India 3.5 on their Corruption Perception Index. The CPI ranges from 0 to 10, with lower scores indicating higher corruption.

[2] See Rose-Ackerman (1998), discussing how some cultures interpret bribery as an expression of legitimate obligations of gift exchange based on personal connections between bribe givers and takers.

©2008 The Aristotelian Society
Proceedings of the Aristotelian Society Supplementary Volume LXXXII
doi: 10.1111/j.1467-8349.2008.00166.x

ceptualize the theoretical foundations of egalitarianism. For my point is not simply that unequal social relations pose instrumental obstacles to achieving equal distributions. A normative assessment of these relations should lead us to the view that they are objectionable over and above whatever bad consequences they have for patterns of distribution. Compare the following states of affairs: in *A*, the poor are poor because the land they work is naturally poor in nutrients, their tools are too primitive to significantly raise productivity, and their geographic isolation poses costly barriers to trade. In *B*, the poor are poor because their social superiors use violence to keep them in inferior positions, extract the lion's share of their production through exploitative credit and employment contracts, and exploit their vulnerability to abuse by forcing them into a condition of servile dependency. I claim that, even if the levels of poverty in *A* and *B* are equal, *B* is far worse than *A*. While natural poverty is unfortunate, poverty induced by oppressive social relations is inherently degrading, humiliating, and assaultive of individuals' status as beings entitled to moral standing before others. To get what they need to survive, the individuals in *B* are reduced to grovelling, begging for mercy before their social superiors, and bound by obligations of deference and loyalty to whoever grants them the favour of subsistence. They must live at others' beck and call, humble themselves in their presence, and live in fear of their arbitrary wrath.

Such social relations are objectionable from an egalitarian point of view, *even if the social inferiors in question are materially well-off*. Consider state *C*, which includes the members of an absolute monarch's court. He feeds them generously at his table, grants them lavish gifts, and offers them well-paid sinecures. Nevertheless, they live at his mercy. Since they owe their station and material well-being to the monarch's gratuitous acts, they could lose their standing at his whim. Hence, they are reduced to mere sycophants, bootlickers. The monarch may spare them self-abasement through his own gracious condescension. But mutual recognition of the gratuitousness of the monarch's conduct still extracts humbling deference from his dependents—at least in a society not yet challenged by an egalitarian ethos.

Reflection on cases like these should reorient egalitarian thinking. The dominant trend in post-Rawlsian egalitarian thought defines the goal of egalitarianism as eradicating distributive inequalities due to factors, such as geographical location and acci-

©2008 The Aristotelian Society
Proceedings of the Aristotelian Society Supplementary Volume LXXXII
doi: 10.1111/j.1467-8349.2008.00166.x

dents of birth, that are mere matters of luck, and hence arbitrary from a moral point of view.[3] This formula obscures the vast moral difference between states *A* and *B*. It has a hard time explaining why a class of people who are materially well off, as in *C*, should be objects of egalitarian concern. It presumes, rather than arguing for, the moral privilege of patterns of equal distribution (Hurley 2003, pp. 150–1). In other work (Anderson 2007*a*), I have argued that not only does justice not require the eradication of distributive inequalities due to arbitrary factors such as luck, it actually requires institutions that guarantee that luck will affect distributions, and condemns institutions that would attempt to compensate for this. Hence the bare fact that one person has less than another due to undeserved bad luck generates no claim to compensation. Egalitarians therefore need to seek some other aim. The cases I have just discussed suggest such an aim: the eradication of unjust social hierarchy. On this view, egalitarians should aim at ending oppressive social relations (which are inherently relations of inequality) and at realizing society conceived as a system of cooperation and affiliation among equals (Anderson 1999).

When we reconceive equality as fundamentally a kind of social relationship rather than a pattern of distribution, we do not abandon distributive concerns. Rather, we give such concerns a rationale. Some goods, such as basic liberties and rights to vote, bring legal suits and testify in court, need to be distributed equally because equal distributions are constitutive of equal social relations. People need adequate levels of other goods, such as income and wealth, so as to be able to avoid or escape oppressive social relations, and to participate in all domains of social life as an equal—which means (in part) without shame or stigma, and with the human, social and cultural capital needed to perform adequately in those domains. Ceilings on distributive inequality may be necessary to avoid the conversion of wealth into social inequality. For example, progressive income and inheritance taxes may be needed to prevent the rich from capturing formally democratic institutions and turning the state into a plutocracy. Such considerations give us instrumental reasons to promote more equal distributive patterns. Distributions may also be objectionable if they are caused by oppressive social relations. For example, compensation may be due to people exploited

---

[3] Cohen (1989, pp. 906, 908, 932) offers a classic statement of this view.

©2008 The Aristotelian Society
Proceedings of the Aristotelian Society Supplementary Volume LXXXII
doi: 10.1111/j.1467-8349.2008.00166.x

by subjection to slavery or debt peonage.[4]

Instead of further discussing the connections between relational equality and distribution, however, the rest of this paper will consider non-distributive egalitarian tools. We have already seen that the standard distributive tools do not have their desired effects in the context of pervasive relational inequalities. An account of these types of unequal relationship and what sorts of relations can replace them must play a central role in an egalitarian programme.

II

Types of Unequal Social Relations. My plea to reorient egalitarians toward equality in social relations is a plea to return to egalitarians' traditional aims. Unjust social hierarchy has traditionally been the prime enemy of egalitarians. Rousseau opposed plutocracy, or rule by the rich over the working classes. Feminists from John Stuart Mill to Catharine MacKinnon oppose patriarchy, or domination of men over women. Marx opposed capitalist productive relations, whereby the owners of capital lord over workers within the firm. B. R. Ambedkar, the author of India's democratic constitution, campaigned against hierarchical caste relations. W. E. B. DuBois campaigned against America's similar system of racial caste. Each of these egalitarians took the eradication of oppressive social relations as their central concern.

Egalitarians are hostile to or suspicious of at least three types of social hierarchy. There are hierarchies of *standing*, whereby those at the top are entitled to make claims on others in their own right, and to enjoy rights and privileges, while those below are denied rights or granted an inferior set of rights and privileges, and denied voice to make claims on their own, or given an inferior forum in which to make their claims. There are hierarchies of *esteem,* whereby those on the top command honour and admiration, while those below are stigmatized and held in contempt, as objects of ridicule, loathing, or

---

[4] Egalitarianism, understood as aiming at ending unjust social inequality and promoting equality in social relations, does not offer a comprehensive theory of distributive justice. Other non-egalitarian concerns make independent distributive claims. For example, humanitarianism tells us to end suffering, whether this is caused by natural or social factors. This requires distributing food, income-generating opportunities, and other goods to the victims of floods, droughts, and other natural disasters.

©2008 The Aristotelian Society
Proceedings of the Aristotelian Society Supplementary Volume LXXXII
doi: 10.1111/j.1467-8349.2008.00166.x

disgust. And there are hierarchies of *command*, of domination and subordination, whereby those at the top issue orders to those below, who must defer and obey. Egalitarians aim, to the extent possible, to abolish such hierarchies and replace them with relations of equality. This is fully possible with respect to hierarchies of standing, which are incompatible with the dignity and rights of human beings. Hence, egalitarians oppose such hierarchies absolutely.

In the case of the other two types of hierarchy, matters are not so simple. Where wholesale replacement is not possible, egalitarians aim to sharply limit the grounds on which social hierarchy can be based, and the scope of its authority. For instance, egalitarians reject hierarchies of esteem based on property and the circumstances of one's birth—race, ethnicity, caste, tribe, family line, gender, and so forth. They also oppose *official*, state-sponsored hierarchies of esteem, such as orders of nobility, that are based on purported normative assessments asserted to be authoritative for all. Esteem and contempt are an inescapable part of human life. But *liberal* egalitarians, at least, can take advantage of the fact of pluralism: the fact that, under conditions of liberty, there will be always be a plurality of conceptions of the good and hence of rival standards of merit and esteem (Rawls 1993, p. 36). Liberal egalitarians prefer that individuals be free to judge who merits esteem and contempt for themselves, without being held to a single official standard of worth. The expected and preferred outcome of such liberty is a plurality of conceptions of the good, which generate rival and cross-cutting orders of esteem, such that no social group comes out on the top or on the bottom of everyone's rankings, all are free to establish or seek a social circle in which they enjoy the esteem of their peers, and no esteem ranking counts as official, as one to which everyone is expected to defer. Against tendencies for people to erect oppressive esteem hierarchies in civil society, based on birth, property, or forms of cultural capital over which the snobbish self-appointed arbiters of manners and taste have assumed monopoly control, egalitarians deploy various tools. Among the most powerful such tools is 'upward contempt' directed by lower classes against upper classes, joined with the democratic norm that legitimizes such contempt and delegitimizes the traditional downward contempt that is directed by upper classes upon the lower (Miller 1997, pp. 206–34).

Henceforth I shall be exclusively concerned with command hierarchies. These are always suspect from an egalitarian point of view. To

©2008 THE ARISTOTELIAN SOCIETY
Proceedings of the Aristotelian Society Supplementary Volume LXXXII
doi: 10.1111/j.1467-8349.2008.00166.x

be subject to another's command threatens one's interests, as those in command are liable to serve themselves at the expense of their subordinates. It threatens subordinates' autonomy, their standing as self-governing individuals. Without substantial controls on the content of legitimate commands, subjection can also be degrading and humiliating.[5] Even when superiors permit subordinates wide scope for acting, the latter may still live at the mercy of the former. Such a condition of subjection to the arbitrary wills of others is objectionable in itself, and has further objectionable consequences: timidity and self-censorship in the presence of superiors—or worse, grovelling and self-abasement.

The proper egalitarian response to command hierarchies depends on the function of the command. Where commands regarding a particular action are not needed to coordinate conduct among different persons, egalitarians hold that adults should be free to make decisions for themselves, without having to ask anyone else's permission. In such cases, the remedy for subjection to another is social arrangements that secure each adult's personal independence. Egalitarians are concerned here with inequality, understood as a personal, face-to-face relation to superiors, that reduces subordinates to a condition of servile dependency on particular others. The egalitarian remedy for this relation helpfully reminds us of the close connection between ideals of freedom and equality. In the classic republican formula, to be unfree is to be subject to the arbitrary will of another (Pettit 1997, p. 5). This is the state of subordination, of inequality. To cast off relations of domination is to live as a free person. Thus, the quest for freedom is the quest for a mode of relating to others in which no one is dominated, in which each adult meets every other adult member of society eye to eye, as an equal.

The solution of letting each choose for himself, however, cannot be generalized to the case where commands are needed to coordinate conduct among different persons. Anarchists hoped that it could be generalized. They hoped that effective coordination would arise from the spontaneous mutual aid of independent persons (Kropotkin 1906). Anarchy, however, has not proven to be a reliable arrangement for securing stable, peaceful cooperation on terms of equality among large numbers of people.

---

[5] 9-to-5, The National Association of Working Women, publicized a case some years ago in which a boss ordered his secretaries to hold out their hands while he tipped his cigar ashes into them.

©2008 THE ARISTOTELIAN SOCIETY
Proceedings of the Aristotelian Society Supplementary Volume LXXXII
doi: 10.1111/j.1467-8349.2008.00166.x

Suppose then, that some command relations are needed to secure cooperation. How can these be reconciled with egalitarian aspirations? Participatory democracy offers one model for doing so that has long been appealing to egalitarians. Where commands cannot be eliminated, the idea is to ensure that command relations are reciprocal, with everyone participating in making the rules that govern them all. All shall meet face to face in a legislative assembly that determines what laws should prevail and that selects the executive officers who administer the laws.

This strategy also has serious limits. Once the scale of cooperation extends beyond a face-to-face community, where everyone knows everyone else, effective rules of coordination can no longer be chosen in a fully participatory fashion. Only a subset of the people will directly enact the rules that apply to others. In addition, a hierarchically organized administrative staff will be needed to promulgate and enforce the rules. Most of the members of this staff will not be directly accountable to the people subject to the rules, even though the rules grant discretionary power to members of the executive. The infeasibility of large-scale participatory democracy led Rousseau (1762, Book III, ch. 15) to insist that republics remain very small. This restriction comes at grave costs, however, among which are the difficulties of sustaining peaceful cooperation among numerous small city-states.

These challenges do not mean that egalitarians must give up. Where command relations are necessary, they can be subject to searching egalitarian constraints. To see what these involve, it helps to step down from the grand scale of states to smaller units of government, and to shift from units that exercise formal sovereignty to units that exercise lesser, but still considerable powers. I speak of the little governments that constitute our hierarchically organized private firms. It is no anomaly to regard the internal relations of the firm as little governments: although they operate within the constraints of laws passed by sovereign governments, they still consist in hierarchical command relations whereby employers boss workers around. I shall suppose that in the sphere of economic production, no less than in the sphere of sovereign government, the anarcho-syndicalist hope that command relations could be abolished is not generally feasible. Here too, once the scale of required cooperation rises above a modest scale, the demands of coordination become too complex for matters of internal governance to be settled by New

©2008 THE ARISTOTELIAN SOCIETY
Proceedings of the Aristotelian Society Supplementary Volume LXXXII
doi: 10.1111/j.1467-8349.2008.00166.x

England town meeting-style decision-making.

We can approach our problem by considering what egalitarian complaints remain after certain basic constraints on command relations within the firm are established. Call these, in order from less to more demanding, (1) libertarian, (2) capitalist, and (3) liberal constraints. These common types of egalitarian constraint on command relations concern (i) the conditions of entry to and exit from such relations, and (ii) the rules for assigning individuals to superior and subordinate positions.

Libertarians place only one constraint on command relations within the firm: that they be freely entered in a voluntary contract. This constraint excludes slavery, serfdom and caste as inherited conditions consigning one to a particular occupation and enterprise. However, it neglects the importance of freedom of exit. Hence it permits contracts into slavery, debt peonage, and other forms of bonded labour, conditions that affect tens of millions of workers across the world (Nozick 1974, p. 331). These relationships are incompatible with a conception of society as a community of equals. They are also incompatible with a conception of society as a community of free individuals.

Capitalism as it was originally understood—a competitive market system based on private property and *free* labour—goes beyond the libertarian model in also insisting on the right of workers to freely *exit* any employment relationship. Capitalism, on this view, is incompatible with any form of slavery, debt peonage or bonded labour. However, it too places insufficient constraints on command relations internal to the firm. Even if workers are formally free to exit some particular abusive relation with their bosses, they may have no reasonable alternative to signing an employment contract that permits some boss to abuse and humiliate them. Laissez-faire capitalism is indifferent to the background condition of reasonable alternatives needed for individuals' consent to legitimize the content of any particular contract. In addition, exit and entry constraints alone are insufficient to guard against the construction of *de facto* caste systems, whereby one group monopolizes positions of command and denies one or more outgroups access to such positions, and to the means to qualify themselves for such positions. This of course was long the position of blacks in the United States, who were effectively constituted as a lower caste of menial labourers through the joint operation of systematic employment discrimina-

©2008 The Aristotelian Society
Proceedings of the Aristotelian Society Supplementary Volume LXXXII
doi: 10.1111/j.1467-8349.2008.00166.x

tion and state deprivation of adequate schooling.

Liberalism, understood narrowly in terms of the classical liberal ideas that legitimizing consent requires reasonable alternatives (Hume 1948) and that careers should be open to talents, provides remedies for the two capitalist defects just mentioned. Suppose workers are guaranteed a decent minimum wage, unemployed workers are guaranteed unemployment insurance, and the state runs fiscal and monetary policies with the aim of promoting full employment. This *might* be enough to make all jobs reasonable alternatives, at least as judged by their external benefits. Suppose further that capitalist enterprises operate under the constraint of effective anti-discrimination laws, and that the state itself provides decent schooling to all groups. These constraints would jointly undermine the conditions that relegate some groups to a lower caste status, destined always to submit to commands issued by others.

Should egalitarians be satisfied with these types of constraints— on entry, exit and the allocation of individuals to superior and inferior positions—alone? I think not. Nothing has yet been said about the *content, scope* and *grounds* of employers' authority over employees. To be sure, the joint realization of freedom of entry and exit and reasonable alternatives is likely to limit the commands employers can get away with. Nevertheless, egalitarians are directly interested in the content of such commands, and not just in the procedures whereby employers come to have the power to issue them. We are interested in whether the content of the commands themselves humiliate or degrade subordinates, or reduce them to servile dependents.

An extreme case of such subjection may be found in company towns, and their contemporary sweatshop equivalents. The town of Pullman, Illinois was one such town in the US, devoted to the production of Pullman sleeper cars. The sole employer in town also owned all the real estate, retail stores and the sole church permitted in town. Workers had to rent houses from their employer, who not only set the rent but regulated workers' private lives in their homes in detail, right down to their housekeeping standards. They were paid in scrip, redeemable only in company stores with prices fixed by the employer. Pullman, the factory owner, set himself up as mayor of the town without free elections, and limited townspeople's religious options to his own church (Walzer 1983, pp. 295–7). Conditions are not much different in some contemporary sweatshops in places such as Anshan, China (Kahn 2003). Factories there recruit teenage girls

©2008 The Aristotelian Society
Proceedings of the Aristotelian Society Supplementary Volume LXXXII .
doi: 10.1111/j.1467-8349.2008.00166.x

from the countryside, promising them high wages. Once the workers arrive, however, they learn that their employer has limited their housing options. They must pay the employer room and board charges (set by the employer at high rates), and are not permitted to leave the factory grounds where their dormitories are located. This empowers the employer to exercise detailed control over their lives, including subjection to sexual harassment.

It might be argued that defects in the conditions of entry and exit account for all of the defects of the command relations in such cases. The Pullman workers, it might be argued, had no reasonable alternatives to signing a contract with Pullman. The teenage workers of Anshan, while promised high wages, are never told upon recruitment that these will be whittled away by exploitative room and board charges, and that they will have to live locked behind gates. They must pay a draconian training fee in order to free themselves of the labour contract. Yet I would argue that the command relations just described would be objectionable even if the workers were fully informed of them, could quit without paying a fee to their employer, and had reasonable employment alternatives that did not tie their consumption options to their employers' whims. What is objectionable here is the content of the employers' commands themselves—especially their regulation of workers' private lives. Such regulation reduces the workers to servile dependents. There is no time of the day when they are free to make significant choices for themselves, without asking their employers' permission. Even when they are off-duty, they remain under their employers' thumbs. This would be objectionable from an egalitarian point of view even if the workers in question were highly paid.

Can egalitarians offer a systematic analysis of the proper *content* and *scope* of command relations in the domain of work (including the administrative branches of government), granting that, given the scale and complexity of modern production, some kind of command hierarchy is necessary? I shall offer here only *part* of the egalitarian answer to this question. I shall argue that *bureaucracy* offers a vital tool for egalitarians that helps us address the objections to command relations that I have just discussed.

©2008 The Aristotelian Society
Proceedings of the Aristotelian Society Supplementary Volume LXXXII
doi: 10.1111/j.1467-8349.2008.00166.x

III

Bureaucracy vs. Patrimonial Domination. Recall the inegalitarian social relations illustrated in Mistry's novel, which are widely instantiated in the developing world. Most of these relations embody a form of domination that Max Weber called 'patrimonial'. This term refers in the first instance to the origin and supposed ground of legitimation of the command relation in question—namely, its basis in tradition. Yet when Weber spelled out the principles by which patrimonial domination operates he went far beyond merely locating authoritative rules in a long-remembered (or perhaps long-forgotten) past. He focused rather on the particular nature of the command relations subjectively legitimated by tradition (Weber 1968, pp. 226–35). One such type of relation is of special interest here, due to its continuing power in developing countries, even when they have adopted much of the formal apparatus of democracy and human rights. This is the patron–client relation. This relation underlies many of the inegalitarian practices mentioned above, including corruption and the chronic resort of the vulnerable to wealthy rescuers, which forces them to subordinate themselves to the wealthy.

The patron–client relation consists in a relation of personal dependence of the client on the patron, secured by the patron's gratuitous gifts or favours to the client. In return for credit or material goods (often paid in kind, as in the form of meals from the patron's table) or in liberation from abuse at the hands of some other powerful person, clients pledge their personal loyalty and submission to their patron. They become the patron's retainers. Like other forms of patrimonial domination, the patron–client relation grants superiors wide scope for arbitrary discretion over their subordinates. Few rules constraint the patron's power. Subordinates' roles are *ad hoc*. They are selected for positions of greater or lesser responsibility on the basis of personal favouritism and judgements of loyalty. Cronyism, not competence, determines subordinates' access to such positions.

Patrimonial domination connects private property to political power in two ways. First, wealthy patrons use their private property to ensnare their clients in subordinating patron–client relationships with domains of authority that we now ascribe uniquely to sovereign states. In the classic case of feudal estates, landowners exercised judicial and military authority over their retainers, servants, and

©2008 The Aristotelian Society
Proceedings of the Aristotelian Society Supplementary Volume LXXXII
doi: 10.1111/j.1467-8349.2008.00166.x

tenants, setting up their own courts to adjudicate disputes among them, and setting themselves up as militia commanders over them in wartime. Even in the colonial United States, creditors commonly assumed command of militias mustered from the ranks of their debtors (Wood 1993, p. 74). Employment contracts that bind employees to arbitration panels controlled by employers, without opportunities to resort to state-run courts, similarly amount to the conversion of private property into sovereign power over employees.

Second, regimes based on patrimonial domination tend to treat political offices of sovereign states as a kind of private property. This is explicit in the cases of tax farming, private customs houses, and other public offices that were literally put up for sale by states that lack, or allow the decay of, a substantial administrative apparatus under the direct management of state officials. (The privatization of prisons and armed military services raises similar questions today.) It is implicit in the corrupt use of the discretionary powers of state office for private ends, as when public officials operating under the 'Licence Raj' extorted bribes from microentrepreneurs, and state officeholders treat civil servants as personal retainers, commanding them to work for their political campaigns, repair their homes and perform other personal services unrelated to discharging the duties of office.

There are many things that can be said against relations of patrimonial domination. When they underlie state offices, the public is likely to be ill-served, since the powers of office are appropriated to private ends. They tend to be inefficient, because they appoint administrators to positions of power on the basis of loyalty rather than merit. They tend to lead to fragmented and conflicting authorities, liable to war against one another, because subordination is based on bonds of loyalty to particular persons who tend to be rivals, rather than to offices unified under a single hierarchy.[6]

From an egalitarian point of view, however, the main objection to such systems of patrimonial domination is that they subject subordinates to the arbitrary wills of their social superiors. Clients bear all the marks of servile dependency on their patrons that are abhorrent to egalitarians: cringing deference, grovelling, subjection to humili-

---

[6] In an important confirmation of these claims, Rashid Khalidi (2006) ascribes the incompetence, fragmentation and near anarchy that has beset the Palestinian authority in part to the reliance of Palestinian leadership on command through patron–client relationships rather than bureaucratic authority.

©2008 THE ARISTOTELIAN SOCIETY
Proceedings of the Aristotelian Society Supplementary Volume LXXXII
doi: 10.1111/j.1467-8349.2008.00166.x

ating commands, perpetual anxiety over what their superiors might do to them, or make them do, self-censorship, the degrading need to resort to begging, lack of freedom to form relationships independent of their patrons' scrutiny and control, living at the mercy of others. What egalitarians need is a sociologically informed understanding of what social arrangements could effectively underwrite the personal independence of individuals.

What could those arrangements be? Weber (1968, pp. 212–23, 983–6) famously counterposed patrimonial domination with bureaucratic domination. Can egalitarians find any satisfaction in command relations run on bureaucratic principles? Images of the dreary *de facto* egalitarianism of the queues we form to get our drivers' licences at Secretary of State offices immediately come to mind. Yet the constitutive rules of such queues should not be disparaged. There persons of all social classes must take their turns in the same line, with no one entitled to assert privileges over others or jump the queue, and with all entitled to their licence upon demonstrating their impersonal qualifications, without having to bribe or cajole the civil servant on the other side of the desk. My interest, however, lies more in the command relations structuring the powers and responsibilities of offices *within* a bureaucratic system, here understood to include not just state offices but the fully formalized large corporations characteristic of advanced capitalist societies. Weber insightfully argued that common principles of bureaucratic legitimation underwrote these systems of internal command. Here, too, we find egalitarian goals advanced by bureaucratic principles. Consider the egalitarian aims advanced by the ideal typical features of bureaucratic authority, as Weber characterized it.

Separation of offices (as places of work) from the home of superiors. This separation enables subordinates to function as employees rather than personal servants to their superiors. It also implies that employees live in homes distinct from that of their bosses. Hence, when they leave work for home, they enter a space under their own authority, not subject to their bosses' rules of the house.

Employee wages paid in cash, not in kind. Employees do not receive subsistence by dining at their superior's table or living on his personal estate, as personal servants do. This entails that subordinates are free from the entanglements of the gift relation, which, as anthropologists have long noted, involves the trade of personal favours for subjection to the magnanimous man's authority (Mauss

©2008 THE ARISTOTELIAN SOCIETY
Proceedings of the Aristotelian Society Supplementary Volume LXXXII
doi: 10.1111/j.1467-8349.2008.00166.x

1967), and which forms the foundation of the patron–client relation. The cash nexus thus frees subordinates of slavish dependence on their superiors. It also equips them with resources needed to exercise autonomy in personal consumption decisions. In the marketplace, consumers meet as equals in the sense that none need ask anyone else's permission or favour to consume whatever commodities lie within their budget constraint. The cash wage principle also excludes payment in scrip and employer provision of room and board on his own property—modes of payment that systematically invite both exploitation and off-duty subordination to employers.

Employee rights of exit. In light of the contrasting mode of patrimonial domination, the right to quit one's job represents not merely a right not to be subject to slavery, debt peonage, or bonded labour. It amounts to liberation from patron–client relationships. It means that employees owe no personal loyalty to their bosses as individuals. Their obligations of obedience arise merely in virtue of their job, not in virtue of any personal relationship they may have to their bosses.

The person–office distinction. All of the above bureaucratic principles serve to underwrite the fundamental distinction between persons and the offices they occupy. Subordinates owe obedience to their superiors in virtue of relations of office (as documented, say, in an organization chart) rather than in virtue of obligations of personal loyalty to named superiors. Individuals thus enjoy powers of command only in virtue of their office. When a particular person resigns his office, he gives up entirely any authority he may have had over subordinate officeholders. When he acts outside the colour of his office, he also has no authority over subordinates. Bureaucrats, unlike feudal lords, are not entitled to *droît de seigneur,* or indeed any kind of personal service. Off-duty in civil society, supervisors and employees meet as formal equals, even if rarely as friends.

Meritocracy. Individuals gain access to positions of responsibility and command—of supervision, administration and decision-making power—in virtue of merit, rather than demonstrations of personal fealty to those occupying the highest levels of command. Bureaucracy is thereby opposed to nepotism and cronyism. From an egalitarian point of view, this means that (when the system is working as designed) people do not have to fawn over, flatter and toady to their superiors in order to advance their careers.

Offices not a form of private property; entailing an anti-corruption principle. Positions of command are not for sale to the highest

bidder, nor are their discretionary powers to be used for the private
ends of the officeholder. Rather, the ends and powers of office are
defined by institutional objectives. From an egalitarian point of
view, these constraints function to prevent superiors from using
their discretionary power to turn subordinates into personal servants, to convert citizens into clients, or to extort bribes by threaten-
ing those whom they are supposed to be serving.

The rule of law, tied to a principle of efficiency. The powers of office are not arbitrary, but limited by rules rationalized by institutional rather than personal objectives. Closely tied to the rule of law
is the principle of efficiency. Long before Weber, Locke offered this
crucial insight into the connection between bureaucratic command
relations and equality:

> [T]he Preservation of the Army, and in it of the whole Common-
> wealth, requires an absolute Obedience to the Command of every Sup-
> eriour Officer, and it is justly Death to disobey or dispute the most
> dangerous or unreasonable of them: but yet we see, that neither the
> Serjeant, that could command a Souldier to march up to the mouth of
> a Cannon, or stand in a Breach, where he is almost sure to perish, can
> command that Soldier to give him one penny of his Money; nor the
> General, that can condemn him to Death for deserting his Post, or for
> not obeying the most desperate Orders, can yet with all his absolute
> Power of Life and Death, dispose of one Farthing of that Soldiers Es-
> tate, or seize one jot of his Goods; whom yet he can command any
> thing, and hang for the least Disobedience. Because such a blind Obe-
> dience is necessary to that end for which the Commander has his Pow-
> er, viz. the preservation of the rest; but the disposing of his Goods has
> nothing to do with it. ... [E]ven absolute power, where it is necessary,
> is not arbitrary by being absolute, but is still limited by that reason
> and confined to those ends which required it. (Locke 1980, ch. 11,
> par. 139)

Locke is pointing to a fundamental bureaucratic constraint on
powers of command: it is not arbitrary, but limited to the ends of office. Officers may only exercise powers over others that are instrumentally necessary to (efficiently) achieving the objectives of office,
which in turn can only be justified in terms of their service to the
public interest.

A corollary of this constraint on legitimate command is that individuals are free to decide for themselves how to lead their lives in
domains outside the scope of their superior's authority. They are

©2008 THE ARISTOTELIAN SOCIETY
Proceedings of the Aristotelian Society Supplementary Volume LXXXII
doi: 10.1111/j.1467-8349.2008.00166.x

personally independent of their superiors in their private, off-duty lives. And even when they are on the job, their duties of obedience are limited by an explicit or implicit job description. This entails substantial constraints on the powers of command. For example, it entails a strict prohibition on sexual harassment of employees.

IV

Two Egalitarian Cheers for Bureaucracy. Weber (1968, pp. 973–5) argued that bureaucratic authority was our main alternative to patrimonial authority. Once installed, it supplies a comprehensive replacement for patron–client relations and other relations of patrimonial domination. This, I have argued, constitutes a major advance toward the fulfillment of egalitarian aims in domains where commands are needed to coordinate the conduct of different people, and the scale and complexity of cooperative relations is such as to overwhelm the coordinating capacities of spontaneous solidarity (impulses of mutual aid) and face-to-face participatory democracy, in which commands are directly authorized by the whole class of those commanded. In these domains, there is necessarily a distinction between those who issue commands and those who must obey, and hence a threat to the egalitarian aim of abolishing unjust social hierarchy. Bureaucratic principles show how hierarchy can be tamed, by instituting a sharp person–office distinction, limiting discretionary commands by the rule of law and the principle of efficiency (tied to institutional rather than personal objectives), prohibiting the conversion of offices to private property, regulating access to office according to merit, and securing the personal independence of subordinates through measures such as the separation of office from home, payment in cash, and exit rights.

If bureaucratic principles were comprehensively instituted, the abuses of inferiors by superiors that are illustrated in *A Fine Balance* and widely instantiated in developing countries would not occur. Local headmen would not be able to corral the votes of their tenants, servants, clients, and lower-caste residents of villages under their control. Police would not be able to extort bribes from poor microentrepreneurs. Teachers would have to show up for work, and teach allcomers, regardless of their caste or class status. The poor would not have to beg for favours from the rich, and thereby lose

©2008 THE ARISTOTELIAN SOCIETY
Proceedings of the Aristotelian Society Supplementary Volume LXXXII
doi: 10.1111/j.1467-8349.2008.00166.x

their personal independence, in order to escape arbitrary abuse at the hands of authorities.

Weber (1968, pp. 973–5) thought that bureaucracy was a juggernaut, crushing all rival forms of authority in its path in virtue of its overwhelmingly superior ability to coordinate individuals' powers toward common ends. If Weber were right, then egalitarians could just sit back and let history take them for a ride at least part way toward their goal. But Weber, like Marx, appears to have been over-confident about the ultimate direction of history. Creating bureaucracies requires not just huge investments in formal institutions and human capital, but overturning deeply entrenched social norms that tie up individuals in parochial relations of personal domination. Bureaucracy offers a way out of many inegalitarian ills, but it is expensive medicine to obtain, and hard to administer to recalcitrant patients.

Egalitarians must also recognize the limitations of bureaucratic principles. Three are of particular interest. First, Weber (1968, p. 989) observed that bureaucracy, despite its deep connection with 'the levelling of economic and social differences', runs the risk of capture by 'crypto-plutocracy'. The dominance of the rich in party-based mass democracies permits them to seize control of the bureaucratic apparatus of the state. He could have added that bureaucratic meritocracy also leads to crypto-plutocracy to the extent that the rich monopolize access to merit-creating training, which in most cases is higher education. Egalitarians need to counter this tendency by providing decent educational opportunities to disadvantaged groups of all kinds.[7]

Second, the efficiency principle itself can threaten egalitarian objectives. Inegalitarian relations are characteristically expressed by treating adults as something other than autonomous persons: they are treated as children, as beasts of burden, as vermin, as spiritual pollution, as sex objects. The efficiency principle, taken to its extremes, threatens a similar degradation of persons to a lower grade of being—in this instance, to cogs in a machine. 'Efficient' production mechanizes human movements, reducing it to its simplest, de-skilled, indefinitely repeated components, ignoring the body's biological rhythms, its tendencies to tire, workers' needs for stimu-

---

[7] I have further argued (Anderson 2007b) that training a managerial and professional elite to be responsive to the interests of all social classes requires comprehensive integration of all groups at all levels of schooling.

©2008 THE ARISTOTELIAN SOCIETY
Proceedings of the Aristotelian Society Supplementary Volume LXXXII
doi: 10.1111/j.1467-8349.2008.00166.x

lation and social affiliation at work, and relief from tedious, mind-numbing, time-pressured, high-speed labour. When a cog wears out, it is simply thrown away, replaced by an identical cog. While such conditions have mostly been superseded for middle-class workers in rich countries, they prevail in sweatshop and manual agricultural labour today, as they did in the satanic mills of the original Industrial Revolution. Egalitarians must insist on dignitary and humanistic constraints on efficiency, narrowly construed. These include, for example, rights of workers to urinate during working hours—rights shockingly denied to many workers today, even in rich countries (Linder and Nygaard 1998).

Third, egalitarian constraints must be placed on the ends of institutions themselves. This paper has focused on the internal operations of institutions, and the importance of avoiding face-to-face relations of *personal* domination and subordination. But objectionable forms of domination also have an impersonal face, as when the ends of public office are set undemocratically, and the laws governing people's interactions in civil society are rigged to favour privileged groups. To address these difficulties we must engage the branch of egalitarian thought known as democratic theory, and consider its application not just to sovereign states, but to the little governments of our workplaces. Such an examination, however, lies beyond the scope of this paper.

Today's egalitarian toolbox is dominated by policies largely generated from a conception of equality conceived as a pattern of distribution. These policies tend to be stymied when they are overlain on pervasive background relations of personal domination and subjection. Such inegalitarian social relations are not only instrumentally objectionable, as obstacles to equal distribution. Egalitarians should regard them as inherently objectionable, and take their eradication as a fundamental end, to which redistributive policies are largely instrumental. We should thus reconceive the ultimate egalitarian aim in relational rather than distributive terms: it is to constructing a society in which persons relate to one another as social equals. This aim faces a challenge in light of the fact that large-scale cooperation requires a distinction between those who issue commands and those who obey them. Egalitarians can reconcile themselves to this condition in part by recovering the egalitarian potential of bureaucratic modes of authority. Bureaucracy offers an alternative mode of structuring command relations that, when it operates properly, liberates

©2008 THE ARISTOTELIAN SOCIETY
Proceedings of the Aristotelian Society Supplementary Volume LXXXII
doi: 10.1111/j.1467-8349.2008.00166.x

people from personal subjection to others. It adds a vital tool to the egalitarian toolbox. The remedy it offers is only partial, however. Hence egalitarians should give bureaucracy only two cheers, not three.

Department of Philosophy
University of Michigan
2239 Angell Hall 1003
435 S. State Street
Ann Arbor, MI 48109-1003
USA
eandrsn@umich.edu

REFERENCES

Anderson, Elizabeth 1999: 'What is the Point of Equality?' *Ethics*, 109, pp. 287–337.
——2007*a*: 'How Should Egalitarians Cope with Market Risks?' *Theoretical Inquiries in Law*, 9, pp. 61–92.
——2007*b*: 'Fair Opportunity in Education: A Democratic Equality Perspective'. *Ethics*, 117, pp. 595–622.
Cohen, G. A. 1989: 'On the Currency of Egalitarian Justice'. *Ethics*, 99, pp. 906–44.
Hume, David 1948: 'Of the Original Contract'. In Henry Aiken (ed.), *Hume's Moral and Political Philosophy*. New York: Hafner.
Hurley, Susan 2003: *Justice, Luck, and Knowledge*. Cambridge, MA: Harvard University Press.
Kahn, Joseph 2003: 'Chinese Girls' Toil Brings Pain, Not Riches'. *New York Times*, 2 October 2003, A1.
Khalidi, Rashid 2006: *The Iron Cage: The Story of the Palestinian Struggle for Statehood*. Boston, MA: Beacon Press.
Kremer, Michael, Nazmul Chaudhury, F. Halsey Rogers, Karthik Muralidharan, and Jeffrey Hammer 2005: 'Teacher Absence in India: A Snapshot'. *Journal of the European Economic Association*, 3, no. 2–3, pp. 658–67.
Kropotkin, Peter 1906: *The Conquest of Bread*. New York and London: G. P. Putnam's & Sons.
Linder, Mark and Ingrid Nygaard 1998: *Void Where Prohibited: Rest Breaks and the Right to Urinate on Company Time*. Ithaca, NY: ILR Press.
Locke, John 1980: *Second Treatise of Government*. Indianapolis: Hackett.

©2008 THE ARISTOTELIAN SOCIETY
Proceedings of the Aristotelian Society Supplementary Volume LXXXII
doi: 10.1111/j.1467-8349.2008.00166.x

Mauss, Marcel 1967: *The Gift*, trans. I. Cunnison. New York: Norton.

Miller, William 1997: *The Anatomy of Disgust*. Cambridge, MA: Harvard University Press.

Mistry, Rohinton 2001: *A Fine Balance*. New York: Vintage.

Narula, Smita 1999: *Broken People: Caste Violence Against India's 'Untouchables'*. New York: Human Rights Watch.

Pettit, Philip 1997: *Republicanism*. New York: Oxford University Press.

Rawls, John 1993: *Political Liberalism*. New York: Columbia University Press.

Rose-Ackerman, Susan 1998: 'Bribes and Gifts'. In Avner Ben-Ner and Louis Putterman (eds.), *Economics, Values, and Organization*, pp. 296–328. Cambridge: Harwood Academic Publishers.

Rousseau, Jean-Jacques 1762/1913: *The Social Contract*, ed. G. D. H. Cole. London: J. M. Dent.

Transparency International 2007: *Corruption Perceptions Index, Regional Highlights: Asia Pacific Region*, <http://www.transparency.org/content/download/23975/358245>.

Walzer, Michael 1983: *Spheres of Justice*. New York: Basic Books.

Weber, Max 1968: *Economy and Society*, ed. Guenther Roth and Claus Wittich. Berkeley and Los Angeles: Univeristy of California Press.

Wood, Gordon 1993: *The Radicalism of the American Revolution*. New York: Vintage.

©2008 THE ARISTOTELIAN SOCIETY
Proceedings of the Aristotelian Society Supplementary Volume LXXXII
doi: 10.1111/j.1467-8349.2008.00166.x

II — John Skorupski

Equality and Bureaucracy

Elizabeth Anderson argues for civic as against distributive egalitarianism. I agree with civic egalitarianism understood as a public ideal, and welcome her interest in the sociological conditions under which it may best flourish. But I argue that she is mistaken in opposing what she calls 'hierarchies of esteem' and proposing that where the egalitarian ideal has insufficient hold on civil society it should be implemented by an efficient bureaucracy. We should learn a different lesson from Max Weber. What the ideal of equality needs is not more bureaucracy but more influential advocacy—and that requires healthy 'hierarchies of esteem'.

The egalitarianism propounded in Elizabeth Anderson's paper has real moral influence in liberal democratic societies (and beyond). It is neither a merely academic discussion topic nor a hopelessly sectarian cause. I too believe in it, as will emerge. My aim will be to reflect a little on its normative content and standing (§§I–III) and then (§§IV–V) probe the social conditions that favour its healthy flourishing.

To endorse this egalitarianism, I shall argue, is to endorse a political ideal of how to live together that goes beyond the universal requirements of justice. I am not a Rawlsian: I have no problem of principle with political positions that are committed to advancing this or other conceptions of the good. That is what they should do. What *is* true, and of great importance to a liberal, in the sense of someone who believes in freedom, is that no political ideal is immaculate. Political ideals are uncertain things. They coarsen, unexpectedly transmute, or harden into the doctrinaire. That applies to the ideal of equality that Anderson supports and I support. What then are the social conditions most likely to keep it live and true to itself? I shall argue that Anderson's opposition to hierarchies of esteem and her two cheers for bureaucracy gets it the wrong way round—and does so just because her version of the ideal is doctrinaire.

©2008 The Aristotelian Society
Proceedings of the Aristotelian Society Supplementary Volume LXXXII
doi: 10.1111/j.1467-8349.2008.00167.x

I

Civic Egalitarianism. As Anderson conceives it, egalitarianism is not about a 'distributive conception of equality' (Anderson 2008, p. 139). It is not concerned with achieving equal distribution of goods, on any non-trivial conception of distributable goods, although it is indeed concerned with ensuring that everyone has certain basic liberties and rights. Anderson rejects what she has elsewhere (1999, p. 289) called 'luck egalitarianism', according to which inequalities that result from brute luck are unjust. There are other versions of the distributive conception, such as the view that there is *pro tanto* reason to prefer more equal distribution of whatever it is that is worth having just because it is a more equal distribution.[1] But I take it that she does not rest the value of her kind of equality on these either.

To eschew such arguments is, as she notes, quite compatible with endorsing indirect or extrinsic arguments against certain kinds of distributive inequality: for example, that poverty removes access to forms of participation that it is important for everyone to have, or that great wealth can be used to acquire objectionable power over others.

I agree with Anderson that a distributive conception of equality has no intrinsic moral claim. That an inequality is not deserved, that it is a matter of brute luck, that it does not make the worst off better off—none of these, in my view, on their own show it to be *prima facie* wrong or bad. Nor do I believe that a shift towards equal distribution is *pro tanto* good in itself.[2] So I am not going to pursue the debate between distributive egalitarianisms of these kinds and egalitarianism of Anderson's kind.

What then of Anderson's kind? Egalitarians, she says (Anderson 2008, p. 143), should aim at 'the eradication of unjust social hierarchy' and 'ending oppressive social relations'. Anyone could agree with that, including believers in hierarchy. It soon turns out, however, that she considers *any* form of hierarchy that is not absolutely un-

---

[1] See Temkin (1993).

[2] I agree that desert is the right criterion in contexts of evaluation, penalty and reward; that distributive constraints play a role in our notion of general welfare (of what is a better overall outcome); that we should collectively provide the necessaries that allow everyone to be an equal citizen. Nonetheless, hard as it is to give a comprehensive account of these distinct considerations, I don't think any form of distributive egalitarianism is the right account.

©2008 THE ARISTOTELIAN SOCIETY
Proceedings of the Aristotelian Society Supplementary Volume LXXXII
doi: 10.1111/j.1467-8349.2008.00167.x

avoidable to be oppressive and unjust. This, in fact, is what her egalitarianism is: radical opposition to hierarchy. Any form of hierarchy is at best a necessary evil, and any diminution of hierarchy is at least *pro tanto* good.

In spelling this out, she usefully distinguishes between hierarchies of standing, esteem and command (Anderson 2008, pp. 144–5). Egalitarians, she says, should aim 'to the extent possible, to abolish such hierarchies and replace them with relations of equality'. Hierarchies of standing 'are incompatible with the dignity and rights of human beings'; they can and should be completely abolished. Hierarchies of esteem and of command pose a greater problem. Esteem and contempt, as Anderson recognizes, 'are an inescapable part of human life'. However, 'liberal' egalitarians favour a competing plurality of such hierarchies—they oppose official hierarchies of worth and more generally any tendency to 'oppressive esteem hierarchies in civil society'. Command hierarchies, she accepts, are to some degree indispensable in coordinating worthwhile social action. So here she concentrates on how their tendency to produce oppressive social relations may be mitigated.

II

Authoritarianism and Justice. This kind of civic egalitarianism is the product of an impressive history. Its roots lead back from the present at least to early modern Europe, and the history of arguments and struggles by which it has been achieved is an illustrious one. Nowadays it has become an almost universally held tenet in liberal democracies, a major constituent of their entrenched political settlement. It is worth remembering, for sure, just how recent this settlement is, how geographically limited it remains, how far, some would argue, from proper implementation. Still, virtually no present-day politician would disagree with the statement 'I am in favour of equal civil and political rights and against all forms of discrimination'—or even follow it with much of a 'but'.

Closer inspection reveals controversy about what such equality means. Not about equality of civil rights, if that means that no one has greater civil rights or civil authority in virtue merely of their birth, sex, religion, charisma, or traditionally, as against meritocratically, allocated role. Nor about political equality, if that simply says

that each citizen has the right to a political say that is neither en-
larged nor diminished by any of the characteristics just ruled out. So
far these two doctrines could have been accepted by a 1789 liberal.
We have moved on to a stronger doctrine of political equality: one
person–one vote irrespective of property, tax-paying or educational
qualifications is now a settled part of liberal-democratic culture
(though the remit of elected as against appointed institutions remains a matter of dispute).

Controversy starts when we consider the implications of non-discrimination. Here too we have moved on: non-discrimination now
goes beyond the old idea of positions open to talents to wider principles. This raises a question about their scope. If a Catholic adoption charity refuses to place children for adoption with same-sex
couples because it thinks they cannot provide a morally sound upbringing, is that discriminatory? Or is it, on the contrary, discriminatory to refuse these charities a licence? If we do that are we
discriminating against Catholic moral convictions?

Still, neither side in this particular debate would accept that it is
rejecting civic equality. It is a question of how to interpret its demands. What then about the larger question of how one might explicitly *oppose* equality—I mean philosophically, rather than by
brute force?

Let's call someone who opposes civic and political equality on
such grounds a philosophical authoritarian. Authoritarians argue
for hierarchical social order of some kind. It might be feudal order,
or theocratic order, or a Comtean order of rule by bankers with ad-
vice from Positivist priests, or a Leadership principle.

For present purposes we can set aside a defence of hierarchy on
grounds that are theistic, or that posit some kind of normativity of
the natural simply *qua* 'natural', or on quasi-magical appeal to the
power of a person or a god. These defences cannot make headway
with anyone who regards the claims on which they are based as at
best false and at worst incoherent. Those of us who feel that way
may indeed accept that feudal and theocratic hierarchies enable distinctively valuable ways of life, and allow distinctive personal virtues to flourish—loyalty, reverence, trust, the sense of being part of
something sacred. Nevertheless, for us they don't begin to be genuine options, and so to us those ways of life are lost.

It is otherwise if the case for hierarchy is made on more empirical
grounds, say on the grounds that it leads to greater human good

Proceedings of the Aristotelian Society Supplementary Volume LXXXII
doi: 10.1111/j.1467-8349.2008.00167.x

(understood in some non-transcendental way). This we should consider more closely.

Suppose we encounter a secular authoritarian society which is
proactively non-discriminatory in the civil sphere, but non-demo-
cratic in the political sphere. Call it Positania. It reserves political
authority to specialists with professional qualifications awarded by
examination. This political elite rules with the help of an administrative bureaucracy, and perhaps with institutionalized ways of con-
sulting the people. Positania is not a democracy, but everyone has
equal rights; in particular, everyone has equal access, on the basis of
examined competence alone, to all positions. We can suppose that
the ruling aim of the political elite is general welfare, and that their
rule in fact leads to considerable equalization of income and wealth
in comparison to the liberal-democratic societies that we know. We
can assume that Positania nurtures talent through a universal and
non-discriminatory system of education; also that it guarantees
rights of emigration, perhaps with generous grants, and that there
are neighbouring democratic states that accept immigrants on decent terms. So leaving is a genuine option.

Positanians agree with Anderson that hierarchy is corruptible.
They don't pretend that corruption is absent from their state, and
they agree that it must be fought. But, they say, one should compare
like with like: what is most likely to happen under their kind of political hierarchy with what is most likely to happen under democracy. On the one hand, it is true, there are unjust abusers of legitimate
authority and subordination, who have to be put down. On the other hand, there is anarchy and anomie, or conformism and mediocri-
ty of opinion—or quite possibly both—and these cannot be put
down, because they are systemic. Furthermore, abuse of power still
exists in all democracies, for it is universal.

If Anderson tells them that their relationships of subordination
are humiliating, they have a reply. 'Authority', they say, 'is not to be
confused with tyranny or arbitrariness. In Positania everyone has
equal intrinsic rights, and the abuse of rights is severely punished
when it is detected. Our political inequality is not based on privilege
but on merit. In your society a political consensus has emerged
around democracy. You would greatly resent even an educational
test for the vote—though one of your ancestral liberal sages favoured it. You find such tests humiliating, disrespectful; for you indeed they *would* be, because of the social expectations that have

built up around your political settlement. Something you call
"equality of worth" has for you acquired a politically dominating, if
philosophically inexplicable, meaning. Your society works well
enough in its way. It defuses resentments as well as creating them.
But we think allowing everyone a say in matters of great social importance, without any test of their qualification, is as unreasonable
as letting people drive on the road without a driving test.'

What is wrong with Positania? Let me say, first of all, that I do
not think Positania is unjust simply in virtue of its political structure. Since this not the place for a general discussion of justice, allow me to resort to assertion. I believe that injustice is violation of
rights. And while there are universal rights, democratic rights are
not among them; they are among the *non*-universal rights. What
grounds some of these non-universal rights is a universal principle
that says something like this: *A legitimate collective decision made
within a group to pursue some common aim binds its members, by
a duty of right to each other, to play a fair part in that pursuit.*[3] The
question is whether it is possible that the political arrangements of
Positania are based on a legitimate collective decision of Positanians. I think it is possible.

To dramatize, let's suppose that Positania used to be a one person–one vote democracy, but that Positanians voted in the new authoritarian political structure. I am not saying that this is the only
way that structure could emerge by legitimate collective decision.
Nonetheless, a democratic vote does constitute a legitimate collective decision, so long as its content is not unjust. Furthermore, having made their decision, Positanians do not now wish to reverse it.
They have a stable structure they are happy with.

It may be replied that democratic rights are both universal and inalienable, so that the Positanian collective decision was indeed illegitimate because unjust. Against that stands the view, which I share, that
democracy is not a universal inalienable right, but simply, in sufficiently developed social circumstances, the best political system—
because in these circumstances it best promotes ideal human flourishing. Our tradition expresses a legitimate collective decision to live
democratically, and we are at home with the democratic rights and
duties of right that decision confers.

---

[3] For some detail, see Skorupski (2008).

©2008 The Aristotelian Society
Proceedings of the Aristotelian Society Supplementary Volume LXXXII
doi: 10.1111/j.1467-8349.2008.00167.x

III

Equality as an Ideal. So authoritarian societies are not necessarily unjust. That does not mean that they are not objectionable. But why are they? Specifically, what is wrong with Positania?

I believe, as I say, that democracy best promotes human flourishing; hence I believe the Positanians, human beings like us, are not on the path that is best for them. Given humans' limitations, one would expect dysfunctions to emerge, such as attempts by the professional political elite to corrupt the tests required for political qualification (in favour of supporters, relatives, etc.), an increasingly biased account on their part of what the general good was, and growing disaffection among the politically unqualified, with no remedy through the ballot box. I shall say that a case for democratic equality that rests on these and similar points alone, without appealing either to justice or to ideals, is a *pragmatic* case.

More viscerally, however, I would hate to live there—and I guess Anderson would hate to live there too. Positania offends an ideal of personal independence, of freedom as dignity, that I strongly believe in, as Anderson does. I would certainly find it, to use one of the telling words she often uses, *humiliating* to have to take the orders of a political elite over which I shared no democratic control. Moreover, I (at least like to) think that I would not want that kind of authority. Even if there are times when one must undertake it, it is never a blessing.

The ideal of personal independence is an ideal of equality in freedom. Mill gives forceful expression to it when he contrasts the love of domination with the love of liberty:

> [P]ower over others, power of coercion and compulsion, any power other than that of moral and intellectual influence, even in the cases where it is indispensable, is a snare, and in all others a curse, both to the possessor and to those over whom it is possessed; a burthen which no rightly constituted moral nature consents to take upon itself, but by one of the great sacrifices which inclination ever makes to duty. (Mill 1963–91, vol. XIX, p. 610)

This, one might say, is the idealistic and not merely pragmatic case against Positania.

Personal independence is an *ideal* because it is not directly about whether people are happy but about whether they are right to be happy. Thus it needs something like Mill's notion of a 'rightly constituted moral nature' to back it up. In general, a notion of that kind is indispensable to any discourse of ideals. There must be an epistemic criterion that supports our judgement that a given ideal is something admirable, and not merely a personal preference. The criterion must be what some human beings when freely educated, not indoctrinated, tend to admire, and in many cases want for themselves (bearing in mind that what is recognized as admirable and what one has reason to want for oneself are distinguishable issues).

The dignity of independence is, furthermore, a public ideal for society and not merely a private ideal for the individual—like, say, an ideal of minimalist decoration for one's apartment. It says that everyone has the capacity and responsibility to live their freedom and not merely take advantage of it. The responsibility is not to others but to themselves as free, 'rightly constituted' human natures. Those who believe in it want society to recognize it and value it in concrete terms—for example, in its system of education—and to give it political standing.

If we propound freedom as dignity in this way, as a universal public ideal for all citizens, we are committed to thinking that almost every rightly educated human being, at least in the social conditions of democracy, would not only admire it but want it for him or herself.

But, to take a reality check, this ideal is not as widely honoured as one would like, certainly in practice. In fact people behave in ways that are subservient and undignified all over the place—for money, advancement, a bit of celebrity, or just to be part of the crowd. For example, they humiliate themselves in front of a television audience from some of these motives, etc. That is a problem for those who want to propound the dignity of independence as a public ideal. It has two aspects, epistemological—are all these people somehow unfree, not fully self-realized?—and political—what is one supposed to do about it? (If you think I am exaggerating, imagine that democracies develop much further in that direction.)

If someone does not realize that they are behaving in a personally humiliating, undignified way, or realizes but doesn't care, what right do we have to stop them, or to stop the people who are humiliating them? What is the objection to humiliation among consenting adults? If they have a real option not to make fools of themselves, they are not being oppressed. The same applies to the company towns that Anderson condemns (2008, pp. 149–50). What she says

©2008 The Aristotelian Society
Proceedings of the Aristotelian Society Supplementary Volume LXXXII
doi: 10.1111/j.1467-8349.2008.00167.x

here is that even if the Pullman workers had reasonable alternatives to working with Pullman, and yet were happy to do so and to live in Pullman, Illinois, the objection that they were reducing themselves to 'servile dependents' would still stand (Anderson 2008, p. 149).

I agree that they wouldn't be measuring up to the ideal of personal independence. But what political significance does this objection have? Should we be trying to stop them, and if so, how? Could these workers legitimately reply that our personal ethico-aesthetic ideals are our own business, and have no place in the public arena of politics?

The classical origins of Anderson's ideal lie in what is proper to an independent 'free man' as against a slave, or even a dependent servant. In this regard her condemnatory vocabulary for hierarchical relations is telling: 'humiliating', 'undignified', 'degrading', 'demeaning', 'servile', 'grovelling', 'self-abasing'.[4] The terms are familiar from Kant[5] and Mill. But from within a certain democratic culture, that is, a certain culture fostered by democracy—one of easy-going familiarity and cosy togetherness—they smack of cold, unbending contempt. That sort of democratic culture can still think it important to provide equality of access for people who are in one way or another disadvantaged, but it will do so on the basis of an ideal of inclusion rather than an ideal of independence. The differences between these ideals can be subtle; however, inclusion does not object to the Pullman way of life in the way that Anderson's ideal of equality-in-dignity does. Not that inclusion is a worthless ideal—but it is, inevitably, a mutable ideal. To a lover of independence and dignity, democratic inclusion has a worrying potential for shading into conformity—the popular tyranny that the old 'aristocratic' liberals worried about.[6] A merely inclusivist democratic culture, they feared, could seriously undermine personal independence.

Freedom-as-dignity is an ideal of equality, equality among all those to whom it is accessible, who can feel its appeal. If it is accessible to all it becomes an ideal that supports democracy, a public ideal of democratic equality. Let's suppose it is. That does not mean that it is the only possible and defensible ideal, or that we have a right positively to prevent people who want to live by another. Con-

---

[4] I have taken a couple of these from Anderson (1999).

[5] 'Be no man's lackey ... one who makes himself a worm cannot complain afterwards if people step on him' (Kant 1996, pp. 558–9; Akademie edition, vol. 6, pp. 436–7). (The whole passage is remarkable.)

[6] I take the term from Kahan (1992).

©2008 THE ARISTOTELIAN SOCIETY
Proceedings of the Aristotelian Society Supplementary Volume LXXXII
doi: 10.1111/j.1467-8349.2008.00167.x

sider someone who from a religious ideal joins a monastery and swears vows of obedience. This ideal is not a purely private one, raising no political questions, in the way that the ideal of minimalism in interior decoration is. So long as monasteries exist within society and not 'outside' it in a private sphere, they effectively demand and receive a certain public deference to their ideal, even if they are not propounding universal ideals.[7] It is important to recognize that such ideals can have public normative force, whether they are merely different to equality-as-dignity, or positively hostile to it, seeing it perhaps as an individualistic fantasy.

One can give, to repeat, a pragmatic defence of democracy. Given sufficient prosperity and material equality it produces peaceful compromise; in its liberal form it lets people get on with their own lives; because people like that it is stable. To see democracy in this way is to see the vote as an insurance policy rather than an expression of one's standing as a free being. Pragmatic people who think in this way still don't want to be Positanians. The pragmatic defence could further argue—with considerable plausibility, indeed quite temptingly—that in a democracy the wisest liberal course is to leave great ideals severely alone and focus on blocking threats to liberty from whatever direction they may come.

I think this doctrine aims too pessimistically for the second best. Even if the presence or absence of the ideal of democratic equality doesn't actually make a very big difference to democratic stability, it might well make a difference to what kind of democracy we get. In any case, if we think this ideal is the best, or one of the best, for all or most people, we have a right, even a responsibility, to advocate it publicly. We should seek to persuade people of its value to them. That leads me to what Anderson has to say about hierarchies of esteem.

IV

Hierarchies of Esteem. A thematic problem for nineteenth-century liberals was that of reconciling the political and civic freedom they favoured with liberal influence in the domain of ideals. Prosperous democracies could be expected to accept expert judgement in recog-

---

[7] They may be losing that public status, but they certainly used to have it. To be a monk was publicly accepted as a high vocation, though not the only vocation. If we now see it as a matter of personal 'lifestyle', do we gain or lose?

©2008 The Aristotelian Society
Proceedings of the Aristotelian Society Supplementary Volume LXXXII
doi: 10.1111/j.1467-8349.2008.00167.x

nized professional and technical fields. But could they be expected
to recognize good judgement and worthwhile creativity in philosophical, spiritual, moral, and aesthetic questions? Or would they
be seduced by the comforting, the conformist, the controversy-
avoiding?

Liberals of this kind did not doubt that some individuals were better judges on questions of meaning and value—wiser, more penetrat-
ingly critical, or more positively creative. They did not doubt that
questions of meaning and value were public questions with political
significance. They appreciated the need for public recognition of high
ideals—their own liberalism was founded on substantive ideals of
self-realization and of living in freedom. Finally, they had a realistic
sociological understanding of the issue. In Anderson's terms, they
thought that influence in the domain of ideals could not take effect
without the existence of socially recognized 'hierarchies of esteem'.

The development of democracy has made it increasingly difficult
to acknowledge these truths in a clear and upfront way. The old liberals in fact predicted that. A more curious sociological puzzle is
that it is liberalism itself, as a political tradition, that has had greatest difficulty in acknowledging them, with important consequences
for what it now stands for. While socialism for some time into the
twentieth century kept up an old-liberal ideal of the free person, liberal thought fell into an alliance with subjectivist and populist
stances, or into the *faux*-liberal notion that ideals and values belong
entirely to the private domain. Once the philosophical side of the
old position had been abandoned, the sociological question of how
to implement it fell into neglect.

It is tempting to sympathize with the philosophy of freedom while
neglecting the sociology. Can we not, *should* we not, distinguish respect and deference for high ideals themselves from respect and deference for particular people? That is one of those neat distinctions
that make conceptual sense, but not psychological or sociological
sense. Ideas influence through concrete relations between people.
Respect for great values is socially embodied in respect for people
who are seen to live them, and in deference to their judgement. Of
course, in these ultimate questions of value, free debate that excludes
no one is essential (essential, I would argue, as a matter of the epistemology of the normative, not just of the ethics of democratic respect). It is not true, however, that every voice carries equal weight.
In a free and inclusive debate about values, natural hierarchies of in-

fluence emerge. So long as the debate is genuinely free and inclusive, it is important that they should—that authoritative voices should not be muffled, or hesitant in taking the lead. It was robustly realistic on Mill's part (in the passage quoted) to *exempt* the exercise of 'moral and intellectual influence' from the power over others that, even when indispensable, constitutes a snare. Putting it the other way round, it is no diminution of one's independence or dignity to recognize moral and intellectual authority freely when one finds it. On the contrary, it is a mark of inward freedom.

We are talking about the importance of non-authoritarian hierarchies of esteem. They are a much deeper phenomenon than the 'official' rankings Anderson dislikes, so easily influenced by respectable thinking and captured by busy cliques. Spontaneous structures of esteem always exist, as Anderson agrees. The question is how to develop and support, within civil society and the state, those structures that favour recognition of worthwhile notions of excellence rather than contemptible or servile ones. In so far as it dismisses this crucial question, Anderson's egalitarianism becomes doctrinaire.

Moreover, it undermines itself. If democracy erodes the distance between great and petty ideals, or between ideals and mere preferences, it erodes a non-trivial part of its own normative foundation. At least, that is so if the foundation is idealistic as well as pragmatic. One of these great ideals is the ideal of personal independence or equality in freedom; its distinctive value for democracy is that it can give principled support to democratic institutions. Not that this is an argument for its *intrinsic* value; the whole point is that that has to be publicly advocated on its own terms. It is, nonetheless, certainly an argument in favour of finding the sociological conditions within which such advocacy is more likely, not less likely, to be effective. And since we are not talking indoctrination here, the general question must be how to provide, within the settled culture and practices of a democratic state, a social underpinning that allows *all* great ideals to be debated and acknowledged, and to recruit freely, i.e. within the limits set by everyone's liberty.

In view of these points, Anderson's treatment of 'hierarchies of esteem' is seriously inadequate. 'Liberal egalitarians', she says,

> prefer that individuals be free to judge who merits esteem and contempt for themselves ... The expected and preferred outcome of such liberty is a plurality of conceptions of the good, which generate rival and cross-cutting orders of esteem, such that no social group comes

out on the top or on the bottom of everyone's rankings, all are free to establish or seek a social circle in which they enjoy the esteem of their peers, and no esteem ranking counts as official, as one to which everyone is expected to defer. (Anderson 2008, p. 145)

She then launches into some familiar material about 'snobbish self-appointed arbiters of manners and taste' who want to assume 'monopoly control' over 'cultural capital', and the egalitarian need for '"upward contempt" directed by lower classes against upper classes' (Anderson 2008, p. 145). I stand ready to condemn snobs and to despise the 'upper classes' (who they?) whenever they deserve it. But this is not the issue, and it gets in the way of serious thinking about the issue. The egalitarian who wants hierarchies of esteem to cancel each other out, and fall back into the preferences of private social circles, is making a serious mistake. Public ideals should be argued for as public ideals. I don't believe Anderson *really* prefers that the ideal of freedom as dignity should be no more than the private preserve of her chosen social circle, while other social circles pursue the servile ideal of celebrity and followership, say, or the vulgar ideal of flaunted wealth, and despise her circle for its uptight ways.

I realize that these cultural issues are not her main preoccupation in the present paper. But given the nature of her project, it seems to me that they should be her preoccupation somewhere. Since she is herself advancing a high ideal for democracies, she should be interested in the social conditions that favour democratic respect for high ideals. So now we turn to the subject of bureaucracy.

V

Bureaucracy—Resignation, No Cheers. Since one of my themes has been the need for sociological realism in political philosophy, I appreciate and applaud Anderson's Weberian interest in this subject. But I confess that the notion that bureaucracy is the answer to oppression made my jaw drop.

Backtrack a little to Weber's seminal work on 'rationalization'. Famously, he thought it would be an imprisoning, not an emancipatory force, a force that would eventually dominate modern societies completely. Of course we shouldn't swallow this pessimism uncritically. To get a balanced assessment, we should notice that Weber put 'rationalization' on insufficiently clear conceptual foundations. He did not distinguish systematically enough between

    (i) 'rationalization' as the development of rule-governed, formally codified and role-specialized forms of social organization.

    (ii) 'legal rationality' versus tradition or charisma as sources of normative legitimation.

It is obviously the case that (i) can exist without (ii): in traditionally legitimated social orders, such as church hierarchy or caste society, or in charismatically based orders such as fascism; and in fact Weber describes such cases.

Moreover there is an important inadequacy in his account of (ii). Legal rationality is, Weber thinks, the product of the seventeenth-century jurists, who thereby gave birth to the modern Occidental state. But he never inquires enough into what these jurists were up to in *philosophical* terms, or puts their work into the general context of the seventeenth century's epistemological questions about what it is to appeal to reason as a fundamental normative source, or, crucially, how reason connects to freedom. 'Legal rationality' is fitted into no general account of rationality. His picture of it as a legitimating source thus becomes a picture of clearly stated and codified rules of behaviour which somehow acquire normative authority *just through* their clarity and codification, in the way that tradition acquires normative authority just through being tradition, and charisma just through being charisma. This makes it more plausible to think that, over time, the process of 'rationalization' tends to produce, by its own momentum, legal rationality as an independent normative source—and that this is the essential causal factor.

Against this one should insist that it is not 'legal rationality' but Reason[8] as such that should have been counterposed to tradition and charisma. It it is not by oversight that Weber did not do so. Since he did not believe there are objective truths about reasons, the next question, of how such truths can play a role in history, could not for him arise. His sociology gives plenty of space for rationalization as a force for modernity, but no space for Reason as a force for freedom.

Yet Weber sees 'rationalization' from the emancipatory humanist

---

[8] I give it a capital letter to indicate that I mean something broader than the conception involved in the contrast between reason and experience, or between reason and sentiment, and to allude to German idealism's emancipatory concept of reason.

©2008 THE ARISTOTELIAN SOCIETY
Proceedings of the Aristotelian Society Supplementary Volume LXXXII
doi: 10.1111/j.1467-8349.2008.00167.x

standpoint, even though his own sociology provides this standpoint with no lasting or commanding place to stand. He thinks that rationalization in all its forms, including bureaucratization and commercialization, produces a new form of servitude whose essence is the decline of humanism and the ascendancy of the expert. These forces do, it is true, generate a certain sort of equality, one which undermines placement in positions by virtue of mere status or relationships, and destroys hierarchies of esteem—not least the authority of cultivated humanist elites—as against technical qualifications. But this equality, he expects, will be the equality of servitude, not the equality of freedom.[9]

This picture is far from being completely misleading; it shows us real dangers. But I am optimistic enough to believe that it is too dark, just because it misses out the emancipatory force of Reason. True, we are depressingly familiar with purportedly subversive but objectively complicit philosophies that seek to undermine this force. Furthermore, Weber would have been right to challenge those who *philosophically* defend Reason's emancipatory power to explain what *sociological* forms its power can take. This is the broadest form of the challenge that I described in the previous section, of showing what social relations and practices are required for great ideals to influence society and politics.

In this light, how much or little attention should we give to bureaucracy as an 'egalitarian tool', and how much or little to trying to advance good as against bad 'hierarchies of esteem'?

Bureaucracy is an indispensable tool of modernization, and has the equalizing tendencies noted. Anderson (2008, pp. 157–8) recognizes some of its limitations. Nonetheless, she seems to underestimate both its own systemic tendency to oppression, and how easily it coexists with independently oppressive social structures. Bureaucracy is a powerful instrument that democracies struggle more or less successfully to control, but autocracies can dominate with ease. Even at its best-intentioned, under good democratic controls, it can hardly avoid turning nuanced principles into doctrinaire tenets and

---

[9] As Gerth and Mills say in their classic introduction to *From Max Weber*, 'Weber is a nostalgic liberal, feeling himself on the defensive. He deplores the type of man that the mechanization and routine of bureaucracy selects and forms. The narrowed professional, publicly certified and examined, and ready for tenure and career. His craving for security is balanced by his moderate ambitions and he is rewarded by the honor of official status. This type of man Weber deplored as a petty routine creature, lacking in heroism, human spontaneity, and inventiveness ...' (Gerth and Mills 1948, p. 50).

©2008 THE ARISTOTELIAN SOCIETY
Proceedings of the Aristotelian Society Supplementary Volume LXXXII
doi: 10.1111/j.1467-8349.2008.00167.x

then applying them in a pettifogging way. With autocratic backing, it can become one of the worst forms of oppression. Anyone with experience of Eastern Europe in the communist period knows how naturally, apparently inevitably, the relationship between official and supplicant becomes humiliating, degrading, grovelling, etc. The same applies in developing countries, with some mitigation from bribery and inefficiency. Unquestionably the impersonal oppression of office can be at least as bad as the personal oppression of a face-to-face authoritarian hierarchy.

Nor is the remedy of democracy adequate on its own. Given how powerful the 'rationalized' instruments of control available to a modern state are, it is quite easy to envisage that a democracy could have a populist culture of formal equality but a power structure dominated by bureaucratic and commercial elites. The *only* bulwark against that outcome is a civil society which generates commercially and politically undominated hierarchies of value. Democratic equality itself, when understood as a positively conceived ideal, can flourish only through the influence of such hierarchies of esteem. Without them, everything shrinks into an exploitable means. Take cultural pluralism, for example. Philosophically speaking, it emerges from a deeply thought-through understanding of the plurality and contestability of values; but whether it actually becomes a force for good or for bad depends on its social expression. From the point of view of the managerial capitalist or the political official, it is a useful tool for divide-and-rule, a way of breaking down structures of social influence other than those of market demand and technical expertise.

There has to be a free culture of criticism in civil society, and that means models of value whose standing and influence is completely independent of bureaucratic and commercial requirements. It is sociologically naïve to think that such self-standing models of value can be maintained without strong 'hierarchies of esteem' which are not subordinated to commerce, bureaucracy or politics, but which, on the contrary, influence these. Anderson believes that the failures of democratic equality in India

> are systematic because they conform to reigning norms, rather than deviating from them. The situation in India, as in many other countries in the developing world, consists in a formal apparatus of democracy and human rights overlain on feudal, caste, and other hierarchical social relations, the constitutive norms of which deeply contradict the official legal norms. (Anderson 2008, p. 141)

©2008 The Aristotelian Society
Proceedings of the Aristotelian Society Supplementary Volume LXXXII
doi: 10.1111/j.1467-8349.2008.00167.x

Exactly so. Given the diagnosis, it is surprising to find her apparently suggesting that a more efficient delivery of bureaucratic legal norms is the remedy. It may be desirable, but it is not the remedy. The problem is the continuing life and influence of traditional norms, though another important part of it is that these norms, while still powerful, are falling into a state of exploitable decay. I certainly don't have a solution to the problem, but I do know that the essential normative contest of ideals will have to work itself out within civil society. For those on the side of 'democratic equality' (in Anderson's sense) it is a task of advocacy, best done with an understanding of how the old culture's constitutive norms have a fortifying as well as an oppressive side, how they still give existing civil society resilience and substance, how they have nonetheless been undermined and opened to corruption by loss of certainty about their sources—how, in short, they might be positively superseded rather than merely destroyed.

Department of Moral Philosophy
University of St Andrews
St Andrews
Fife KY16 9AL
Scotland
UK

REFERENCES

Anderson, Elizabeth 1999: 'What is the Point of Equality'. *Ethics*, 109, pp. 287–337.
——2008: 'Expanding the Egalitarian Toolbox: Equality and Bureaucracy'. *Proceedings of the Aristotelian Society Supplementary Volume* 82, pp. 139–60.
Gerth, H. H. and C. Wright Mills (eds.) 1948: *From Max Weber.* London: Routledge & Kegan Paul.
Kahan, Alan 1992: *Aristocratic Liberalism: the Social and Political Thought of Jacob Burckhardt, John Stuart Mill, and Alexis de Tocqueville.* Oxford: Oxford University Press.
Kant, Immanuel 1996: *Metaphysics of Morals.* In Mary Gregor (ed. and trans.), *Practical Philosophy.* Cambridge: Cambridge University Press.
Mill, John Stuart 1963–91: 'Centralisation'. In John M. Robson (ed.), *The Collected Works of John Stuart Mill*, vol. XIX. Toronto: Toronto Univer-

©2008 THE ARISTOTELIAN SOCIETY
Proceedings of the Aristotelian Society Supplementary Volume LXXXII
doi: 10.1111/j.1467-8349.2008.00167.x

sity Press.

Skorupski, John 2008: 'Human Rights'. In Samantha Besson and John Tasioulas (eds.), *Philosophy of International Law*. Oxford: Oxford University Press.

Temkin, Larry 1993: *Inequality*. Oxford: Oxford University Press.

©2008 THE ARISTOTELIAN SOCIETY
Proceedings of the Aristotelian Society Supplementary Volume LXXXII
doi: 10.1111/j.1467-8349.2008.00167.x

VIRTUES OF ART
PETER GOLDIE AND DOMINIC MCIVER LOPES

I — PETER GOLDIE

VIRTUES OF ART AND HUMAN WELL-BEING

What is the point of art, and why does it matter to us human beings? The answer that I will give in this paper, following on from an earlier paper on the same subject, is that art matters because our being actively engaged with art, either in its production or in its appreciation, is part of what it is to live well. The focus in the paper will be on the dispositions—the virtues of art production and of art appreciation—that are necessary for this kind of active engagement with art. To begin with, I will argue that these dispositions really are virtues and not mere skills. Then I will show how the virtues of art, and their exercise in artistic activity, interweave with the other kinds of virtue which are exercised in ethical and contemplative activity. And finally, I will argue that artistic activity affords, in a special way, a certain kind of emotional sharing that binds us together with other human beings.

I

Introduction. The central idea that I want to argue for is that artistic virtues—virtues of art production and of art appreciation—are as much genuine virtues as ethical and intellectual virtues, and that, as such, their exercise, like the exercise of these other virtues, is done for its own sake and is constitutive of human well-being.[1]

In a recent paper, 'Towards a Virtue Theory of Art' (Goldie 2007a), I began to explore this idea, in an Aristotelian spirit, by drawing an analogy between ethics and art. This paper picks up from where that one finished. The concern I want to address now is, roughly, whether the exercise of the virtues of art really is an exercise of *virtue*, and thus partly constitutive of human well-being, or whether instead what I claim to be the virtues of art are really not virtues proper. Rather, the concern is, they are more like local skills

---

[1] Unless the context suggests otherwise, by intellectual virtues I mean the virtues which are expressed in what Aristotle called contemplative activity or *theōrein*, thus excluding practical wisdom, which I will subsume under the ethical virtues. I will say more about contemplation later.

©2008 THE ARISTOTELIAN SOCIETY
Proceedings of the Aristotelian Society Supplementary Volume LXXXII
doi: 10.1111/j.1467-8349.2008.00168.x

whose exercise is by no means constitutive of human well-being.

This is a real challenge. Art and artistic activity, when well done, are, we might all accept, a Good Thing. But there are many good things in a human life that are not themselves constitutive of well-being and that are not sought after for their own sake. Some of these are luxuries, such as excellent food, designer clothes and private swimming pools, which we often delight in partly because we have them and others do not. Others are skills and the products of skills, such as the ability of a cobbler to make a good shoe, something which is good of its kind. And yet other good things are necessities, such as nourishment, sleep, leisure, protection from the elements and good health. But, at least for Aristotle, leading an ethical and intellectual life is more than just necessity, skill or optional extra; it is what living well or well-being consists of. The challenge, then, is to show that artistic activity, whether of production or appreciation, is really expressive of the virtue of art, and really is just as much part of what well-being consists of.[2]

Why does this matter? What would be materially different if artistic activity were just a luxury or a skill, or, like sleeping, just a necessary condition for leading a good life? The central concern here is that artistic activity should be both non-instrumentally valuable and partly constitutive of human well-being.[3] But the point is not just an abstract one about the kind of value in artistic activity. The point is also one about human psychology, about motivation. Having a good night's sleep is instrumentally valuable, valuable only in so far as it enables one to lead a good life. Shoes are valuable only for the purpose of wearing on your feet, and the exercise of the skill of making them is valuable only for this purpose and is not valuable for its own sake. A luxury item (a mink coat for example) might be valued for its own sake as well as for its purpose (of keeping out the cold), but still it should be thought of as an optional extra, so that its possession and use is neither necessary for leading a good life nor a constituent part of it.[4] In contrast, if I am right, the activities of art-making and of art appreciation are part of a good life, and are

---

[2] Aristotle drew an analogy between art and ethics, but did not himself include artistic activity in his account of well-being—although see my remarks about *theōrein* later.

[3] I will leave intrinsic value to one side, and will not consider what the relation is between non-instrumental and intrinsic value.

[4] Christine Korsgaard (1983) discusses examples such as these, of what she calls 'mixed value'. The mink coat is, in fact, her example.

©2008 THE ARISTOTELIAN SOCIETY
Proceedings of the Aristotelian Society Supplementary Volume LXXXII
doi: 10.1111/j.1467-8349.2008.00168.x

not done for some further end, but for the sake of art, under the concept of art, as I put it in my earlier paper, following Richard Wollheim.[5] So, if I am right, in engaging in artistic activity, of production and of appreciation, one would be as mistaken to be motivated only by some further end as one would be if one were to think that a contemplative activity such as doing philosophy should be done only for some further end—valuable only in so far as it gives rise to a pleasant feeling perhaps, or enables one to make a living or impress one's colleagues.[6] This, then, is why the challenge matters.

To begin with, I will consider, and respond to, a concern that the dispositions—what I claim to be virtues—of art-making and art appreciation seem intuitively to be unlike the ethical virtues in two important respects. First, they are much more *local* than the ethical virtues, which require a high degree of what is called *cross-situational consistency*. Putting it very roughly, we have no problem with someone who has only a very local artistic ability, but we expect more of ethics—it is not enough just to be honest with one's friends, say, one should be honest *period*. This might seem to imply that the virtues of art are not really virtues but skills—abilities that have only a very limited range of application. I will argue that this is not the case: one of the marks of the dispositions of art-making and art appreciation being virtues (and not mere skills) is that they do have a wider range of application within the arts than might at first appear. And yet this still reveals a difference with the ethical virtues—a difference now that is one of degree. I will argue that this difference of degree is one important feature of the artistic virtues which they share with the intellectual virtues, rather than with the ethical virtues.

Secondly, what I claim to be the virtues of art seem to be unlike the ethical virtues in another respect: the ethical virtues are motivationally *demanding* in ways that the artistic virtues are not. The point is a familiar one. If someone fails on an occasion to do what is required of his ethical virtue, honesty for example, then we will think the less of him, whereas this does not seem to apply where the

---

[5] In Goldie (2007a), I discussed the difficulties surrounding motivation, and in particular what kinds of motivation can reasonably be included as falling 'under the concept of art'.

[6] The 'only' is important here. Much artistic (and intellectual) activity is done both for its own sake and for some further end, and will thus be examples of Korsgaard's mixed value. For example, shields, swords and religious artefacts can be made under the concept of art, as well as for some further end.

©2008 The Aristotelian Society
Proceedings of the Aristotelian Society Supplementary Volume LXXXII
doi: 10.1111/j.1467-8349.2008.00168.x

artistic virtues are concerned. In this respect, again, they seem more like skills, which one can exercise on an appropriate occasion if one chooses, but which one is not *required* to exercise. But I think that the answer to this concern is very much along the same lines as the first, namely that there is a kind of demandingness in relation to the artistic virtues, but that, in this respect too, the artistic virtues are analogous more to the intellectual virtues than to the ethical virtues. If one were to insist that these other kinds of virtue must be like the ethical virtues in *all* respects if they are to be virtues proper, then one will find oneself excluding not only the artistic virtues but also the intellectual virtues that are expressed in contemplation.[7]

The next part of my response is to show that, in spite of there being important normative and psychological differences between the three broad kinds of virtue, the exercise of the virtues of art-making and art appreciation are, in important ways, intimately interwoven with the exercise of both the ethical and the intellectual virtues, and this has important consequences for the virtues of art. In particular, I will show how our use of certain thick concepts has application across all three domains. The differences between the virtues, then, should not mask these important connections—connections made manifest in the fact that the exercise of all kinds of virtue is constitutive of well-being.

Finally, I will try to develop a discussion of something which I think is distinctive of the virtues of art that I touched on at the end of my last paper: the idea that the exercise of the virtues of art-making and art appreciation, when properly virtues and not mere skills, binds us together, unites us, in emotional sharing with our fellow human beings.

II

The Virtues of Art: Cross-Situational Consistency and Demandingness. When we think about someone's ethical virtue, such as honesty, we expect it to be expressed in thought, feeling and action across

---

[7] It might be suggested here than an appeal to contemplation as a virtuous activity will only be persuasive to someone who has already bought into an Aristotelian picture of what a virtuous life consists of. Perhaps. But one should not forget here that my notion of contemplation, which I discussed in Goldie (2007a), is a broad and ecumenical one, of putting to use an enquiring mind, and with this notion in place, contemplation does seem more intuitively to be partly constitutive of a human being's good life.

©2008 The Aristotelian Society
Proceedings of the Aristotelian Society Supplementary Volume LXXXII
doi: 10.1111/j.1467-8349.2008.00168.x

a wide domain within the ethical. But this does not seem to be the case with the virtues of art, a fact which seems to threaten the claim that the virtues of art really are virtues, rather than more localized skills.

Consider someone who is honest only with friends and loved ones. She cannot be said to be an honest *person*, or to have the character trait or virtue of honesty, for we expect more of such a person. This is what Rosalind Hursthouse says we should expect of the honest person:

> [W]e expect a reliability in their actions; they do no lie or cheat or plagiarize or casually pocket other people's possessions. You can rely on them to tell you the truth, to give sincere references, to own up to their mistakes, not to pretend to be more knowledgeable than they are; you can buy a used car from them or ask for their opinion with confidence ... [W]e expect them in conversation to praise or defend people, real and fictitious, for their honesty, to avoid consorting with the dishonest, to choose, where possible, to work with honest people and have honest friends, to be bringing up their children to be honest ... [W]e expect them to uphold the ideals of truth and honesty in their jobs ... (Hursthouse 1999, pp. 10, 11, 12)[8]

Hursthouse's point can be put like this. An honest person's disposition, his virtue, which is expressed in honest thoughts, motivations, feelings and actions, must not be restricted in its domain; rather, it must be expressed consistently, and in a fully engaged way, across a wide range of different ethical situations, just as her examples illustrate. If it were restricted just to friends and loved ones, for example, or just to one's colleagues, or just to matters of claiming one's expenses, it would not be a virtue proper but a more localized disposition. This idea of *cross-situational consistency* does, indeed, seem to capture what we expect of an honest person: a tendency to be honest only in certain aspects of one's ethical life does detract from our willingness to ascribe the virtue.

One worry here which I should mention, and then put to one side, might seem to threaten across the board the very idea of the virtues. The worry is that is our virtue ethics expects more than is psychologically possible of the honest person; that it is not psychologically realistic to expect such cross-situational consistency as Hursthouse's discussion seems to require. Much work has been

---

[8] I cite and discuss this passage in Goldie (2004).

©2008 THE ARISTOTELIAN SOCIETY
Proceedings of the Aristotelian Society Supplementary Volume LXXXII
doi: 10.1111/j.1467-8349.2008.00168.x

done recently in social psychology which seems to show that these expectations are indeed unrealistic, and these finding have been adopted by a number of philosophers recently to support the claim that there are no virtues of the kind that virtue ethics postulates; and so virtue ethics is in deep trouble.[9] My reply to this, which I have argued for elsewhere, is that this degree of cross-situational consistency implied by our notion of the ethical virtues arises because we are *idealistic* about them: we consider, of ourselves and of others, that if we are an honest person we *ought* to think and act honestly in all these diverse kinds of situation, and not just when it concerns our friends and loved ones, or when it concerns our expenses claims.[10] And it is for this reason that failure to be honest in one domain detracts from our willingness to call the person honest.

Now, this might rescue the virtues, and virtue ethics, but it might seem also to result in even more pressure being put on the idea of the virtues of art. For we are not idealistic about these in at all the same way as we are in respect of the ethical virtues. Consider the artist who is an excellent sculptor, or the art appreciator who is a knowledgeable and sensitive appreciator of the works of the impressionists. According to me, these are virtues of art-making and art appreciation, activities pursued for their own sake, and constitutive of well-being. And yet we do not expect cross-situational consistency from these people: if the excellent sculptor cannot paint or play music, or if the appreciator of impressionism fails to appreciate baroque music or German expressionism, then this does not detract from our willingness to call them excellent at art-making or excellent at art appreciation.

I think this is true: we do hope for cross-situational consistency in ethics more than we do in art.[11] But I do not agree that this implies that the relevant artistic traits are not virtues.

The first part of my response is that cross-situational consistency is a matter of degree, and that the virtues of art also require a certain degree of consistency. What is required, I think, is that the possessor of the trait, the putative virtue of art, has what might be summarized as a certain artistic *receptivity*, sensitivity, or openness outside their particular local domain of interest—such as sculpting

---

[9] See, for example, Harman (1999) and Doris (2002).

[10] See my discussion in Goldie (2004, chs. 3 and 4).

[11] There are a number of reasons for this, connected to a general need for reliability in virtues which directly involve the concerns of others, which I will not consider here.

©2008 THE ARISTOTELIAN SOCIETY
Proceedings of the Aristotelian Society Supplementary Volume LXXXII
doi: 10.1111/j.1467-8349.2008.00168.x

or impressionism. Let me explain what I mean.

In my earlier paper on this, I mentioned a wide range of traits that we are concerned with when considering a virtue of art: traits such as imagination, insight, sensibility, vision, creativity, wit, authenticity, integrity, intelligence, persistence, open-mindedness, and courage (Goldie 2007a, p. 383). Many of these underlying traits will be clustered in constituting the trait of being a good artist or being a knowledgeable and sensitive appreciator of art. Now, what would we say of the person who had this latter trait of art appreciation, specialized in impressionism, but who was unwilling to make any effort to deploy the range of underlying traits in relation to other aspects of art appreciation outside his local domain of interest, refusing to consider even the possibility of any merit in, for example, German expressionism, or in early Sienese painting, let alone in music or any of the other arts? If he was not in any way open to the possibility of merits in these areas, if his receptiveness were restricted only to the local domain of impressionism, then I think we would be inclined to say that what he has is just a skill, with a very narrowly focused domain of application. And the same kinds of comments would apply to an unreceptive sculptor. Moreover, as a matter of psychology, I suspect that such a person, lacking the required kind of receptivity, would characteristically be pursuing his artistic activity not for its own sake (under the concept of art), but rather would be doing what he does merely for some instrumental reason—as a pastime, perhaps (that is, as a way to pass the time), or as a way to make money. For if one's goal is merely to make money, or merely to pass the time, one's interest in the arts will typically be limited to those activities that serve this further purpose.

To sum up the first part of my response to the challenge of cross-situational consistency, we do, after all, expect a certain amount of cross-situational consistency in the exercise of the virtues of art—more than might appear at first sight. The second part of my response to this challenge is concerned with the fact that, in spite of what I have said, there does remain a significant difference of degree of cross-situational consistency in the ethical virtues and the virtues of art. For example, we do not expect the same level of ability from a sculptor across a range of other media, or the same level of knowledge from the expert on impressionism across other styles of painting. I readily acknowledge this fact, but I do not accept that this remaining difference in degree with the ethical virtues implies that the artistic virtues are really not virtues proper. For the difference in degree with the ethical virtues is to be found also in relation to the intellectual virtues. For example, if a good, intellectually virtuous philosopher specialized in modal realism or the philosophy of religion, we would not expect them to have the same level of knowledge and ability in other spheres of philosophy. However, the first point remains, that receptivity or open-mindedness are required of the philosopher, just as they are of the artist or art appreciator. It is, one might say, part of intellectual and artistic virtue to see how different areas of activity connect with each other, and to be open to what is worthwhile outside your area of specialization; it would be a mistake to think that what is worthwhile is restricted to what *you find to be* worthwhile.

Now let us turn to the *demandingness* of virtue, the second important respect in which the virtues of art (as I claim them to be) are different from the ethical virtues. Philippa Foot (1978, pp. 7–9) has argued that a virtue, unlike a skill, is not a 'mere capacity', but a disposition that 'must actually engage the will'.[12] Kindness is a virtue. If someone is a kind person, and yet is not motivated to act in a kind way on an occasion when kindness is appropriate, just because she does not feel like it, then we would think the less of her; the disposition, kindness, has failed actually to engage the will. Whereas if someone plays the violin very well, and on an occasion chooses not to play it because she does not feel in the mood, we do not think any the less of her, or of her violin-playing ability. Violin-playing is not demanding in the same way as kindness. So, it is said, violin-playing must be a skill rather than a virtue.

This distinction, though, very much like the one regarding cross-situational consistency, is not as sharp as might at first appear. For there really is a kind of demandingness in relation to violin-playing which applies on occasions where one is fully engaged.[13] It is one thing suddenly to decide that you are not in the mood to play the violin to entertain your fellow guests after a dinner, and another thing to choose to stop playing during a string quartet concert perform-

---

[12] For a detailed discussion of the contrasts between virtue and skill, see Zagzebski (1996, pp. 106–16).

[13] I discuss this idea of being fully engaged in Goldie (2007*b*, pp. 347–62). Marcia Eaton (1989) discusses the idea that 'it is useful to view the aesthetic person as one who sees what is required in the way of attention and reflection' (p. 163), and that 'You *should* enjoy trees and sunsets and music, where again the *should* is the "meaning-of-life" should' (p. 175). So Eaton too finds a certain demandingness in art.

ance. Moreover, there is another kind of demandingness that comes with artistic virtue: the demand to *care* about what one is engaged in; mere virtuosity of performance is not enough.

But still, it is clear that there is here too a remaining difference of degree with the ethical virtues. And, again as in the earlier discussion, there is a similarity with the intellectual virtues that are expressed in contemplation. Must doing philosophy, for example, 'actually engage the will' in the way that Foot says it must if it is to be expressive of a virtue? Surely not—or there is no hope for many of us. Surely it is not a condition of having intellectual virtue that one must engage in doing philosophy when the moment is appropriate even if one is not 'in the mood' (although there is again the possibility of being fully engaged in the activity). And again, we expect more than just cleverness or virtuosity of argumentation; there is here too the demand to *care*, and to care for the right reasons. As Aristotle said, having the right feelings is part of what it is to be virtuous, part of what it is really to be committed to the activity for its own sake.

It is beginning to look as if there are a number of respects—we have seen two so far—in which the virtues of ethics, of the contemplative intellect, and of art should not all be seen as having the same normative or psychological structure; and in these respects, the virtues of art seem to be closer to the virtues of the intellect than to the ethical virtues. There is a third respect in which this is the case, and this is in our overall judgement of the character of a person. If someone is lacking in an ethical virtue then we are inclined to make a judgement that he is, at least in this respect, not a good *person*, whereas if someone is lacking in an intellectual virtue that is required for contemplation, or is lacking a virtue of art, we are not inclined to make the same judgement of him as a person. Once again, it seems, we should not always take the ethical virtues as the paradigm in our analysis of the notion of virtue, against which all other kinds of virtue must be measured.

But, in spite of these important differences, the three broad kinds of virtue do not each stand alone, normatively or psychologically. Indeed, as I now want to show, the exercise of the virtues of art-making and art appreciation are, in important ways, intimately interwoven with the exercise of the more familiar ethical and intellectual virtues, and this has important consequences for the virtues of art.

©2008 The Aristotelian Society
Proceedings of the Aristotelian Society Supplementary Volume LXXXII
doi: 10.1111/j.1467-8349.2008.00168.x

III

The Interweaving of the Virtues of Art with the Other Virtues. A rather quick route to the adoption of the virtues of art as virtues proper would be to identify them with the ethical virtues, somewhat in line with the familiar saying that beauty is goodness and goodness beauty. Recently, for example, Colin McGinn has advanced what he calls the aesthetic theory of value, which holds 'that virtue coincides with beauty of soul and vice with ugliness of soul' (McGinn 1999, p. 93).[14] However, even disregarding the normative and psychological differences that I have just been discussing, I would prefer a more cautious route, drawing on what McGinn says, without adopting his aesthetic theory of value. Let me try to map out that route.

The notion of thick and thin ethical concepts (Willams 1985) is now a familiar one. Thick ethical concepts, concepts such as 'brave', 'brutal', and 'compassionate', are concepts which have both an evaluative and a descriptive content, and their application typically provides the thinker with reasons for action. In contrast, thin ethical concepts such as 'good' and 'right' are evaluative, but have minimal descriptive content, and they are less directly connected to action. In addition to these thick and thin ethical properties, McGinn draws our attention to a third category of ethical concepts, concepts which are thick, in the sense that they have more descriptive content than concepts such as 'good' and 'right', but which also have a distinctive aesthetic flavour. McGinn says this:

> These are almost wholly neglected in standard discussions of moral concepts, for reasons that go deeper than mere arbitrary selectivity— since they suggest a conception of moral thought that is alien to the entire outlook of twentieth-century philosophical ethics. There are many terms of this type: for example, on the positive side, 'fine', 'pure', 'stainless', 'sweet', 'wonderful'; and on the negative side (which is richer), 'rotten', 'vile', 'foul', 'ugly', 'sick', 'repulsive', 'tarnished'. These words, or their uses in moral contexts, have certain distinguishing characteristics. They are highly evaluative or 'judgemental', expressing our moral attitudes with particular force and poignancy, somewhat more so than words like 'generous' and 'brave'. Correspondingly, they are less 'descriptive' than those words, telling us less about the specific features of the agent, though they are more descriptive than words like 'good' and

---

[14] My position is closer to that of Eaton, who argues that 'moral value and aesthetic value really come together at the deep, meaning-of-life level' (Eaton 1989, p. 171).

©2008 THE ARISTOTELIAN SOCIETY
Proceedings of the Aristotelian Society Supplementary Volume LXXXII
doi: 10.1111/j.1467-8349.2008.00168.x

'right'. They convey a moral assessment by ascribing an aesthetic property to the subject'. (McGinn 1999, pp. 92–3)

There is a converse point to be made in relation to the artistic domain, a point which McGinn mentions, and also in relation to the intellectual domain: we use many concepts that would seem to be primarily ethical in our artistic and intellectual thought and talk: ethical concepts such as 'brave', 'gentle', 'brutal', 'generous', 'sensitive' and 'dishonest', as well as concepts that are ethical in a broader sense of the ethical, such as 'nervous', 'tentative', 'clumsy', 'offensive' and 'thorough'. In and across all three domains, these interweaving concepts can be applied to a variety of things: to persons, to states of character, to motives, to actions, to the product of actions in states of affairs or in artworks or in intellectual works of philosophy, and so on. We can as readily call the brushstrokes in an artwork brutal or the philosophical argument crude as we can call the action of a generous person fine.[15]

So there seems to be an interweaving of our conceptual repertoire across these three domains. Let me focus for a moment on the use of ethical concepts in the intellectual and in the artistic domain, and return in particular to my earlier example of honesty. In the intellectual domain of philosophy, for example, we can have an honest argument or a dishonest approach to a difficult counter-argument; and in the artistic domain, we can have an honest depiction of the hardship of life, or a dishonest approach to the problem of painting a portrait of one's patron. Now, where intellectual and artistic activities have these kinds of ethical connections, we also tend to find that the degree of cross-situational consistency and demandingness is greater, closer to what one would expect in the ethical domain. So if someone is an honest person, we would expect him to be honest in his intellectual or artistic activity as well as in his ethical dealings with other people, and we would think less of him if he was not. And this would apply even where the thick concept is being used in a rather metaphorical sense, as for example, in the sense that a picture can be dishonest. Similar remarks apply to the virtue of integrity, and to many others.[16] It begins to look as if the virtues of honesty,

---

[15] Notably, 'fine' is often the translation given for the Greek word *kalon*, which is ascribed both to ethical actions and to, for example, the action of an athlete as he returns to his place after throwing the discus.

[16] Integrity is discussed in Zagzebski (1996, p. 162), where she discussed the connections between the intellectual and the moral virtues.

©2008 THE ARISTOTELIAN SOCIETY
Proceedings of the Aristotelian Society Supplementary Volume LXXXII
doi: 10.1111/j.1467-8349.2008.00168.x

integrity and so on have application across the whole field of human
activity, and not just in the directly ethical sphere, the sphere which
is directly concerned with our dealings with other people.[17]

Similar issues arise in relation to intellectual concepts when used
in the ethical and the artistic domain. Dominic McIver Lopes says
this in relation to the cognitive value of pictures: 'One demand that
fine pictures obviously make of us is that we be "fine observers".
Here there is a symmetry between what is required of pictures' makers and what is required of their viewers' (Lopes 2006, p. 148). Being a fine observer demands 'delicacy of discrimination', 'accuracy in
seeing', and 'adaptability of seeing', and fine observation, he says, is
'one intellectual virtue fostered or reinforced by looking at pictures'
(Lopes 2006, p. 150). Fine observation, then, is an intellectual virtue, and yet a connected thick concept such as 'delicacy of discrimination' has a home in art production and art appreciation just as
much as it does in an intellectual activity such as doing philosophy.
And, of course, delicacy of discrimination has a home too in the ethical domain: for example, it is an integral part of the virtue of kindness or of generosity—the ability to see what is the kind thing to do
to help an independently-minded person, or to see what is the right
sort of generosity to the friend who has little money of her own.[18]

I now want to turn to my final task: to develop the idea that the
exercise of the virtues of art-making and art appreciation, when
properly virtues and not mere skills, binds us together, unites us,
with our fellow human beings in shared emotional experience.

IV

Artistic Activity, Well-Being, and Emotional Sharing. Virtues, so I
maintain, are dispositions which are valued as necessary for virtuous activity, and virtuous activity is what well-being consists of.
One such virtuous activity is contemplative activity, or what Aristotle called *theōria*—the 'theoretic life'. In my earlier paper, I suggest-

---

[17] With thick ethical concepts having application across the whole field of human activity,
the concern might arise that, in the end, all virtues will be subsumed under the ethical. If the
ethical is understood broadly, as concerned with how one should live, this might well be
correct, but I would maintain that under this meta-category one would still need a category
of the ethical, narrowly understood as being directly concerned with our dealings with others. Thanks to M. M. McCabe for raising this concern.

[18] For discussion, see Goldie (2007*b*).

©2008 THE ARISTOTELIAN SOCIETY
Proceedings of the Aristotelian Society Supplementary Volume LXXXII
doi: 10.1111/j.1467-8349.2008.00168.x

ed a broad, ecumenical understanding of this, as 'putting to use an enquiring mind, engaging in, and discoursing about, the vast range of deeply important things with which Aristotle was himself concerned' (Goldie 2007a, pp. 384–5).

This paper is not intended as exegesis of Aristotle's views, but it is instructive, I think, to see just how inclusive Aristotle's notion of *theōrein* (the activity of contemplation) is, and even how artistic activity might be assimilated into it. Sarah Broadie interprets Aristotle's notion as one which 'covers any sort of detached, intelligent, attentive pondering, especially when not directed to a practical goal' (Broadie 1991, p. 401). And she then goes on to add something which brings it closer to including artistic activity than does my earlier suggestion: 'Thus it can denote the intellectual *or aesthetic* exploration of some object, or the absorbed following of structures as they unfold when we look and stay looking more deeply, whether by means of *sensory presentations* or abstract concepts' (Broadie 1991, p. 401, my italics). And Terence Irwin, in his translation of the *Nicomachean Ethics*, notes that *theōrein*, the activity of contemplation, is 'cognate with "*theasthai*" ("gaze on") and indicates having something in clear view and attending to it'; his translation of *theōrein* as 'study', then, is 'study in the sense in which I study a face or a scene that I already have in full view; that is why the visual associations of *theōrein* are appropriate' (Aristotle 1985, p. 427). So why could the object of contemplation in *theōrein* not be an artwork just as much as a Pythagorean theorem or a philosophical argument? I leave that question hanging.

Earlier on in this paper, I suggested that, in a number of respects, the virtues of art are closer to the intellectual virtues than they are to the ethical. We can now see that this is also the case when we turn to the related activities which are expressive of these two kinds of virtue: contemplative activity is closer to art appreciation and art-making than it is to ethical activity. First, the way in which the intellectual virtues and the virtues of art are, and should be, expressed by an individual will depend on a number of factors relating to that particular individual, including, for example, what skills and other abilities he has; whereas this is not so in the same way with ethical activity. Secondly, contemplative activity is closer to art appreciation and art-making than to ethical activity in that the first two can directly yield, in profoundly important ways, self-understanding. (The 'directly' is important here: the ethical virtues can also yield self-understanding, in the sense that one might come to understand that one is selfish as a result of having done a selfish thing.) Contemplation, such as engaging in a philosophical exploration of the nature of virtue, whether ethical, artistic or contemplative, can deepen our understanding of ourselves and of what makes a good life. And thinking about these things can in turn lead us to change our life. Similarly, engaging in artistic activity can deepen our self-understanding and change our life, enhanced perhaps by a theoretical understanding of the role of art in human well-being.[19] Artistic contemplation of Picasso's *Guernica* can yield a deeper and fuller understanding of the awfulness of war, especially wars which cause mass death of civilians. And this might lead us to conduct our lives accordingly, standing out against the promotion of such wars. These remarks, recalling Lopes's discussion of what he so nicely calls 'fine observation', are 'symmetrical' between the virtues of art-making and of art appreciation: the artist too can change his life by doing what he does.

However, and this is my last point, I do want to claim that there is something valuable about artistic activity that is not in the same way shared by contemplative intellectual activity, nor by ethical activity, although it substantially contributes to the latter. Artistic activity also involves *emotional sharing*: as expressed in Joseph Conrad's marvellous words, the artist speaks to 'the subtle but invincible conviction of solidarity that knits together the loneliness of innumerable hearts; to the solidarity in dreams, in joy, in sorrow, in aspiration, in illusions, in hope, in fear, which binds men to each other, which binds together all humanity—the dead to the living and the living to the unborn' (Conrad 1897/1963, p. xlviii).[20]

Emotional sharing arises where two or more people experience an emotion of a certain kind, directed to a particular shared object or to a shared kind of object, and those people are aware that they are experiencing the same emotion towards the same object (see Goldie 2000). For example, you and I are on a rollercoaster, and we share the same thrills, as well as the knowledge that we each have this shared emotion. That we each know this may well enhance the ex-

---

[19] Amelie Rorty makes this point about the relation between contemplation and the exercise of the more practical virtues: 'The *phronimos* who has also contemplated the species has perfected his knowledge' (Rorty 1978, p. 350); 'contemplating humanity and the *energeiai* that are its proper functions and ends perfect and fulfil that life' (Rorty 1978, p. 351).

[20] In the preface to his *The Nigger of The 'Narcissus'*. I discuss this passage in Goldie (forthcoming).

©2008 The Aristotelian Society
Proceedings of the Aristotelian Society Supplementary Volume LXXXII
doi: 10.1111/j.1467-8349.2008.00168.x

perience of the emotion, and our screams and yells may well be more extreme than they would have been if we had been on our own.

Of course this is a familiar thing in our experience of plays and films: we tend to find the experience of the good comedy or the good tragedy more worthwhile in a full theatre, with all the members of the audience fully engaged in what is being enacted.[21] But I intend much more than that, and I read much more than that into Conrad's words. What we have in artistic activity is an intimate awareness of the *permanent possibility* of emotional sharing. When appreciating a picture such as *Guernica*, for example, alone in the gallery, we are aware that the artist, and the picture, 'speaks to' our shared human responses, as Conrad puts it—to responses that we know we can and do share with others. We share them not only with the artist, through our artistic engagement with the work that is the product of his virtuous activity. We share them also with those to whom we are closely connected and with others of our own culture, and yet more widely, across cultures and generations, to include 'all humanity'.[22] This, I believe, is what is special about artistic activity.

Again, there may be analogies here with contemplative intellectual activity, for this too might well yield up shared intellectual emotions, such as a shared feeling of amazement at the subtlety of a Pythagorean theorem, or a shared wonder at the complexity of the double helix.[23] Nevertheless, what may well be unique about artistic activity is that it can reach out to the full gamut of human experience and human emotion, to everything that is part of the human condition, not just our rational nature, but including our many sillinesses, our irrational fears and hopes, our unethical envies, our illusions of our own immortality, our fantasies. This kind of emotional sharing, as part of artistic activity, is valuable in its own right, and, of course, it is also valuable in so far as it plays a role in the deployment of our ethical virtues, in leading a good ethical life in our inter-

---

[21] A point is worth making briefly here, about tragedy. In our engagement with tragedy, we may experience, and share with others, painful emotions, such as grief and desolation. It is no paradox for me to say that the experience of these painful emotions, *as part of the expression of the virtue of artistic appreciation*, is partly constitutive of well-being. For my account of well-being is not in any way hedonistic.

[22] And here again, to echo Lopes's earlier remarks, there is a 'symmetry' between artist and viewer.

[23] For discussion of the intellectual emotions, see Stocker (2004).

©2008 THE ARISTOTELIAN SOCIETY
Proceedings of the Aristotelian Society Supplementary Volume LXXXII
doi: 10.1111/j.1467-8349.2008.00168.x

action with others, and in our self-knowledge.

We might finally note here that Aristotle thought that one of the reasons why a life of contemplation was the supreme virtuous activity is that it is a God-like life: 'For someone will live it not in so far as he is a human being, but in so far as he has some divine element in him' (Aristotle 1985, 1171b27). I think this is something that would finally and definitively mark out artistic activity from purely intellectual contemplation. One might even be tempted to say that what is marvellous about artistic activity is its very humanness—its being something that *cannot* be shared by the gods, for they cannot appreciate from the inside what 'binds together all humanity' in the same way that we humans can.[24]

Department of Philosophy
Room 4.048, Arthur Lewis Building
University of Manchester
Manchester M13 9PL
UK
peter.goldie@manchester.ac.uk

References

Aristotle 1985: *Nicomachean Ethics*, trans. T. Irwin. Indianapolis: Hackett.

Broadie, Sarah 1991: *Ethics with Aristotle*. Oxford: Oxford University Press.

Conrad, Joseph 1897/1963: *The Nigger of The 'Narcissus'*, ed. C. Watts. London: Penguin.

Doris, J. 2002: *Lack of Character: Personality and Moral Behaviour*. Cambridge: Cambridge University Press.

Eaton, M. 1989: *Aesthetics and the Good Life*. London and Toronto: Associated University Presses.

Foot, Philippa 1978: 'Virtues and Vices'. In her *Virtues and Vices and Other Essays in Moral Philosophy*. Berkeley, CA: University of California Press.

Goldie, Peter 2000: *The Emotions: A Philosophical Exploration*. Oxford: Clarendon Press.

——2004: *On Personality*. London: Routledge.

——2007a: 'Towards a Virtue Theory of Art'. *British Journal of Aesthetics*, 47, pp. 372–87.

---

[24] Many thanks to Dom Lopes and to M. M. McCabe for kindly reading earlier drafts and for making such wonderfully helpful comments and suggestions.

©2008 The Aristotelian Society
Proceedings of the Aristotelian Society Supplementary Volume LXXXII
doi: 10.1111/j.1467-8349.2008.00168.x

——2007*b*: 'Seeing What is the Kind Thing to Do'. *Dialectica,* 61, pp. 347–62.

——forthcoming: '*La Grande Illusion* as a Work of Art'. In W. Jones and S. Vice (eds.), *Ethics in Film.* Oxford: Oxford University Press.

Harman, Gilbert 1999: 'Moral Philosophy Meets Social Psychology'. *Proceedings of the Aristotelian Society,* 99, pp. 315–31.

Hursthouse, Rosalind 1999: *On Virtue Ethics.* Oxford: Oxford University Press.

Korsgaard, Christine M. 1983: 'Two Distinctions in Goodness'. *Philosophical Review,* 92, pp. 169–95.

Lopes, Dominic McIver 2006: *Sight and Sensibility.* Oxford: Oxford University Press.

McGinn, Colin 1999: *Ethics, Evil, and Fiction.* Oxford: Oxford University Press.

Rorty, Amelie 1978: 'The Place of Contemplation in Aristotle's *Nicomachean Ethics'. Mind,* 87, pp. 343–58.

Stocker, M. 2004: 'Some Considerations About Intellectual Desire and Emotions'. In Robert C. Solomon (ed.), *Thinking about Feeling: Contemporary Philosophers on Emotion,* pp. 135–50. Oxford: Oxford University Press.

Williams, Bernard 1985: *Ethics and the Limits of Philosophy.* London: Fontana Press.

Zagzebski, Linda Trinkaus 1996: *Virtues of the Mind.* Cambridge: Cambridge University Press.

©2008 THE ARISTOTELIAN SOCIETY
Proceedings of the Aristotelian Society Supplementary Volume LXXXII
doi: 10.1111/j.1467-8349.2008.00168.x

II — Dominic McIver Lopes

Virtues of Art: Good Taste

If good taste is a virtue, then an account of good taste might be modelled on existing accounts of moral or epistemic virtue. One good reason to develop such an account is that it helps solve otherwise intractable problems in aesthetics. This paper proposes an alternative to neo-Aristotelian models of good taste. It then contrasts the neo-Aristotelian models with the proposed model, assessing them for their potential to contend with otherwise intractable problems in aesthetics.

Suppose that, unlike skills, which have instrumental value, a virtue is intrinsically good for its possessor. Thus, good taste is a virtue only if

(v) Good taste is intrinsically good.

But although (v) is plausible, and although it promises to pull some weight in aesthetics, nobody has attempted explanations of (v) that might contribute to accounts of art or the aesthetic. Until now, that is.[1] Professor Goldie gets us to (v) from the claim that the exercise of good taste is partly constitutive of human well-being. Broadly speaking, this approach is neo-Aristotelian. However, there is another route to (v), which follows G. E. Moore in finding intrinsic value in the 'appreciation of what has great intrinsic value' (Moore 1903, p. 204). Call this approach 'neo-Moorean'. Both approaches deserve to be put on the table as we begin to think about virtue, art and aesthetics.[2]

I

Good Taste as a Virtue. Embracing (v) marks something of a break with traditional theories of taste like those of David Hume and Frank

---

[1] See also Goldie (2007) and Kieran (MS).

[2] A third approach, not discussed here, is that of Slote (1992).

©2008 The Aristotelian Society
Proceedings of the Aristotelian Society Supplementary Volume LXXXII
doi: 10.1111/j.1467-8349.2008.00169.x

Sibley. Whereas these explain how good taste can have a measure of instrumental value, (v) says that good taste has intrinsic value.

A principal concern of early modern aesthetics is judgements of taste, viewed as occurrent states which arise from the perception of an item, attribute value to it, and involve pleasure. Hume takes judgements of taste to be concerned with beauty, and so, given his theory of beauty, to be grounded in a pleasurable perception of the item judged. He goes on to say why these judgements vary from judge to judge and then to argue that the judgements are warranted to the extent that they conform to a standard, the joint verdict of true judges, who have 'strong sense, united to delicate sentiment, improved by practice, perfected by comparison, and cleared of all prejudice' (Hume 1985, p. 241). Strong sense and delicate sentiment are clearly abilities; they are strengthened by practice and comparison and they operate properly when free from prejudice. The true judge is one having the right cluster of traits.

Moving closer to the present, Sibley (1959, 1969) is most closely linked with appeals to a notion of taste. He accepts that the aesthetic features of an item (e.g. its elegance) supervene on its non-aesthetic, perceptible features; but he also argues that no attribution of non-aesthetic, perceptible features implies an attribution of aesthetic features. In part, the idea is that an item's elegance is a gestalt of its non-aesthetic features—it is a way of organizing them in perception into an elegant whole. Two people looking at some Japanese calligraphy may disagree as to its elegance, even though they see it as having all the same non-aesthetic features, because they differ in taste, an ability which carries the one but not the other from seeing the non-aesthetic features of the brushwork to seeing its elegance. So Sibley gives the nod to taste as 'an ability to discern the aesthetic qualities of things' (Sibley 1969, p. 68).

Presumably Sibleyan taste is a good thing to have, and Hume (1985, p. 242) writes that 'it will be agreed in by all mankind' that the character of the true judge 'is valuable and estimable'. The question is what kind of value good taste has, given the resources available in their accounts.

The accounts can easily credit good taste with instrumental value. Any trait that promotes good states of affairs is instrumentally good; and good taste promotes good aesthetic responses or behaviours, whatever they are. If a good aesthetic response assembles an aesthetic gestalt of non-aesthetic qualities, then good taste is good in so far as it assembles these gestalts. Likewise, if what makes judgements of taste good is that they are warranted, then taste is good in so far as it delivers warranted judgements of taste; and if what makes judgements of taste good are the pleasures they deliver, then the true judge enjoys pleasures that add value to her life. Finally, the character of the true judge is valuable as a gauge of the taste of other judges and of the quality of their judgements, since the joint verdict of true judges provides 'a rule, by which the various sentiments of men may be reconciled; at least, a decision, afforded, confirming one sentiment, and condemning another' (Hume 1985, p. 220).

It is harder to see how these accounts might explain (v), the claim that good taste is intrinsically good. Needless to say, it is a fraught question what intrinsic value is, so let us say that a state has intrinsic value if it has some non-instrumental value. Given this weak reading, (v) is true if good taste has some non-instrumental value. Thus (v) is consistent with good taste having a mix of non-instrumental and instrumental value, and it is consistent with the claim that good taste is valued as an end, for its own sake. Traditional discussions of taste supply no resources to explain why any of these claims are true. Nevertheless, some intuitions support (v).

Moore's (1903, pp. 83–5, 187–8) 'isolation test' is one way to bring out the intuitions. In part, the test is a product of Moore's relatively strong conception of the intrinsic value of a state as determined only by its intrinsic, non-relational properties. Since the intrinsic properties of a state are the same in all conditions, the state's intrinsic value is the same in all conditions, including the condition of isolation, where it is the only state that obtains (so instrumental value is factored out). But although Moore's strong conception of intrinsic value led him to the isolation test, any state that passes the isolation test has intrinsic value in the weaker sense identifying it with non-instrumental value. Moore saw this, writing that 'if we isolate such things, which are mere means to good, and suppose a world in which they alone, and nothing but they, existed, their intrinsic worthlessness becomes apparent' (Moore 1903, p. 187). So a situation that is good in isolation is non-instrumentally good.

Imagine two worlds—call them 'Felix' and 'Oscar'—that are identical except in respect of the taste of their inhabitants. Felix contains persons of good taste, able to appreciate beauty, whereas Oscar contains persons lacking this ability. Felicians are capable of fine discriminations, can detect aesthetic features like elegance, and can get pleasure from beauty where it is to be found. Oscaroons cannot tell an oboe from a trombone, mistake exquisite proportion for humdrum regularity, and can find no pleasure in beauty. But apart from this, the populations are identical, for both worlds are 'plain vanilla' through and through—neither contains anything beautiful or ugly—and so neither population exercises its taste. Intuition holds good taste to have intrinsic value if it judges Felix better than Oscar.

Perhaps this application of the isolation test is indecisive. Perhaps no character trait is good unless it is exercised. Since the test applies Moore's strong conception of intrinsic value, it is no surprise if the test is indecisive if good taste has intrinsic value only in some weaker sense. The question is whether intuitions attribute some weakly intrinsic value to good taste in ecological conditions.

So far, taste has been characterized as an ability to form aesthetic judgements or perceptions of aesthetic gestalts, but it also includes a motivational component. Such a component comes as standard in neo-Aristotelian views of virtue and also in the view of virtue adopted by Moore (1903, pp. 175–7). Linda Zagzebski sums up the consensus that a virtue is a 'deep and enduring acquired excellence of a person, involving a characteristic motivation to produce a desired end and reliable success in bringing about that end' (Zagzebski 1996, p. 136).

With that in mind, consider this scenario sketched by Matthew Kieran (MS). Two individuals arrive at the same aesthetic judgements because they pick up on the same features of the objects judged, yet they have very different motivations. One is a 'snob' who engages with art in order to cement his image of himself as 'high class'. The other is an 'amateur' who engages with art caring about it 'for its own sake'. Although, as a rule, motivations make a difference to judgements and aesthetic perceptions, there are circumstances where the judgements and aesthetic perceptions of the snob are no different from those of the amateur. In these circumstances, the snob will have acquired a character just like that of the amateur in all respects except motivation. Thus (v) enjoys intuitive support if we hold that the character of the amateur is better than that of the snob even when they issue all the same judgements.

Goldie (2008, p. 180) makes a point that may further amplify intuitions in favour of (v). Whereas taste is traditionally a trait concerned with receptive states, Goldie also views it as figuring equally in productive states (e.g. making art, and maybe its 'packaging' by curators and others). This idea harnesses intuitions that creative character is intrinsically valuable, and these intuitions could be probed by variants on the isolation test and Kieran's case of the snob and the amateur. Moreover, it may be worthwhile (on another occasion) to exploit elements of the influential strand of aesthetics which holds the traits responsible for art-making to be intrinsically valuable (especially Kant 2000).

That (v) is backed by intuition does not prove its truth. However, virtue-theoretic approaches in aesthetics are worth developing if, by explaining (v), they contribute to accounts of art and the aesthetic. So we might supplant or supplement traditional theories of taste if they do not supply resources to explain (v).

II

Recursive Theories of the Value of Taste. Traditional theories of taste parallel consequentialist theories of moral virtue, which are some-times put down as unable to allow moral virtue anything but instru-mental value. Against this, consequentialists like Moore argued that moral virtues have intrinsic value. The neo-Moorean arguments rely on general principles that explain the intrinsic value of good taste.

According to Moore, if a state of affairs, p, is intrinsically good, then a state of affairs that includes a pro-attitude to p is also intrin-sically good. Thomas Hurka (2001, pp. 11–19) explicitly represents this idea as a recursive theory of intrinsic goods (and evils).[3] The theory begins with a base clause laying down which states of affairs are intrinsically good:

(B) p is intrinsically good.

We must substitute into this schema a list of basic intrinsic goods such as pleasurable and beautiful states of affairs. Next, a recursion clause:

(R) If p is intrinsically good then V-ing p for itself is intrinsically good,

where V-ing p involves a pro-attitude towards p. Suppose that beau-tiful states of affairs are intrinsically valuable according to (B) and

---

[3] See also Nozick (1981, p. 430).

©2008 THE ARISTOTELIAN SOCIETY
Proceedings of the Aristotelian Society Supplementary Volume LXXXII
doi: 10.1111/j.1467-8349.2008.00169.x

that admiring is *V*-ing. It follows from (R) that admiring some beauty is intrinsically good. Now that admiring the beauty is intrinsically good, it follows from a second application of (R) that admiring the admiration of the beauty is intrinsically good. Hurka (2001, p. 17) also proposes that attitudes to instrumental goods are intrinsically valuable:

(1) If *x* is instrumentally good at promoting intrinsic good *y* then *V*-ing *x* for promoting *y* is intrinsically good.

If the MoMA is instrumentally good at arranging beautiful states of affairs which are intrinsically good, then it is intrinsically good to admire the MoMA for arranging these states of affairs.

Adapting this theory to explain (v) means taking up two tasks. The first is to hone in on some goods that are the objects of the attitudes taken in the exercise of taste. The second is to correctly characterize *V*-ing—that is, to characterize it as constitutive of good taste.

Starting with the first, if (R) explains why good taste is intrinsically good, then the objects of the attitudes that are involved in good taste must show up in (B) or (I). For present purposes, treat beauty as a thin concept equivalent to aesthetic goodness rather than a thick concept according to which, for example, being shocking counts against being beautiful. Obviously, then, one may list beautiful states of affairs in (B) as basic, intrinsic goods. That is the most straightforward view.

Aesthetic empiricists deny that beauty is intrinsically good in Moore's strong sense, and insist instead that it is good only when experienced.[4] On one version of aesthetic empiricism, beautiful states of affairs are good only because they afford intrinsically good experiences. Beauty's value is instrumental. A second, more palatable, version of aesthetic empiricism can be stated using the notion of organic unity. Moore's notion of organic unity is a product of his strong conception of intrinsic value. The intrinsic value of a unity is not the sum of the intrinsic value of its parts, which retain the same intrinsic value whether or not they are parts of the unity. Dropping the strong conception of intrinsic value gives us another notion of organic unity (Hurka 1998). The intrinsic value of an organic unity is determined by the intrinsic value of its parts, where the value of

---

[4] For example, Budd (1995) and Stecker (1997, pp. 251–8).

some parts is conditional upon the presence of other parts. If some beauty and the experience of it are parts of an organic unity, then the value of one or both is conditional upon the presence of the other. The beauty's value may depend upon its being experienced, or the value of the experience may depend on the presence of the beauty itself. Conditional value is not intrinsic value on Moore's strong conception of intrinsic value. He held that beautiful states of affairs have little or no intrinsic value, though the organic unity of them with experiences of them has great intrinsic value. Those who reject the strong conception of intrinsic value and doubt only that beautiful states of affairs have much unconditionally intrinsic value may credit them with considerable conditional value as parts of organic unities with experiences.

The options are to list beautiful states of affairs in (B) or to credit them with value instrumental to an end with intrinsic value. Either way, (R) or (I) explains the intrinsic value of episodes of V-ing. If beautiful states of affairs are intrinsically good, either conditionally or unconditionally, then V-ing them for themselves is intrinsically good. If they are instrumentally good because they afford intrinsically good experiences, then V-ing them for affording these experiences is intrinsically good.

How does the neo-Moorean approach explain the intrinsic value of good taste, where good taste is a trait of character? Let good taste be a disposition for V-ing beautiful states of affairs. Such a disposition is intrinsically good according to (R) if having the disposition itself counts as a case of V-ing—that is, if V-ing need not be occurrent. This idea has some appeal. Encouraging creativity, seeking truth, and admiring good prose seem to be intrinsically good stances that are not always occurrent as actions. Those who do not see the appeal of this suggestion are free to supplement (R) with a second recursion clause:

(RD) If p is intrinsically good then a disposition for V-ing p for itself is intrinsically good.

So if beautiful states of affairs are intrinsically good, then it is intrinsically good to have an admiring stance towards them. Together with (R), (RD) generates new intrinsic goods. For example, if it is intrinsically good by (RD) to be prone to admire beautiful states of affairs, then it is intrinsically good by (R) to admire a person who is prone to admire them. Likewise, (I) is easily adapted if beautiful states of affairs are good only as instruments to intrinsically good experiences:

> (ID) If x is good at promoting intrinsic good y then a disposition for V-ing x for promoting y is intrinsically good.

It is intrinsically good to have an admiring stance towards any beauty which affords intrinsically good experiences.

The second task is to give a convincing characterization of V-ing. For Moore, V-ing includes contemplating, appreciating, enjoying, admiring, and loving (Moore 1903, pp. 177, 204, 208–9, 217). Robert Nozick (1981, pp. 429–30) issues a longer list: bringing about, maintaining, saving from destruction, prizing, contemplating, valuing, caring about, accepting, supporting, affirming, encouraging, protecting, guarding, praising, seeking, embracing, serving, adoring, revering, ... and so on. Hurka (2001, pp. 13–14) abstracts three overarching categories. V-ing p is desiring or wishing for p when it does not obtain; or acting with the aim of making it the case that p obtains or that p continues to obtain; or taking pleasure in p, whether it did obtain, does obtain, or will obtain. In all of these cases, V-ing p involves a pro-attitude towards p.

Not every episode of V-ing is an exercise of good taste, and not every disposition for V-ing is the same character trait as good taste. Good taste involves V-ing beautiful states of affairs. Moreover, the trait is expressed by V-ing beautiful states of affairs either for themselves (apart from their consequences) or for their affording intrinsically good experiences. This is why the snob described earlier does not act from good taste when he supports the ballet not for itself but in order to cement his image of himself as 'high class'. By explaining why this snob fails to have good taste, the recursive theory makes sense of some of the intuitions favouring (v). This result suggests the following constraint: V-ing expresses good taste only in acts of V-ing beautiful states of affairs either for themselves or as means to intrinsically good states of affairs.

Again, not every instance of V-ing that satisfies this constraint expresses good taste. Imagine a movie fan who admires a beautiful movie only because she is impressed by the fame of the cast. Although her propensity to admire what is worth admiring is good, it fails to express good taste because it is not grounded in the right features of the movie. There is more to exercising good taste than V-ing some beauty for itself. Let 'appreciation' name the activity that fills in the gap. An act of V-ing a beauty-including state of affairs exercises good taste only if it involves appreciation. Admiration without appreciation fails to express good taste.

In the end, the neo-Moorean approach leans on an account of appreciation. A good starting point is the observation that there is more to appreciation than believing or even knowing. Traditional theories of taste identify the perceptions, discriminations and inferences that go into good taste. Maybe good taste requires an ability to assemble aesthetic gestalts of non-aesthetic qualities, or maybe it involves good sense and delicate discrimination. A recursive theory of good taste may build on traditional theories of taste.

Recursive theories explain the intuitions for (v) that are brought out by the isolation test—they explain why it seems intrinsically good to be equipped to appreciate beauty. Although the isolation test is meant to bring out this intuition, one might worry that verdicts about isolated states of affairs are very poor indicators of intuitions about ecologically realistic states of affairs. For one thing, in imagining Felix we are to consider whether a good state of affairs obtains (the presence of the character trait) in the absence of what determines its value (the existence of beautiful things). However, this worry is misplaced.[5] The recursive theory implies that the intrinsic value of good taste is determined by the intrinsic value of beautiful states of affairs, but it does not require the existence of those states of affairs. Compare: a person's desire for peace is intrinsically good even in a world without peace because peace is intrinsically good (of course, the desire for peace and good taste are even better when there is some peace and beauty). Recursive goods are unconditional goods, so the isolation test usefully indicates intuitions about recursive goods. An explanation of (v) that appeals to (R) or (RD) explains why good taste is unconditionally good, if it is unconditionally good.

The neo-Moorean approach sets up a framework for constructing recursive theories of the value of good taste. It leaves room for different views of the aesthetic goods listed in (B) and for an instrumental view of the value of beauty. It leaves a choice between (R) and (RD) as recursion clauses, and it calls for an account of appreciation. Moreover, it says nothing about bad taste or about varieties of good taste that consist in rejecting ugliness. Nor does it say how

---

[5] See Hurka (2001, pp. 49–50) and Regan (2003, p. 671).

to measure degrees of good taste or the right fit between the intensi-
ty of appreciating beauty-involving states of affairs and the amount
of beauty in those states of affairs. Finally, it keeps silent on the value of good taste compared to other virtues or other goods—it certainly does not imply Moore's own view that good taste is 'by far'
one of 'the most valuable things' (Moore 1903, p. 188).

III

Good Taste and Why Art Matters. Like its neo-Moorean counterparts, neo-Aristotelian theories handily explain why good taste is intrinsically good. If the exercise of good taste partly constitutes
human well-being, then, plausibly enough, good taste is intrinsically
good because human well-being is intrinsically good. However, the
main attraction of virtue-oriented approaches in aesthetics (as in
ethics) depends on their solving problems that confound traditional
approaches. So in choosing between the approaches, we should assess how each contributes, by explaining (v), to understanding art
and the aesthetic.

The two approaches propose opposite orders of explanation. One
takes as basic the value of beautiful states of affairs, using it to explain the intrinsic value of episodes of appreciation and the virtue of
good taste. The other makes human well-being the basic, intrinsic
good and takes its value to explain the value of good taste and ultimately the value of the objects of taste. In this spirit, Goldie suggests
an explanation of why art matters—or (take it to be equivalent) of
the value of beauty. Art matters because it affords the exercise of
good taste, which is part of human well-being.

According to one line of objection, the neo-Aristotelian approach
wrongly implies that art only matters instrumentally. Art is instrumentally good if its aesthetic value consists solely in its affording
certain goods. But surely art is not a purely instrumental good. The
reply is that the claim that art affords certain intrinsically good activities does not imply that its aesthetic value consists solely in its affording them. A neo-Aristotelian may either assert that art has
intrinsic value in Moore's strong sense or, if she is impressed by the
thought that art has no value in a world bereft of taste, that the value of art is conditional and so intrinsically good in a sense weaker
than Moore's. Either way, the intrinsic value of art is determined by

©2008 The Aristotelian Society
Proceedings of the Aristotelian Society Supplementary Volume LXXXII
doi: 10.1111/j.1467-8349.2008.00169.x

the intrinsic value of good taste.

Is she free to bite the bullet and grant that art or beauty are instrumentally good? Only at a price. It is common ground that good taste has a characteristic motive. Someone exercises good taste in writing a song only if his composing is a case of appreciating the song for its own sake—'under the concept of art', as Goldie (2008, p. 185) puts it. The songwriter makes an error if he thinks of the song's value as intrinsic when its value is wholly instrumental. In general, the motive required in exercising good taste commits us to error (and maybe that diminishes the value of the virtue). The choice is to accept that we are systematically mistaken when we exercise good taste, to amend the content of the motive characteristic of good taste, or to deny that art and beauty are instrumentally good.

Setting the objection aside, let us return to what is to be gained by following the order of explanation taken by the neo-Aristotelian approach. Good taste is intrinsically good because (1) its exercise is part of human well-being, and (2) human well-being is intrinsically good. Grant (2) as basic. It is possible to treat (1) as basic too, so that there is no further explanation of why human well-being includes the exercise of good taste.[6] Even so, the neo-Aristotelian approach treats only (2), not (1), as basic. It proposes to explain (1) via an independent account of human well-being—an account that does not rely on prior notions of appreciation, beauty, or art. Thus a theory of appreciation falls out of an independent account of human well-being. The latter will explain why good taste is expressed in certain activities, such that art matters for its role in these activities.

The promise to deliver a theory of appreciation is enormously attractive, but it also poses a pretty hefty challenge. Consider the teeming variety of activities listed above—bringing about, maintaining, saving from destruction, prizing, contemplating, valuing, caring about, accepting, supporting, affirming, encouraging, protecting, guarding, praising, seeking, embracing, serving, adoring, revering, and so forth. These activities target objects of many kinds in many different contexts. People appreciate songs by listening intently for their large-scale structural properties, by singing along, or by dancing; and they appreciate paintings by scrutinizing them visually, copying them, using them as motifs in new paintings, or writing ekphrastic verse. What makes these appreciative activities? In an-

---

[6] Cf. Slote (1992).

©2008 THE ARISTOTELIAN SOCIETY
Proceedings of the Aristotelian Society Supplementary Volume LXXXII
doi: 10.1111/j.1467-8349.2008.00169.x

swering this question, traditional theories of appreciation appeal in one way or another to a prior notion of beauty. The neo-Aristotelian approach does not thread the needle in this way. It extracts a theory of appreciation from a conception of human well-being, without appeal to a prior notion of beauty. Can we expect any conception of human well-being to be up to the task?

Goldie makes a start. A part of human well-being is interpersonal emotional sharing, and appreciative activities are ones through which we share emotionally. Consequently, art matters for its role in emotional sharing. This nicely illustrates the kind of story that must be told to cash in the promise of the neo-Aristotelian approach. In the course of explaining why good taste is intrinsically good, an independent conception of human well-being yields an account of appreciation and tells us why art matters (or why beauty is good). As Goldie is the first to acknowledge, though, this is not the whole story about appreciation. Certainly some art is good because it figures in emotional sharing—John Coltrane's 'Alabama', for instance, or any nineteenth-century novel. Just as certainly, not all good art succeeds for the role it plays in emotional sharing. Sol LeWitt's *Floor Plan #4* is a strikingly beautiful cube grid with practically no power to mediate emotional sharing. Going further, the quality of some art lies in its capacity to figure in emotional alienation. Manet's *Olympia* is an example, if it evokes shame, if shame alienates the picture's viewer from himself and others, and if its alienating quality is part of its great aesthetic merit.[7] Appreciation, if it engages with *Olympia* and *Floor Plan #4*, does not always take form as emotional sharing.

A start is only a start, of course. Goldie does not intend emotional sharing to be the whole story, and *Olympia* and *Floor Plan #4* do not scotch the neo-Aristotelian enterprise. They indicate that more must be said to flesh out a conception of human well-being that embraces the full range of activities expressing good taste. In aid of this, theories of art and aesthetic value can be mined, though caution is needed. It will not do to catalogue varieties of aesthetic value simply to project them onto a conception of human well-being, for the procedure would not output an independent conception of human well-being. While it makes sense to look to a catalogue of varieties of aesthetic value for clues to a conception of human well-

---

[7] See Lopes (2005, pp. 181–90).

©2008 THE ARISTOTELIAN SOCIETY
Proceedings of the Aristotelian Society Supplementary Volume LXXXII
doi: 10.1111/j.1467-8349.2008.00169.x

being, that conception must be independently compelling. At this point, one has reason to bet against the enterprise. Goldie asks, why does art matter? The neo-Aristotelian approach bets that the question either has a single answer or multiple answers that are relatively tightly interconnected in a way that makes it compelling to locate them in an independent conception of human well-being.[8] Surely the question has multiple answers. Some art matters just because it figures in emotional sharing, some art matters just because it focuses contemplation of perceptible structures, some art matters just because it embodies profound truths, some art matters just because it is a break from the daily grind, and so on. The more diverse the items on this list, the thinner the element that unifies them, and so the more likely that its place in a conception of human well-being depends on having projected the diverse items onto a picture of human well-being. For example, according to a fine recent attempt to locate the unifying element, appreciating is finding experiencing a state of affairs to be non-instrumentally valuable (Iseminger 2004). By itself, this is hardly a compelling part of a conception of human well-being.[9] The challenge is to locate an account of appreciation which is thick enough to feature in an independent conception of human well-being and yet thin enough to cover all that goes under the banner of appreciation. That is a hefty challenge.

That the challenge is hefty is no reason to shirk. Goldie's question —why does art matter?—is an excellent question. In the traditional order of explanation, the question does not even get off the ground, since it is taken as basic that art (or beauty) matters. Once the question is raised, the traditional order of explanation looks woefully unsatisfactory. The only hope for an antidote to dissatisfaction is to see what gets explained by taking it as basic that beauty (or art) matters.

The neo-Moorean approach adeptly wrangles the fragmentation that is otherwise a challenge. The recursion clauses (R) and (RD) make any act of or disposition for V-ing an intrinsic good for its own sake. These acts and dispositions can be as different from one another as you like, so long as they have intrinsic goods as their ob-

---

[8] Neo-Aristotelian virtue ethics faces no challenge like this. According to the standard line, human well-being includes contemplation, practical reasoning is a kind of contemplation, and the moral virtues express practical reasoning at its best. But our conception of practical reasoning is as sharp as our sense of its place in well-being.

[9] The same is true of the proposal in Lopes (2005, ch. 3).

jects. Moreover, the intrinsic goods themselves—beautiful states of affairs—can also be diverse. Thus the chain of explanation runs like this: episodes of good taste and the character trait of good taste are intrinsically good because beautiful states of affairs are intrinsically good. As already noted, good taste involves appreciation, but the approach says nothing more about appreciation than that it is any properly grounded activity of V-ing beautiful states of affairs for themselves. It stops short of promising a theory of appreciation and builds instead on existing theories, like those of Hume or Sibley and their successors.

Those whose instincts side with fragmentation, should prefer the neo-Moorean approach for its modesty. It explains why (v) is true without committing to theories of appreciation grounded in an independent account of human-well being. Those whose instincts tell them that a thick theory of appreciation can be extracted from an account of human-well being should prefer the neo-Aristotelian approach.

Progress in current value-theoretic aesthetics is seriously hampered by a lack of consensus on explananda, but sometimes explananda come into focus as theories are refined. Explaining (v) permits us to bring in the powerful apparatus of neo-Aristotelian virtue theory in ethics and epistemology, but it also invites us to work up a neo-Moorean recursive theory of the value of taste. Since the choice between the two approaches comes down to the weight they pull in solving traditional problems in aesthetics, the sure-fire strategy is to work on both.[10]

Department of Philosophy
University of British Columbia
Vancouver, BC
Canada
V6T 1Z1
dom.lopes@ubc.ca

---

[10] Thanks to Peter Goldie, Josh Johnston and James Shelley for helpful comments and suggestions.

©2008 THE ARISTOTELIAN SOCIETY
Proceedings of the Aristotelian Society Supplementary Volume LXXXII
doi: 10.1111/j.1467-8349.2008.00169.x

REFERENCES

Budd, Malcolm 1995: *Values of Art: Pictures, Poetry, and Music*. London: Penguin.

Copp, David and David Sobel 2004: 'Morality and Virtue: An Assessment of Some Recent Work in Virtue Ethics'. *Ethics*, 114, pp. 514–54.

Goldie, Peter 2007: 'Towards a Virtue Theory of Art'. *British Journal of Aesthetics*, 47, pp. 372–87.

——2008: 'Virtues of Art and Human Well-Being'. *Proceedings of the Aristotelian Society Supplementary Volume* 82, pp. 179–95.

Hume, David 1985: 'Of the Standard of Taste'. In *Essays Moral, Political, and Literary*, pp. 226–49. Indianapolis: Liberty Classics.

Hurka, Thomas 1998: 'Two Kinds of Organic Unity'. *Journal of Ethics*, 2, pp. 299–320.

—— 2001: *Virtue, Vice, and Value*. Oxford: Oxford University Press.

Iseminger, Gary 2004: *The Aesthetic Function of Art*. Ithaca, NY: Cornell University Press.

Kant, Immanuel 2000: *Critique of the Power of Judgment*, trans. Paul Guyer and Eric Matthews. Cambridge: Cambridge University Press.

Kieran, Matthew (MS): 'Appreciative Virtue: Aesthetic Justification and the Vice of Snobbery' (unpublished).

Lopes, Dominic McIver 2005: *Sight and Sensibility: Evaluating Pictures*. Oxford: Oxford University Press.

Moore, G. E. 1903: *Principia Ethica*. Cambridge: Cambridge University Press.

Nozick, Robert 1981: *Philosophical Explanations*. Cambridge, MA: Harvard University Press.

Regan, Donald H. 2003: 'How to Be a Moorean'. *Ethics*, 113, pp. 651–77.

Sibley, Frank 1959: 'Aesthetic Concepts'. *Philosophical Review*, 68, pp. 421–50.

—— 1969: 'About Taste'. *British Journal of Aesthetics*, 6, pp. 68–9.

Slote, Michael 1992: *From Morality to Virtue*. Oxford: Oxford University Press.

Stecker, Robert 1997: *Artworks: Definition, Meaning, Value*. University Park, PA: Pennsylvania State University Press.

Zagzebski, Linda Trinkaus 1996: *Virtues of the Mind*. Cambridge: Cambridge University Press.

©2008 THE ARISTOTELIAN SOCIETY
Proceedings of the Aristotelian Society Supplementary Volume LXXXII
doi: 10.1111/j.1467-8349.2008.00169.x

online access to the current and all online back files to January 1997, where available. For other pricing options, including access information and terms and conditions, please visit www.black-wellpublishing.com/supa. For information about subscribing to the *Proceedings of the Aristotelian Society*, please visit www.black-wellpublishing.com/pash.

JOURNAL CUSTOMER SERVICES
For ordering information, claims, and any enquiry concerning your subscription please contact your nearest office:
UK: e-mail: customerservices@blackwellpublishing.com; tel: +44 (0) 1865 778315; fax: +44 (0) 1865 471775.
USA: e-mail: customerservices@blackwellpublishing.com; tel: +1 781 388 8599 or +1 800 835 6770 (toll-free in the USA and Canada); fax: +1 781 388 8232 or +44 (0) 1865 471775.
Asia: e-mail: customerservices@blackwellpublishing.com; tel: +65 6511 8000; fax: +44 (0) 1865 471775.

DELIVERY TERMS AND LEGAL TITLE
Prices include delivery of print journals to the recipient's address. Delivery terms are Delivered Duty Unpaid (DDU); the recipient is responsible for paying any import duty or taxes. Legal title passes to the customer on dispatch by our distributors.

The Aristotelian Society Supplementary Volume (ISSN 0309-7013) is published in print in one volume per year. US mailing agent: Mercury Airfreight International Inc., 365 Blair Road, Avenel, NJ 07001, USA. Periodical postage paid at Rahway, NJ. Postmaster: Send all address changes to *Aristotelian Society Supplementary Volume*, Blackwell Publishing Inc., Journals Subscription Department, 350 Main Street, Malden, MA 02148-5020, USA.

BACK ISSUES
Single issues from the current and recent volumes are available at the current single issue price from Blackwell Publishing Journal. Earlier issues may be obtained from Periodicals Service Company, 11 Main Street, Germantown, NY 12526, USA; tel: +1 518 537 4700; fax: +1 518 537 5899; e-mail: psc@periodicals.com.

Blackwell Publishing is now part of Wiley-Blackwell.